Object Recognition in Man and Machine

3

COGNITION Special Issues

The titles in this series are paperback, readily accessible special issues of *COGNITION: An International Journal of Cognitive Science*, edited by Jacques Mehler and produced by special agreement with Elsevier Science Publishers B.V.

Published by The MIT Press:

Visual Cognition
Steven Pinker, guest editor

The Onset of Literacy: Cognitive Processes in Reading Acquisition
Paul Bertelson, guest editor

Spoken Word Recognition
Uli H. Frauenfelder and Lorraine Komisarjevsky Tyler, guest editors

Connections and Symbols
Steven Pinker and Jacques Mehler, guest editors

Neurobiology of Cognition
Peter D. Eimas and Albert M. Galaburda, guest editors

Animal Cognition
C. R. Gallistel, guest editor

COGNITION *on Cognition*
Jacques Mehler and Susana Franck, guest editors

Computational Approaches to Language Acquisition
Michael R. Brent, guest editor

Similarity and Symbols in Human Thinking
Steven A. Sloman and Lance J. Rips, guest editors

Object Recognition in Man, Monkey, and Machine
Michael J. Tarr and Heinrich H. Bülthoff, guest editors

Published by Blackwell:

Lexical and Conceptual Semantics
Beth Levin and Steven Pinker, guest editors

Reasoning and Decision Making
P. N. Johnson-Laird and Eldar Shafir, guest editors

Object Recognition in Man, Monkey, and Machine

edited by Michael J. Tarr and Heinrich H. Bülthoff

A Bradford Book

The MIT Press
Cambridge, Massachusetts
London, England

Reprinted from COGNITION: *International Journal of Cognitive Science,* Volume 67, Numbers 1–2, July 1998. The MIT Press has exclusive license to sell this English-language book edition throughout the world.

Library of Congress Cataloging-in-Publication Data

Object recognition in man, monkey, and machine / edited by Michael J. Tarr and
  Heinrich H. Bülthoff
     p.   cm.—(COGNITION special issues)
  "A Bradford book."
  Includes bibliographical references and index.
  ISBN 0-262-70070-0 (pbk: alk. paper)
   1. Optical pattern recognition. 2. Differentiation (cognition). 3. Computer vision.
4. Three-dimensional display systems. I. Tarr, Michael J. II. Bülthoff, Heinrich H.
III. Series.
TA1650.024   1999
006.4'2—dc21

                                                                98-31766
                                                                     CIP

Contents

1

Image-based object recognition in man, monkey and machine

Michael J. Tarr[a,*], Heinrich H. Bülthoff[b]

[a]*Brown University, Department of Cognitive and Linguistic Sciences,*
P.O. Box 1978, Providence, RI 02912, USA
[b]*Max-Planck-Institut für Biologische Kybernetik, Tübingen, Germany*

Abstract

Theories of visual object recognition must solve the problem of recognizing 3D objects given that perceivers only receive 2D patterns of light on their retinae. Recent findings from human psychophysics, neurophysiology and machine vision provide converging evidence for 'image-based' models in which objects are represented as collections of viewpoint-specific local features. This approach is contrasted with 'structural-description' models in which objects are represented as configurations of 3D volumes or parts. We then review recent behavioral results that address the biological plausibility of both approaches, as well as some of their computational advantages and limitations. We conclude that, although the image-based approach holds great promise, it has potential pitfalls that may be best overcome by including structural information. Thus, the most viable model of object recognition may be one that incorporates the most appealing aspects of both image-based and structural-description theories. © 1998 Elsevier Science B.V. All rights reserved

Keywords: Object recognition; Image-based model; Structural description

1. Introduction

It has been over a decade since *Cognition* published its special issue on 'Visual Cognition' (Pinker, 1984a). That volume addressed topics such as mental imagery, visual attention and object recognition. Since that time there has been tremendous progress in each of these domains, but no where more so than in visual object recognition. In 1984 relatively little was known about the nature of the mental

* Corresponding author. Tel.: +1 401 8631148; fax: +1 401 8632255; e-mail: Michael_Tarr@brown.edu

representations used in human object recognition. Cognitive neuroscientific methods were still in their infancy and computational models of recognition were based primarily on Marr's (1982) work. In 1998 we know much more about object recognition through research in each of these domains. First, psychophysical studies have revealed many facets of the amazing human capacity to recognize objects (Jolicoeur, 1985; Biederman, 1987; Tarr and Pinker, 1989; Bülthoff and Edelman, 1992; Humphrey and Khan, 1992). Second, a wide range of neuroscientific methods have been used to investigate the neural basis of object recognition in non-human primates and brain-damaged humans (Perrett et al., 1987; Farah, 1990; Goodale and Milner, 1992; Logothetis et al., 1995; Tanaka, 1996). Third, there have been significant advances in the sophistication, robustness and ecological validity of computational models (Poggio and Edelman, 1990; Ullman and Basri, 1991; Hummel and Stankiewicz, 1996b).

In this special issue we present recent work by some of the most creative scientists studying the problem of visual recognition. Moore and Cavanagh take a classic demonstration, the perception of 'two-tone' images, and turn it into a method for understanding the nature of object representations in terms of surfaces and the interaction between bottom-up and top-down processes. Tarr and Gauthier use computer graphics to explore whether viewpoint-dependent recognition mechanisms can generalize between exemplars of perceptually-defined classes. Goodale and Humphrey use innovative psychophysical techniques to investigate dissociable aspects of visual and spatial processing in brain-injured subjects. Perrett, Oram and Wachsmuth combine neurophysiological single-cell data from monkeys with computational analyses to provide a new way of thinking about the mechanisms that mediate viewpoint-dependent object recognition and mental rotation. Ullman's work also addresses possible mechanisms that may account for viewpoint-dependent behavior, but from the perspective of machine vision. Finally, Schyns synthesizes work from many areas, providing a coherent account of how stimulus class and recognition task interact. What is notable is that this group of contributors brings together a wide range of methodologies to a common problem. Moreover, much of the work presented in this volume provides converging evidence for a common approach – what we refer to as 'image-based' or 'view-based' recognition. The key idea of the image-based approach is that object representations encode visual information as it appears to the observer from a specific vantage point. Note that, although such a claim is actually neutral with regard to particular types of features, including pixel regions, shape contours, texture, etc., it does imply that features, regardless of their content, are viewpoint-dependent. Consequently, the usefulness of a given feature for recognition will diminish as that feature changes its appearance with changes in viewpoint and overall recognition performance will be viewpoint-dependent.

2. Models of recognition

The study of visual object recognition is often motivated by the problem of recognizing 3D objects given that we only receive 2D patterns of light on our retinae. A commonly-held solution, popularized by Marr (1982), is that the goal of vision is to reconstruct the 3D scene. Reconstruction assumes that visual perception is a hierarchical process which begins with local features that are combined into progressively more complex descriptions (also see Pinker, 1984b). Note that the types of features used and how they are combined is completely deterministic. That is, particular types of features and the relations between them are pre-defined and used for reconstruction across all images. Moreover, the presence or absence of a given feature is absolute-there is no 'middle ground' in which there is partial or probabilistic evidence for a feature. Thus, lines are grouped into contours, contours into surfaces, and surfaces into objects. At the endpoint of the reconstruction process Marr and Nishihara (1978) assumed that viewer-centered descriptions (what Marr termed 'sketches') are remapped into 3D object-centered representations. This final step was motivated by Marr and Nishihara's (1978) suggestion that object representations should be relatively stable, that is, they should generalize or be invariant over changes in the retinal image. Otherwise, Marr and Nishihara argued, new, distinct representations would be required for each small variation in the image of a given object, e.g. for each change in 3D position, each change in illumination, etc. More concretely, this meant that object representations should be object-centered rather than viewer-centered-hence their conjecture that objects are represented as configurations of 3D parts or volumes.

Although there is a theoretical elegance to this approach, it has never been obvious that recovering descriptions of 3D parts from 2D images is generally possible. Indeed, during the 1980s numerous machine vision researchers attempted to implement reconstruction algorithms with only marginal success (Nalwa, 1993). Thus, one argument that favors the image-based approach is that it does not require reconstruction. Indeed, given that our visual systems are given viewer-centered images as input, it would not be altogether surprising if visual recognition was based on similar mental representations.

Notwithstanding these potential problems, Marr's work has had tremendous impact on the study of vision, and, in particular, helped to shift the focus of high-level vision research from visual imagery (e.g. Kosslyn, 1980) to visual object recognition during the 1980s. One of the most prominent theories to come out of this era was the 'Recognition-By-Components' model (RBC) by Biederman (1987). The RBC model built on Marr and Nishihara's earlier work on object recognition, proposing that objects are represented as collections of volumes or parts. What RBC added, however, were additional syntactic constraints that specified the allowable types of volumes, how such volumes might be recovered from 2D images, and the types of qualitative spatial relations that connect such volumes. RBC also followed the stricture that object representations should be stable and, consequently, proposed that the configurations of parts that are used to describe objects are invariant across changes in viewpoint (up to significant changes in the visible part structure (Biederman and Gerhardstein, 1993)), illumination, and color (Biederman and Ju, 1988). Thus, the RBC approach, often referred to as a 'structural-description' model, provides a computationally-elegant, but completely deterministic (i.e. the elements of the representation are pre-defined and such elements are either present or absent), answer to the question of how human perceivers recognize objects across changes in viewpoint.

Although RBC has been very influential, it is still not clear that any approach that relies on the recovery of 3D volumes is robust enough to subserve general object recognition. Moreover, the actual evidence for viewpoint-invariance in human visual recognition (as predicted by RBC) is somewhat thin – the most notable experiments that obtain viewpoint invariance for rotations in depth[1] (Biederman and Gerhardstein, 1993) having only limited generalizabilty to other recognition tasks and stimulus sets (Hayward and Tarr, 1995; Tarr and Bülthoff, 1995; Tarr et al., 1997). In contrast, psychophysical and neurophysiological studies from the late 1980s and early 1990s offer a somewhat different conclusion – under a wide variety of experimental conditions, human object recognition performance is strongly viewpoint-dependent across rotations in depth (Bülthoff and Edelman, 1992; Edelman and Bülthoff, 1992; Humphrey and Khan, 1992; Tarr, 1995). Converging evidence for this result has come from single-cell recording studies in the inferior temporal cortex of monkeys (Logothetis et al., 1995). From a computational perspective this result is rather surprising because view-dependent object representations are necessarily less stable than view-invariant representations – yet the data seem to imply that humans rely on image-based representations that are viewpoint-dependent.

On the face of it, the image-based approach to recognition appears to be subject to Marr and Nishihara's criticism of viewer-centered models – that each distinct viewpoint of an object necessitates a separate representation. What Marr and Nishihara omitted was that the stability constraint only holds if there is no means for generalizing from one image to another. For instance, if observers can compensate for changes in viewpoint by a normalization process, they may be able to use a small number of viewer-centered representations to recognize objects in any orientation in space (i.e., a 'multiple-views' representation). Indeed, proponents of the image-based approach have offered a variety of different mechanisms for generalizing from unfamiliar to familiar views, including mental rotation (Tarr and Pinker, 1989), view interpolation (Poggio and Edelman, 1990) and linear combinations of views (Ullman and Basri, 1991). Even more sophisticated (Ullman, 1998) and neurally-plausible (Perrett et al., 1998) generalization mechanisms are presented in this volume.

While generalizing over viewpoints has been accepted as one way of providing stability within image-based models, generalizing over different instances of a perceptually-defined class has been seen as a far more difficult problem (Biederman and Gerhardstein, 1995). Consider that almost every behavioral study that has reported viewpoint-dependent recognition has also used tasks in which subjects must discri-

---

[1]There are several studies that have obtained orientation invariance for rotations in the picture plane (Corballis et al., 1978; Tarr and Pinker, 1990). This result, however, is not considered diagnostic for theories of recognition in that there are both image-based and structural-description models that predict recognition costs over changes in picture-plane orientation (Tarr and Pinker, 1989; Hummel and Biederman, 1992).

minate between visually-similar objects, not object classes. For example, subjects might be asked to distinguish robins from sparrows, but not birds from cars. Thus, there is little data that directly addresses the question of how basic-level (Rosch et al., 1976) or entry-level (Jolicoeur et al., 1984) recognition is accomplished. Although more specific recognition discrim-inations are no doubt important, it is relatively uncontroversial that visual recognition most frequently functions at the basic level. Moreover, with the exception of RBC theory, most models of human visual recognition have failed to provide well-specified mechanisms for class-level recognition. Image-based models seem particularly problematic in this regard-because objects are represented as viewpoint-specific images it is assumed that the representations are also specific to particular exemplars, not object classes. The common claim is that image-based or view-based representations are templates based on inflexible linear coordinates, and, as such, cannot accommodate the varia-tions in image geometry that characterize different exemplars of a single object class (Hummel, 1998). Indeed, as reviewed below, this is only one of several oft-cited critiques of image-based models.

3. Evidence for the image-based approach

Criticisms that portray image-based theories as overly simplistic are no longer tenable as arguments against such theories. This claim is supported by recent exten-sions of the image-based approach (Edelman, 1995b; Beymer and Poggio, 1996; Moses et al., 1996) and by the new work presented in this volume. While it is true that earlier image-based models suffered because of simplifying assumptions (e.g. locating features at fixed x, y coordinates in the image-plane), theorists were well-aware of the problem. For instance, in one of the seminal papers on the image-based approach, Poggio and Edelman (1990; p. 264) state that 'The key issue of how to detect and identify image features that are stable for different illuminations and viewpoints is outside the scope of this paper...[the model] does not require the x, y coordinates of image features as inputs: other parameters of appropriate features could also be used...Recognition of noisy or occluded objects, using realistic feature identification schemes, requires an extension of the scheme...'. What we have wit-nessed over the past several years are serious attempts to extend the image-based approach. For instance, Bricolo et al. (1997) employ features characterized by small brightness regions that can be located at any position within the image, thereby facilitating flexible object representations. Amit and Geman (1997) use similar features, but relate the spatial positions of such features in a manner that allows for a highly robust matching scheme. There have also been attempts to develop models that use less local representations of shape. For example, Hayward and Tarr (1997) found that observers were sensitive to both the metric and qualitative struc-ture of image contours in 3D objects.

Concurrent with efforts to extend the image-based approach, there has been a great deal of scrutiny regarding the biological validity of the structural-description approach. In particular, a variety of labs has tested the specific predictions of RBC and related theories that posit the recovery of view-invariant parts. Behavioral results suggest that such models offer only limited explanatory power. For example, several studies (Bülthoff and Edelman, 1992; Humphrey and Khan, 1992; Tarr, 1995) have demonstrated that, when subjects are trained to recognize novel objects in a small set of viewpoints, not only are the generalization patterns viewpoint-dependent, but, critically, they are related to the distance between an unfamiliar test view and the nearest familiar view. Such results provide strong evidence for object representations based on multiple image-based views matched to input shapes through normalization processes. Supporting this claim, Logothetis et al. (1995) trained monkeys to recognize novel objects similar to those used in Bülthoff and Edelman (1992). Recordings in the inferior temporal cortex of these monkeys reveal 'view-tuned' neurons, that is, cells that are preferentially active for specific instances of these trained objects in specific views. Moreover, for a given object, Logothetis et al. (1995) found that different neurons coded for different views, thereby providing a multiple-views representation similar to that inferred from behavioral data. It should be noted, however, that Logothetis et al. (1995) also found some evidence for view-independent neurons for some objects. The question is whether such neurons arise as a result of the derivation of truly viewpoint-invariant object representations or because multiple view-tuned neurons simply feed into a single neuron.

As mentioned, one criticism of this body of results is that the stimuli used in these experiments were typically drawn from a single visually-similar class, e.g. 'paper-clip objects' (Bülthoff and Edelman, 1992) or 'cube objects' (Tarr, 1995; Fig. 1a). In part due to this limitation, it is popularly held that both structural-description and image-based models explain elements of human visual recognition. For exam-

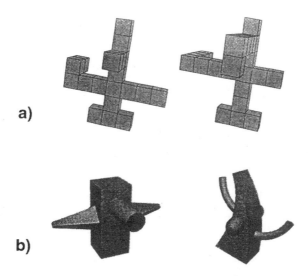

Fig. 1. (a) The top pair of objects are drawn from the same visually-similar class (adapted from Tarr, 1995). (b) The bottom pair of objects are qualitatively dissimilar from one another in terms of both image structure and parts (adapted from Hayward, 1998).

ple, structural-descriptions providing categorical-level access and image-based mechanisms providing within-class or exemplar-specific level access (Jolicoeur, 1990).

Why then can we claim that current empirical results strongly support image-based models and provide little evidence for view-invariant models? The answer lies in a series of recent behavioral studies based on critiques of image-based studies (Biederman and Gerhardstein, 1993, 1995). Specifically, Biederman and Gerhardstein (1993) proposed three 'conditions for invariance' claimed to be 'typical' of human object recognition. Briefly, the conditions are that: (i) objects must be decomposable into parts; (ii) each object in the recognition set must be composed of a distinct configuration of parts; (iii) different viewpoints of the same object must show the same configuration of parts. These conditions attempt to exclude almost all earlier studies, e.g. Bülthoff and Edelman (1992) and Tarr (1995), from consideration as diagnostic of visual recognition. In response to this critique, researchers began to test recognition performance using experimental designs that satisfied Biederman and Gerhardstein's conditions. In particular, each target object is qualitatively different from the other objects in the recognition set (Fig. 1b). Results in these studies strongly support image-based models. In almost every case, even given highly dissimilar objects, recognition performance has been found to be viewpoint-dependent (Liter, 1995; Hayward and Tarr, 1997; Suzuki et al., 1997; Hayward, 1998; Tarr et al., 1997, 1998); but see also Biederman and Gerhardstein (1993).

4. Reconciling image-based and structural-description models

Recent empirical results seem to pose problems for a particular family of structural-description models, and, most notably, RBC. However, they do not indicate that all approaches to structural-descriptions are invalid, only that we need to rethink what kind of structural knowledge is encoded. Indeed, a major goal of vision scientists should be to develop models that provide robust accounts of human performance within a combined image-based/structural-description framework (insofar as the preponderance of behavioral data supports such a framework and that there are computational advantages to both approaches).

What are the challenges in developing such an approach? First of all, we must consider the fact that the spectrum of results measuring viewpoint dependency ranges from almost complete viewpoint invariance (Biederman and Gerhardstein, 1993; Tarr et al., 1998) to extreme viewpoint dependence (Bülthoff and Edelman, 1992; Humphrey and Khan, 1992; Tarr, 1995). What is not the case is that we see a pattern across experiments in which there is simply either invariance or dependence. Rather, depending on the homogeneity of the stimulus class and the particular recognition task, we obtain relatively more or less of an effect (Edelman, 1995a; Schyns, 1998). This is exemplified by the results of nine experiments reported by Tarr et al. (1998). They found that under the specific conditions used by Biederman and Gerhardstein (1993), i.e. match-to-sample recognition of qualitatively-distinct

3D objects and response time feedback on each trial, recognition performance was close to viewpoint-invariant. However, given a different recognition task, e.g. sequential matching or naming, or no feedback, recognition of the same 3D objects was viewpoint-dependent. A viable model of recognition must account for this continuum and the conditions under which different values along it are obtained. Constraining any such account, several recent studies have tested some of the conditions that appear to determine the degree of viewpoint invariance or dependence. For example, Tarr and Pinker (1990) found that performance was viewpoint invariant when subjects recognized 2D shapes that could be discriminated by a unique one-dimensional ordering of features, but was viewpoint-dependent when the shapes could only be discriminated by using 2D relations between features. Similarly, Tarr et al. (1997) found that the recognition of 3D objects containing single unique parts was much less view-dependent as compared to the recognition of objects containing multiple parts that had to be related to one another.

Second, we must consider the fact that human perceivers are capable of recognizing objects at multiple categorical levels, ranging from basic-level (Bartram, 1976; Jolicoeur, 1985; Biederman and Gerhardstein, 1993) to subordinate-level (Gauthier et al., 1997) to item-specific (Bülthoff and Edelman, 1992; Humphrey and Khan, 1992; Tarr, 1995) recognition. Models of recognition must account for how we represent object information that supports multiple levels of access – either through multiple systems that interact (e.g. with structural-descriptions supporting the category level and image-based mechanisms supporting the more specific levels (Jolicoeur, 1990; Tarr and Pinker, 1990; Marsolek and Burgund, 1997) or through a single system that is highly adaptable to varying recognition conditions (Biederman et al., 1997; Edelman, 1995b; Gauthier and Tarr, 1997b).

Third, we must consider the fact that human perceivers vary in the level of expertise they have for a given stimulus class. The degree of experience an individual has had with a class may help to determine the default level of access for recognition, how sensitive recognition is to image transformations, e.g. brightness reversal, and to changes in configural information (Gauthier and Tarr, 1997a; Tanaka and Sengco, 1997; Gauthier et al., 1998). Models of recognition must be sufficiently plastic to adapt as experience with an object class accumulates. Moreover, it is not enough for a model to simply allow recognition at different levels of expertise. There must be an account for why performance across various behavioral measures changes with changes in expertise.

Finally, it is crucial to realize that performance in a given recognition task is actually the product of a complex interaction between all of these factors: homogeneity of the stimulus class; categorical level; and level of expertise (Gauthier, 1998; Schyns, 1998). As a rule, extant models of recognition have tended to focus on only one or two of these factors, for example, comparing face recognition to non-face object recognition (Farah, 1992), or contrasting basic-level with subordinate-level recognition (Biederman, 1987). Recent models have certainly begun to move away from such simple dichotomies (e.g. Edelman, 1995a), but there is clearly still a great deal of work to be done.

5. Current problems with image-based models

It is our contention that new approaches to image-based recognition can account for the complete range of human recognition performance. However, meeting this challenge may necessitate abandoning old notions of what is meant by an image-based or view-based model. In particular, because there is some behavioral evidence to support both image-based representations and structural-descriptions, as well as computational strengths for each, it seems likely that a viable model will encompass elements of both. In order to see why this is the case, let us examine some of the most oft-cited problems with 'traditional' image-based models.

5.1. Class generalization and categorical representation

Image-based models typically represent the appearance of a specific object from a specific viewpoint. As such, they are exemplar-based and seemingly poor candidates for class-level recognition. Moreover, even if it is possible to generalize from familiar exemplars of a class to unfamiliar exemplars, mechanisms for specifying category membership and representing perceptually-defined categories as categories are less than obvious.

5.2. Hyper-sensitivity, inflexibility and combinatorial explosions

Even for the recognition of a single object, an image-based approach may have difficulties in generalizing across slight variations in appearance. Marr and Nishihara (1978) suggested that object representations should be sensitive in order to discriminate between visually-similar objects. However, sensitivity should not be so great that each specific change in the image necessitates a distinct representation. Therefore, if image-based information does not generalize across viewing conditions, an excessive number of representations may be required to capture the appearance of only a single object. Indeed, image-based models often appear prone to this problem in that some approaches have posited inflexible or 'holistic' representations that are ill-suited for generalizing from known to unknown viewing conditions. Although it has been argued that trading 'memory for computation' in this manner is acceptable, it is unclear that there can ever be sufficient memory to compensate for a system that allows for only minimal generalization.

5.3. Matching algorithms and normalization mechanisms

In order for image-based representations to generalize between exemplars or between views, robust matching algorithms must be specified. That is, there must be some mechanism for measuring the perceptual similarity (within some domain) between an input image and known objects. One possibility is that we simply measure local pixel or brightness similarity across images, but it is doubtful that such representations will exhibit the necessary robustness because they are likely to be highly unstable over image transformations. An alternative might be to measure similarity across the output of receptive fields, although it is unclear that what are still relatively local descriptions of the image will suffice. More plausibly, relational information between local features is needed. A second issue is how to match an unfamiliar view of an object to a familiar view of the same object. Image-based models have often appealed to mental transformations or alignment models that seem to beg the question. At issue is that such processes must establish the direction of rotation before executing a rotation or alignment. Determining this information seems to imply that recognition, at least at a coarse level, has already occurred.

6. Extending the image-based approach

6.1. Interpolation across views

How do we extend image-based models to address such problems? As alluded to earlier, there has been increasing interest in developing image-based models that can generalize between familiar and unfamiliar views for a given object and between familiar and unfamiliar exemplars for a given class. Indeed, some of the earliest computational approaches to image-based recognition relied on mechanisms that effectively measured the visual similarity between different views rather than executing a transformation, for example, the view interpolation model of Poggio and Edelman (1990). In this approach, specific object views are described as sets of viewpoint-dependent features (e.g. the output of receptive fields). Each view can then be considered a point in a high dimensional space that captures the appearance of all possible views. Generalization from unknown to known views (those in memory) is accomplished by establishing the location of the unknown view within this space and measuring the similarity of its features relative to the features of the nearest known views, that is, 'interpolating' across the view space. Such models are appealing in that they do not require the precomputation of 'alignment keys' (Ullman, 1989) or other information about the shape prior to recognition (see also Ullman, 1998). Moreover, there is some psychophysical evidence to support the view interpolation approach (Bülthoff and Edelman, 1992; Edelman and Bülthoff, 1992). Critically, more recent computational instantiations of view interpolation have adopted more flexible representations of image features (Bricolo et al., 1997; Riesenhuber and Poggio, 1998) based on neurophysiological results that provide evidence for view-tuned neurons (Logothetis et al., 1995). Reinforcing the biological plausibility of this approach, Perrett et al. (1998) offer specific neurophysiological evidence for 'evidence accumulation' across collections of local features, a mechanism similar to that proposed in some of the recent computational models.

6.2. Interpolation across exemplars

One insight that has helped extend the image-based approach is that interpolation need not only occur between views of an object. It is equally plausible that interpolation can occur between different exemplars of a perceptually-defined object class. Thus, just as an unknown view can be recognized through interpolation to a visually-similar nearby view, an unknown exemplar can be recognized through interpolation to a visually-similar exemplar (Lando and Edelman, 1995; Beymer and Poggio, 1996). Psychophysical evidence for exactly this sort of class generalization has begun to accrue (Moses et al., 1996; Gauthier and Tarr, 1997b) and is discussed in detail by Tarr and Gauthier (1998). Indeed, the neural mechanisms proposed by Perrett et al. (1998) could readily extend to measuring the similarity of local features across class instances[2].

One caveat about image-based generalization processes is that view interpolation is possible because the view space for a given object or class tends to vary smoothly. That is, across a wide range of adjacent viewpoints, there are only small qualitative changes in the projected image of the object. When dramatic changes in the image do occur, such as when a major part comes in or out of view (Biederman and Gerhardstein, 1993; Hayward and Tarr, 1997; Hayward, 1998), it is probable that interpolation mechanisms may fail across this boundary (referred to as a 'visual event' by Koenderink, 1987). Under such conditions it may be that explicit[3] view-invariant structural information is required to map a view of an object onto a qualitatively different view of that same object – a possibility we discuss below.

Similarly, interpolation between different exemplars is only likely when the two are visually similar, that is, when the space of exemplars defining the object class varies smoothly. How likely is the assumption of smoothness? For many basic-level classes, the answer may be quite likely. Several recent computational studies have assessed how easily familiar objects can be categorized into stable visually-defined classes. Using only silhouette or boundary contour information readily extracted from images, it has been found that large numbers of exemplars can be separated into perceptual categories. Critically, these categories correspond quite closely to those that might be delineated by human perceivers (Ullman, 1996; Cutzu and Tarr, 1997). A similar conclusion regarding the perceptual stability of basic-level classes has been reached by developmental psychologists studying the acquisition of visual category information in infants. For example, Quinn et al. (1993) found that 3–4-month-old infants were capable of discriminating images of birds from dogs and cats, as well as images of dogs and cats from one another. Presumably, given the limited experience such young infants have had with these object classes, their performance must be based on visual information available in the images, not on conceptual knowledge acquired through the names assigned to the objects. Indeed, in the original formulation of basic-level categories, Rosch et al. (1976) posited that

---

[2] While the view-tuned neurons reported in Logothetis et al. (1995) appeared to have their highest activation when presented with a specific exemplar, e.g. a particular 'paperclip' object, the same neurons sometimes showed above-resting-level activation for the presentation of visually-similar objects, suggesting that within-class generalization may have occurred.

[3] We use the term explicit here because we mean a distinct, explicitly represented description of an object's structure. As discussed below, we propose that image-based representations also encode implicit structural information in terms of the relative positions of local features.

most classes have a perceptual basis and, in particular, that silhouettes might provide this basis. Overall, these results suggest that generalization within perceptually-defined classes is a plausible extension to image-based models. On the other hand, much as multiple-views are necessary to represent the complete 3D structure of an object (Tarr, 1995), multiple exemplars will be necessary to represent the complete range of object classes.

Multiple-views or multiple-exemplar representations alone do not provide a basis for representing 3D objects. What are needed are organizing principles that provide a 'glue' between qualitatively dissimilar views or exemplars (qualitatively similar views or exemplars may be related on the basis of visual similarity and interpolation mechanisms). For multiple-views representations, two types of information may be available as evidence that distinct and geometrically dissimilar views arise from the same 3D object.

6.3. Temporal associations

Consider that from one moment to the next, the most likely image to follow an image of given object is another view of that same object. Using simple occurrence-based association mechanisms (i.e. Hebbian learning) the visual system could come to associate distinct views. Specifically, the more often that two images temporally co-occur, regardless of image similarity (Miyashita, 1993), the more strongly they will be associated. If we couple this with some measure of perceptual similarity, we have a powerful mechanism for building multiple-views representations. Although the existence this type of temporal association is somewhat speculative, there are recent psychophysical, neurophysiological, and computational results that provide some evidence in this direction (Miyashita, 1993; Wallis, 1996a,b).

6.4. Explicit structural information

Associations between views may also be formed by explicitly represented structural information. We have already alluded to the fact that there are instances for which structural information about an object may be critical. Insofar as a structural-description of a given object is stable over changes in viewpoint, it may provide a mechanism for linking two distinct views. However, given the problems we have raised for structural-descriptions based on 3D parts, what kind of structural information might offer sufficient stability, yet not predict complete invariance? One candidate is a 'medial-axis' representation derived from an object's silhouette, that is, a skeletal description of the object. The idea of using medial-axis representations is quite old, being first proposed in Blum's 'Grassfire' model (Blum, 1967). Blum's idea was that if the edges of an object's silhouette are simultaneously 'ignited', the flames will burn inward until they collide or interfere with one another, thereby leaving a skeleton describing the shape of the object. More recent instantiations of this idea have provided computationally robust methods for recovering skeletal descriptions (Kimia et al., 1995; Zhu and Yuille, 1996). Additionally, there is recent behavioral evidence suggesting that medial-axis representations are computed early in visual processing (Kovacs and Julesz, 1994).

Medial-axis representations are appealing for several reasons. First, they are readily computed from an object's silhouette or bounding contour, a type of information that is recoverable from 2D images (in contrast with 3D part descriptions). Second, they provide a topological description of object shape that allows the representation to remain relatively stable over changes in viewpoint, illumination, color and object configuration (Marr and Nishihara, 1978; Zhu and Yuille, 1996). Third, the topological nature of the representation facilitates fast and efficient matching between object descriptions (Kimia et al., 1995).

Given these positives, why do we claim that explicit structural information only supplements image-based recognition? The answer is that medial-axis representations provide only limited information about an object, that is, a coarse description of its shape. Recognition based on such information would not be entirely reliable and, at best, might provide a 'ballpark' estimate of the category (see the examples provided in Zhu and Yuille, 1996). Moreover, we have already made it clear that recognition may occur at many different categorical levels. Thus, skeletal descriptions may help constrain the search space during recognition, but in and of themselves they are not sufficient for recognition. As an example, consider an observer that has learned to recognize several views of a 3D object; unfamiliar views that are similar to familiar views may be recognized through normalization processes such as interpolation. However, because of qualitative differences between new views and stored views, it may not always be possible to recognize unfamiliar views through interpolation. Therefore, new views should be learned as distinct nodes ('aspects' in Koenderink, 1987) in a multiple-views representation. The question is, a node in *which* multiple-views representation? The answer may be provided by relatively view-invariant structural information: the skeletal description for a given view may be similar enough to the skeletal descriptions derived from other views of the same object or class to help constrain which particular multiple-views object representation is selected.

It is worth noting that other theorists have taken different directions in combining image-based information and explicit structural-descriptions. For example, Hummel and Stankiewicz (1996b) have sought to extend a neural-net implementation of RBC (Hummel and Biederman, 1992) to include both structural-descriptions based on 3D parts and image-based surface information. Their model is motivated by the computational problem of 'binding' together the different component parts that form a structural-description of an object. Interestingly, the representation of surfaces in their model helps to defray the costs of the binding process. Thus, image-based and structural information may be both functionally and computationally complementary. Indeed, their model is much more successful than its predecessor–some specific predictions regarding the need for attention in the binding process and sensitivity to left-right reflection, translation, and scale changes have been born out in behavioral experiments (Stankiewicz et al., 1998).

6.5. Implicit structural information

In contrast to explicit medial-axis descriptions, image-based models may also incorporate what we refer to as implicit structural information. We use the term implicit here to denote the fact that this type of structural information does not provide a global description of object shape, but rather simply codes relations between local features. Consider that images may be described as collections of local measures of the image at different locations (e.g. the output of oriented receptive fields, Edelman, 1993; small pixel regions, Bricolo et al., 1997; Amit and Geman, 1997; qualitative and quantitative measures of shape, color, texture, etc.). At one extreme, it may be possible to represent these features in a completely unordered fashion, thereby losing all information regarding the spatial relation between one local feature and the next. Such a representation would retain only information about the presence of each feature anywhere within the image. It is clear that such a model has severe limitations: for example, randomly scrambling the positions of the features will produce an image that cannot be distinguished from the original. On the other hand, there is computational evidence that even such simplistic representations have a surprising degree of explanatory power in terms of recognizing novel views of 3D objects (Bricolo et al., 1997). At the other extreme, the relations between local features may be completely deterministic, as in a literal image where the point-to-point positions between features are rigidly fixed relative to one another, e.g. described in linear coordinates (Poggio and Edelman, 1990). This is the kind of shape representation often associated with templates and image-based models (Hummel and Stankiewicz, 1996a). Obviously, such rigid and completely deterministic templates where features match absolutely or not at all also have severe limitations: for example, hyper-sensitivity to trivial metric changes in the image (Hummel, 1998).

What we propose is a representation of image features somewhere between completely unordered vectors and rigid templates, that is, a model in which there is implicit structural information regarding the spatial relations between local features. The form of the structural information is not a global description of an object in terms of parts or skeletons, rather, it is a relatively local description that captures the positional certainty between image measurements. In contrast to this type of statistical relation between features, structural-description models such as RBC relate far less local features, i.e. 3D parts, in a purely qualitative fashion (e.g. a part is simply 'above' a second part rather than more or less above). One way of coding these implicit relations is as set of weights within a neural network. For example, both Edelman and Weinshall (1991) and Lades et al. (1993) have proposed taking the output of receptive-field-like image filters and mapping them directly onto a recognition layer (Williams (1997) has developed a similar model that uses individual pixels as input). The weights between the input and output layers effectively code the likelihood of co-occurrence between local features. Thus, the relative positions of features are probabilistic, thereby providing 'flexible' or 'deformable' templates for recognition. Critically, metric variation between a known image of an object and a new image will not be catastrophic–recognition performance will degrade smoothly as the relative positions of features deviate further and further from their associated relations. The fact that the degree of match varies smoothly with changes in the image suggests that models incorporating local features in conjunction with implicit structural information may be compatible with view and class interpolation mechanisms, for instance, by computing the likelihood of each local feature at particular locations within the image (Edelman, 1995b).

The majority of models incorporating local image measurements in neural-network architectures have included only simple mappings between features (Edelman and Weinshall, 1991; Lades et al., 1993; Williams, 1997), e.g. one set of weights between input and output. As such, these implementations are still template models, albeit deformable, in that there is only a one layer description for each shape. One method for increasing the power of this approach is to add compositional structure to the representation (Bienenstock and Geman, 1995). In this framework local image-based features would be organized hierarchically into multiple levels of increasing complexity. For example, highly associated first order relations between image measurements could themselves be associated at the next level. However, in contrast to the reconstruction approach, these assemblies would be based on the statistics of the images shown to the system rather than fixed syntactic constraints.

One appealing aspect of compositionality is that it allows input shapes to be matched to stored representations through randomized tree searches (Amit and Geman, 1997). That is, rather than attempting to match all of the features of the representation during recognition, a series of binary 'queries' are performed. Each of these queries relates the position of one additional feature to the positions of features already queried. Critically, no particular set of features is required for successful identification—queries can begin with almost any feature (more informative features are selected during learning) and can follow many different search paths. Therefore, recognition should be robust over occlusion and other image variations. Equally important is that only a small number queries are likely to be necessary to recognize the input shape (as in the children's '20-questions' game). Thus, recognition should be computationally efficient.

A second appealing aspect of the compositional approach is that it allows for emergent structures at many scales within the image. Thus, more global representational elements, for instance, surfaces or parts, may arise at some level of the hierarchy depending on the co-occurrence of image measurements (Fukushima, 1980; Bienenstock et al., 1997). Indeed, because many image measurements are likely to co-occur repeatedly when one encounters the surfaces of a specific part, it may be possible to capture the part structure of most objects without the need for recovery or deterministic processes. However, such representations are still image-based in that the fundamental units of the representation are measurements of the image from a particular viewing direction—as such they are individually unlikely to remain stable over large changes in viewpoint or other viewing parameters. On the other hand, the inclusion of implicit structural information in the form of compositionality allows for more invariance than would otherwise be possible. To some extent this is precisely the goal of structural-description models (Marr and Nishihara, 1978), and indeed, differences between such models and our extended image-based approach come down to differences in the choice of features and the relations between such features. It is important to note, however, that these choices are critical for how each type of theory accounts for behavioral data.

6.6. Perceptual expertise

Our conjectures to this point have not addressed how the visual system achieves expertise with an object class. Consider the above framework in which object representations are comprised of features for which the spatial positions are more or less strongly related to one another. Two characteristics of this approach indicate that it may help provide an explanation for the phenomenon of perceptual expertise. First, features that co-occur more frequently will become more strongly associated. Second, extensive experience with the same features in a consistent configuration will give rise to more complex features. These simple statistical learning mechanisms offer an explanation for the configural sensitivity found in cases of perceptual expertise, including face recognition (Gauthier and Tarr, 1997a; Tanaka and Sengco, 1997). Consider that the acquisition of expertise is marked by extensive practice differentiating similar instances from within a class. Many class-level features will co-occur in the same configuration with great frequency, for example, the eyes, nose and mouth of human faces. Such oft-seen features will become tightly interdependent as the system is fine tuned by experience. Thus, relocating the position of one such feature will impact the recognition of the other features much as has been found for parts of human faces (Tanaka and Sengco, 1997) and for parts of non-face objects when recognized by experts (Gauthier and Tarr, 1997a). Moreover, because of compositionality, new, more stable configurations of features that have greater discriminatory power may emerge as an observer gains experience discriminating exemplars within a class (Gauthier et al., 1998).

7. Conclusion

Tremendous progress in understanding visual object recognition has been made over the past decade. Models of recognition have become far more computationally sophisticated. New and exciting findings from cognitive neuroscience and neurophysiology have offered insights into the brain mechanisms used during recognition. There has also been an impressive body of behavioral data collected on human recognition performance. Insights from all of these domains suggest that new theories hold great promise for explaining biological object recognition. At the same time, recent work has also illuminated some of the potential pitfalls of these theories. We have identified some of the most notable problems and offer possible solutions. What you will find in this special issue are the ideas of researchers that are working towards this goal, that of understanding visual recognition using a wide range of new methodologies.

Acknowledgements

The authors wish to thank Steven Pinker, Jacques Mehler and Susana Franck for their help and guidance throughout the development of this special issue and Talia Ben-Zeev, Guy Wallis, Chris Christou, John Hummel, and Bosco Tjan for their comments on this paper. This work was supported by a TRANSCOOP grant to MJT and HHB

References

Amit, Y., Geman, D., 1997. Shape quantization and recognition with randomized trees. Neural Computation 9, 1545–1588.

Bartram, D.J., 1976. Levels of coding in picture-picture comparison tasks. Memory and Cognition 4, 593–602.

Beymer, D., Poggio, T., 1996. Image representations for visual learning. Science 272, 1905–1909.

Biederman, I., 1987. Recognition-by-components: a theory of human image understanding. Psychological Review 94, 115–147.

Biederman, I., Gerhardstein, P.C., 1993. Recognizing depth-rotated objects: Evidence and conditions for three-dimensional viewpoint invariance. Journal of Experimental Psychology: Human Perception and Performance 19 (6), 1162–1182.

Biederman, I., Gerhardstein, P.C., 1995. Viewpoint-dependent mechanisms in visual object recognition. Journal of Experimental Psychology: Human Perception and Performance 21 (6), 1506–1514.

Biederman, I., Ju, G., 1988. Surface versus edge-based determinants of visual recognition. Cognitive Psychology 20, 38–64.

Biederman, I., Subramaniam, S., Kalocsai, P., Bar, M., in press. Viewpoint-invariant information in subordinate-level object classification. In: Gopher, D., Koriat, A. (Eds.), Attention and Performance XVII. MIT Press, Cambridge, MA.

Bienenstock, E., Geman, S., 1995. Compositionality in neural systems. In: Arbib, M.A. (Ed.), The Handbook of Brain Theory and Neural Networks. MIT Press, Cambridge, MA, pp. 223–226.

Bienenstock, E., Geman, S., Potter, D., 1997. Compositionality, MDL priors, and object recognition. In: Mozer, M.C., Jordan, M.I. Petsche, T. (Eds.), Advances in Neural Information Processing Systems 9. MIT Press, Cambridge, MA.

Blum, H., 1967. A transformation for extracting new descriptors of shape. In: Wathen-Dunn, W. (Ed.), Models for the Perception of Speech and Visual Form. MIT Press, Cambridge, MA, pp. 362–380.

Bricolo, E., Poggio, T., Logothetis, N.K., 1997. 3D object recognition: A model of view-tuned neurons. In: Mozer, M.C., Jordan, M.I., Petsche, T. (Eds.), Advances in Neural Information Processing Systems 9. MIT Press, Cambridge, MA, pp. 41–47.

Bülthoff, H.H., Edelman, S., 1992. Psychophysical support for a two-dimensional view interpolation theory of object recognition. Proceedings of the National Academy of Sciences of the United States of America 89, 60–64.

Corballis, M.C., Zbrodoff, N.J., Shetzer, L.I., Butler, P.B., 1978. Decisions about identity and orientation of rotated letters and digits. Memory and Cognition 6, 98–107.

Cutzu, F., Tarr, M.J., 1997. The representation of three-dimensional object similarity in human vision. In: SPIE Proceedings from Electronic Imaging: Human Vision and Electronic Imaging II, Vol. 3016. SPIE, San Jose, CA, pp. 460–471.

Edelman, S., 1993. Representing three-dimensional objects by sets of activities of receptive fields. Biological Cybernetics 70, 37–45.

Edelman, S., 1995a. Class similarity and viewpoint invariance in the recognition of 3D objects. Biological Cybernetics 72, 207–220.

Edelman, S., 1995b. Representation, similarity, and the chorus of prototypes. Minds and Machines 5 (1), 45–68.

Edelman, S., Bülthoff, H.H., 1992. Orientation dependence in the recognition of familiar and novel views of three-dimensional objects. Vision Research 32 (12), 2385–2400.

Edelman, S., Weinshall, D., 1991. A self-organizing multiple-view representation of 3D objects. Biological Cybernetics 64, 209–219.

Farah, M.J., 1990. Visual agnosia: disorders of object recognition and what they tell us about normal vision. MIT Press, Cambridge, MA.

Farah, M.J., 1992. Is an object an object an object? Cognitive and neuropsychological investigations of domain-specificity in visual object recognition. Current Directions in Psychological Science 1 (5), 164–169.

Fukushima, K., 1980. Neocognitron: a self-organizing neural network model for a mechanism of pattern recognition unaffected by shift in position. Biological Cybernetics 36, 193–202.

Gauthier, I., 1998. Dissecting face recognition: the role of categorization level and expertise in visual object recognition. Unpublished doctoral dissertation. Yale University.

Gauthier, I., Anderson, A.W., Tarr, M.J., Skudlarski, P., Gore, J.C., 1997. Levels of categorization in visual objects studied with functional MRI. Current Biology 7, 645–651.

Gauthier, I. and Tarr, M.J., 1997a. Becoming a 'Greeble' expert: exploring the face recognition mechanism. Vision Research 37 (12), 1673–1682.

Gauthier, I., Tarr, M.J., 1997b. Orientation priming of novel shapes in the context of viewpoint-dependent recognition. Perception 26, 51–73.

Gauthier, I., Williams, P., Tarr, M.J., and Tanaka, J., 1998. Training 'Greeble' experts: a framework for studying expert object recognition processes. Vision Research, in press.

Goodale, M.A., Milner, A.D., 1992. Separate visual pathways for perception and action. Trends in Neuroscience 15 (1), 20–25.

Hayward, W.G., 1998. Effects of outline shape in object recognition. Journal of Experimental Psychology: Human Perception and Performance, in press.

Hayward, W.G., Tarr, M.J., 1995. Spatial language and spatial representation. Cognition 55, 39–84.

Hayward, W.G., Tarr, M.J., 1997. Testing conditions for viewpoint invariance in object recognition. Journal of Experimental Psychology: Human Perception and Performance 23 (5), 1511–1521.

Hummel, J.E., 1998. Where view-based theories break down: The role of structure in shape perception and object recognition. In: Dietrich, E., Markman, A. (Eds.), Cognitive Dynamics: Conceptual Change in Humans and Machines. MIT Press, Cambridge, MA.

Hummel, J.E., Biederman, I., 1992. Dynamic binding in a neural network for shape recognition. Psychological Review 99 (3), 480–517.

Hummel, J.E., Stankiewicz, B.J., 1996a. Categorical relations in shape perception. Spatial Vision 10, 201–236.

Hummel, J.E., Stankiewicz, B.J., 1996b. An architecture for rapid, hierarchical structural description. In: Inui, T., McClelland, J. (Eds.), Attention and Performance XVI. MIT Press, Cambridge, MA. pp. 93–121.

Humphrey, G.K., Khan, S.C., 1992. Recognizing novel views of three-dimensional objects. Canadian Journal of Psychology 46, 170–190.

Jolicoeur, P., 1985. The time to name disoriented natural objects. Memory and Cognition 13, 289–303.

Jolicoeur, P., 1990. Identification of disoriented objects: A dual-systems theory. Mind and Language 5 (4), 387–410.

Jolicoeur, P., Gluck, M., Kosslyn, S.M., 1984. Pictures and names: making the connection. Cognitive Psychology 243–275.

Kimia, B.B., Tannenbaum, A.R., Zucker, S.W., 1995. Shapes, shocks, and deformations, I: The components of shape and the reaction-diffusion space. International Journal of Computer Vision 15, 189–224.

Koenderink, J.J., 1987. An internal representation for solid shape based on the topological properties of the apparent contour. In: Richards, W., Ullman, S. (Eds.), Image Understanding 1985–86. Ablex, Norwood, NJ, pp. 257–285.

Kosslyn, S.M., 1980. Image and mind. Harvard University Press, Cambridge, MA.

Kovacs, I., Julesz, B., 1994. Perceptual sensitivity maps within globally defined visual shapes. Nature 370, 644–646.

Lades, M., Vorbruggen, J.C., Buhmann, J., Lange, J., von der Malsburg, C., Wurtz, R.P., Konen, W., 1993. Distortion invariant object recognition in the dynamic link architecture. IEEE Transactions on Computers 42, 300–311.

Lando, M., Edelman, S., 1995. Receptive field spaces and class-based generalization from a single view in face recognition. Network 6, 551–576.

Liter, J.C., 1995. Features affecting orientation-invariant recognition of novel objects. Unpublished doctoral dissertation. University of California, Irvine, CA.

Logothetis, N.K., Pauls, J., Poggio, T., 1995. Shape representation in the inferior temporal cortex of monkeys. Current Biology 5 (5), 552–563.

Marr, D., (1982). Vision: a computational investigation into the human representation and processing of visual information. Freeman, San Francisco, CA.

Marr, D., Nishihara, H.K., 1978. Representation and recognition of the spatial organization of three-dimensional shapes. Proceedings of the Royal Society of London B 200, 269–294.

Marsolek, C.J., Burgund, E.D., 1997. Computational analyses and hemispheric asymmetries in visual-form recognition. In: Christman, S. (Ed.), Cerebral Asymmetries in Sensory and Perceptual Processing. Elsevier, Amsterdam, pp. 125–158.

Miyashita, Y., 1993. Inferior temporal cortex: where visual perception meets memory. Annual Review of Neuroscience 16, 245–263.

Moses, Y., Ullman, S., Edelman, S., 1996. Generalization to novel images in upright and inverted faces. Perception 25, 443–462.

Nalwa, V.S., 1993. A guided tour of computer vision. Addison-Wesley, Reading, MA.

Perrett, D.I., Mistlin, A.J., Chitty, A.J., 1987. Visual neurones responsive to faces. Trends in Neuroscience 10 (96), 358–364.

Perrett, D.I., Oram, M.W., Ashbridge, E., 1998. Evidence accumulation in cell populations responsive to faces: an account of generalisation of recognition without mental transformations. Cognition 67, 111–145.

Pinker, S., 1984a. Visual cognition. Cognition 18.

Pinker, S., 1984b. Visual cognition: An introduction. Cognition 18, 1–63.

Poggio, T., Edelman, S., 1990. A network that learns to recognize three-dimensional objects. Nature 343, 263–266.

Quinn, P.C., Eimas, P.D., Rosenkrantz, S.L., 1993. Evidence for representations of perceptually similar natural categories by 3-month-old and 4-month-old infants. Perception 22, 463–475.

Riesenhuber, M., Poggio, T., 1998. Just one view: invariances in inferotemporal cell tuning. In: Advances in Neural Information Processing Systems 10. MIT Press, Cambridge, MA, in press.

Rosch, E., Mervis, C.B., Gray, W.D., Johnson, D.M., Boyes-Braem, P., 1976. Basic objects in natural categories. Cognitive Psychology 8, 382–439.

Schyns, P.G., 1998. Diagnostic recognition: task constraints, object formation and their interactions. Cognition 67, 147–179.

Stankiewicz, B.J., Hummel, J.E., Cooper, E.E., 1998. The role of attention in priming for left-right reflections of object images. Journal of Experimental Psychology: Human Perception and Performance, in press.

Suzuki, S., Peterson, M.A., Moscovitch, M., Behrmann, M., 1997. Viewpoint specificity in the identification of simple volumetric objects (geons) is evident in control subjects and very exaggerated in visual object agnosia. Cognitive Neuroscience Society, Boston, MA.

Tanaka, J.W., Sengco, J.A., 1997. Features and their configuration in face recognition. Memory and Cognition 25 (5), 583–592.

Tanaka, K., 1996. Inferotemporal cortex and object vision. Annual Review of Neuroscience 19, 109–139.

Tarr, M.J., 1995. Rotating objects to recognize them: a case study of the role of viewpoint dependency in the recognition of three-dimensional objects. Psychonomic Bulletin and Review 2 (1), 55–82.

Tarr, M.J., Bülthoff, H.H., 1995. Is human object recognition better described by geon-structural-descrip-

tions or by multiple-views?. Journal of Experimental Psychology: Human Perception and
Performance 21 (6), 1494–1505.

Tarr, M.J., Gauthier, I., 1998. Do viewpoint–dependent mechanisms generalize across members of a
class? Cognition 67, 71–109.

Tarr, M.J., Bülthoff, H.H., Zabinski, M., Blanz, V., 1997. To what extent do unique parts influence
recognition across changes in viewpoint?. Psychological Science 8 (4), 282–289.

Tarr, M.J., Pinker, S., 1989. Mental rotation and orientation-dependence in shape recognition. Cognitive
Psychology 21 (28), 233–282.

Tarr, M.J., Pinker, S., 1990. When does human object recognition use a viewer-centered reference frame?.
Psychological Science 1 (42), 253–256.

Tarr, M.J., Williams, P., Hayward, W.G., Gauthier, I., 1998. Three-dimensional object recognition is
viewpoint-dependent. Nature Neuroscience 1.

Ullman, S., 1989. Aligning pictorial descriptions: an approach to object recognition. Cognition 32, 193–
254.

Ullman, S., 1996. High-level vision. The MIT Press, Cambridge, MA.

Ullman, S., 1998. Three-dimensional object recognition based on the combination of views. Cognition 67,
21–44.

Ullman, S., Basri, R., 1991. Recognition by linear combinations of models. IEEE Transactions on Pattern
Analysis and Machine Intelligence 13 (10), 992–1006.

Wallis, G., 1996a. How neurons learn to associate 2D-views in invariant object recognition (Tech. Rep.
No. 37). Max-Planck Institut für Biologische Kybernetik, Tübingen, Germany.

Wallis, G., 1996b. Presentation order affects human object recognition learning (Tech. Rep. No. 36).
Max-Planck Institut für Biologische Kybernetik, Tübingen, Germany.

Williams, P., 1997. Prototypes, exemplars, and object recognition. Unpublished doctoral dissertation,
Yale University.

Zhu, S.C., Yuille, A.L., 1996. FORMS: a flexible object recognition and modeling system. International
Journal of Computer Vision 20 (3), 187–212.

2

Three-dimensional object recognition based on the combination of views

Shimon Ullman*

Weizmann Institute of Science, Department of Applied Mathematics and Computer Science, POB 26, 76100 Rehovot, Israel

Abstract

   Visual object recognition is complicated by the fact that the same 3D object can give rise to a large variety of projected images that depend on the viewing conditions, such as viewing direction, distance, and illumination. This paper describes a computational approach that uses combinations of a small number of object views to deal with the effects of viewing direction. The first part of the paper is an overview of the approach based on previous work. It is then shown that, in agreement with psychophysical evidence, the view-combinations approach can use views of different class members rather than multiple views of a single object, to obtain class-based generalization. A number of extensions to the basic scheme are considered, including the use of non-linear combinations, using 3D versus 2D information, and the role of coarse classification on the way to precise identification. Finally, psychophysical and biological aspects of the view-combination approach are discussed. Compared with approaches that treat object recognition as a symbolic high-level activity, in the view-combination approach the emphasis is on processes that are simpler and pictorial in nature. © 1998 Elsevier Science B.V. All rights reserved

Keywords: Three-dimensional object recognition; View combinations; Classification

1. Recognition and the variability of object views

   For biological visual systems, visual object recognition is a spontaneous, natural activity. In contrast, the recognition of common objects is still beyond the capabilities of current computer vision systems. In this paper I will examine certain aspects of the recognition problem and outline an approach to recognition based on the

* Tel.: +972 8 9343545; fax: +972 8 9342945; e-mail: shimon@wisdom.weizmann.ac.il

combination of object views. The discussion of the recognition problem will be limited in a number of ways. In particular, it will focus on shape-based recognition, and it will consider primarily object identification rather than classification. In general, objects can be recognized not only by their shape, but also based on other visual cues, such as color, texture, characteristic motion, their location relative to other objects in the scene, context information, and expectation. Here, I will focus on the recognition of isolated objects, using shape information alone.

Why is visual recognition difficult? It may appear that the problem could be approached by using a sufficiently large and efficient memory system. In performing recognition, we are trying to determine whether an image we currently see corresponds to an object we have seen in the past. It might be possible, therefore, to approach object recognition by storing a sufficient number of different views associated with each object, and then comparing the image of the currently viewed object with all the views stored in memory (Abu-Mostafa and Psaltis, 1987). Models of so-called associative memories have been proposed for implementing this 'direct' approach to recognition (Willshaw et al., 1969; Kohonen, 1978; Hopfield, 1982).

Although direct comparison to stored views can play a useful role, especially for the recognition of highly familiar objects, this direct approach by itself is insufficient for recognition in general. One reason is that the space of all possible views of all the objects to be recognized is likely to be prohibitively large. A second, and more fundamental reason, is the problem of generalization, that is, recognizing an object under novel viewing conditions. Object views are highly variable and depend on the viewing direction and distance, the effects of illumination direction, shadowing and highlights, partial occlusion by other objects, and possible changes and distortions in the object itself. As a result, the image to be recognized will often not be sufficiently similar to any image seen in the past.

1.1. An empirical comparison of intra- and inter-object variability

The effects of these sources of variation, in particular, viewing position and illumination direction, were evaluated quantitatively in the domain of face images (Adini et al., 1997). In the study, twenty-six different individuals were imaged from a number of viewing directions and under different illumination conditions. The goal was to compare images of different individuals, with images of the same individual but under different viewing conditions. In this manner, it becomes possible to examine whether the differences induced by mere changes in the viewing conditions are large or small compared with the differences between distinct individuals. The images used were of males, with no glasses, beards, etc., and with the hairline covered, taken under five viewing conditions. The first was from a frontal view, with left illumination (45°), and neutral expression. The other four differed from the first by changing either the illumination (45° right), the viewing direction (17° to the right), or the facial expression. The different images were taken by moving a robotic arm with a TV camera to different locations in space.

To compare the different images, one needs to define a measure of similarity. The study employed a number of commonly used measures for comparing images. The simplest measure used the average absolute difference between the image intensity levels of corresponding points. The face images were normalized in size, orientation, and position, before this measure was computed. A more flexible measure allowed local distortions between the two images: the image intensity value at a given point was compared not only to a single corresponding location in the second image, but to all the points within a given neighborhood, and the best-matching value within this neighborhood was selected. The computation of image differences also included compensation for changes in overall intensity level and linear intensity gradients, so that the difference measure became insensitive to these global parameters. Another type of difference measure used transformed versions of the images, obtained by applying to the images various filters, such as difference-of-gaussians, (DOG) filters (Marr and Hildreth, 1980), Gabor filters (Daugman, 1989), and using directional derivatives of the gray level images (Koenderink and Van Doorn, 1990). Filtering of this kind appears to take place in the early processing stages of the mammalian visual system, and it is also often used in artificial image processing systems. Finally, images were also compared by first obtaining an edge map from each image, and then comparing the resulting contour maps. The use of such edge maps is also a standard procedure in image processing, partly because they are less sensitive to illumination conditions than the original gray-level images. For each of the different measures, comparisons were made between the full face images, but also between partial face images, such as the upper or lower parts.

The main result that emerged from these comparisons is that the differences induced by changes in the viewing conditions are large compared with the differences between different individuals. An example is illustrated in Table 1 (after Moses, 1993), comparing the effects of changes in illumination and in viewing direction, with differences between individuals, for 11 different faces (F_1–F_{11}).

Table 1
Distances between face images

FC	IC	VP	Pairs of faces										
			F1	F2	F3	F4	F5	F6	F7	F8	F9	F10	F11
F1	59	25		21	25	26	24	39	25	22	23	22	17
F2	56	23			16	18	27	25	16	14	16	15	21
F3	56	26				17	27	27	14	15	20	16	34
F4	58	27					26	26	18	18	20	20	26
F5	54	30						38	29	26	23	15	15
F6	50	25							26	28	25	24	40
F7	57	30								17	20	17	23
F8	51	23									18	17	22
F9	54	24										7	25
F10	53	21											23
F11	57	25											

Larger values indicate increased dissimilarity, for units see text. Column FC lists 11 different faces. IC, distances between images of the same face, but under different illumination; VP, distances between images of the same face taken from frontal and 17° side view; 'pairs of faces', distances between all 11 face pairs.

Each face is compared to an image of the same face under a different illumination (first column, marked 'IC', for illumination condition), to an image of the same face viewed from a different direction (17° change in direction, column marked 'VP', for viewing position), and then to ten other faces viewed under the original viewing conditions. For example, for the first face, F_1, a change in illumination induced a difference measure of 59 units between the two images, and for a change in viewing direction the difference measure was 25 units. (Units are the average difference between normalized gray level images, other measures were also used, as discussed below.) When this face image was compared with another face image, F_2, the difference measure was 21 units. This means that the changes induced by variations in the viewing conditions were larger than the difference between the two individuals. In fact, for eight out of the ten face images, the differences due to viewing conditions were the same or larger than the differences between distinct individuals.

One conclusion from these comparisons is that in this domain recognition based on direct view-comparisons will result in severely limited generalization to viewing direction and illumination. Suppose, for example, that we attempt to identify the faces of just the limited set of 26 individuals in the study by comparing an input image to a set of 26 images, one for each face, stored in memory, and then selecting the stored image that most closely resembles the input image. The results show that such a scheme will be highly inadequate: for the images in the face database, the wrong answer will often be selected. For the best performing comparison scheme (of a total of 107 tested) the error rates were above 20% for illumination changes and about 50% for changes in viewing direction. These results were also compared with the performance of the human visual system, using the same as well as additional test images (Moses et al., 1996). It was found that the variations tested in the study, as well as larger ones (up to 51° in viewing positions) were easily compensated for by human observers.

Similar results were reached in a study by Liu et al. (1995). The study, described in Section 5 below, also concluded that generalization to novel views cannot be explained in terms of independent comparisons to stored views.

Taken together, these results indicate that the differences induced by changes in the viewing conditions are large compared with the differences between different individuals, and that direct image comparisons, even in combination with the pre-normalization used for size, orientation, position, and intensity level, are not sufficient for recognition. To obtain reliable recognition, some processes that can compensate for the effects of viewing conditions are required. The nature of these processes is a fundamental problem in the study of visual recognition. A review of the main approaches to this problem, including the use of invariances and the construction of object-centered structural description can be found in (Ullman, 1989, 1996). In this paper I will focus on an approach that compensates for the effects of viewing directions by comparing the novel image with certain combinations of previously stored views. The approach is somewhat similar to the direct comparison scheme in that it is based on the comparison of picture-like representations. However, by using previously stored views not independently but in certain combinations, significant generalization across viewing direction can be obtained.

The discussion will focus on theoretical aspects of the scheme. Psychophysical and physiological aspects of this approach are reviewed in Section 5.

2. The combination of object views

2.1. The view-combination property

In many recognition theories it is assumed that the visual system somehow stores and manipulates 3D object models (Biederman, 1985; Lowe, 1985; Ullman, 1989). When confronted with a novel 2D image of the object, the system deduces whether it is a possible view of one of the already stored 3D objects. In contrast, the method outlined in this section does not use explicit 3D models. Instead, it uses small collections of object views directly, without the need to explicitly recover and represent the 3D structure of objects.

In this approach, a 3D object is represented by the linear combination of 2D views of the object. If $M = M_1,\ldots,M_k$ is the set of views representing a given object, and P is the 2D image of an object to be recognized, then P is considered an instance of M if

$$P = \sum_{i=1}^{k} \alpha_i M_i$$

for some constants α_i.

The linear combination of views has the following meaning. Suppose that (x_i, y_i), (x_i', y_i'), (x_i'', y_i'') are the coordinates of corresponding points (i.e. points in the image that arise from the same point on the object) in three different views. Let X_1, X_2, X_3, be the vectors of x-coordinates of the points in the three views. Suppose that we are now confronted with a new image, and X' is the vector of the x-coordinates of the points in this new view. If X' arises from the same object represented by the original three views, then it will be possible to express X' as the linear combination of X_1, X_2, X_3. That is, $X' = a_1X_1 + a_2X_2 + a_3X_3$ for some constants a_1, a_2, a_3. Similarly, for the y-coordinates, $Y' = b_1Y_1 + b_2Y_2 + b_3Y_3$ for some constants b_1, b_2, b_3. In general, different coefficients will be required for the x and y components, and therefore the total number of coefficients is six. In more pictorial terms, we can imagine that each of the three points x_i, x_i', x_i'' has a mass associated with it. The mass at x_i, x_i', x_i'' is a_1, a_2, a_3, respectively (the same weights are used for all triplets). The linear combination of the points is now their center of mass. The linear combination property is expressed by the following mathematical statement: all possible views of a rigid object that can undergo rotation in space, translation, and scaling, are spanned by the linear combinations of three views of the object.

The proposition assumes orthographic projection and objects with sharp bounding contours. For objects with smooth bounding contours, the number of views required is five rather than three. Objects with smooth bounding contours, such as an egg or a football, require more views because the object's silhouette is not generated by fixed contours on the object. The bounding contours generating the silhouette move continuously on the object as the viewing position changes. Finally, it should be noted that, due to self occlusion, three views are insufficient for representing an object from all orientations. That is, a different set of views will be required to represent, e.g. the 'front' and the 'back' of the same object. For a proof of the proposition and further details of its implications see Ullman and Basri (1991).

Fig. 1 shows an example of using linear combinations of views to compensate for changes in viewing direction. Fig. 1a shows three different views of a car (a VW). The figure shows only those edges that were extracted in all three views; as a result, some of the edges are missing. This illustrates that reliable identification can be obtained on the basis of partial image data (as may happen due to noise and partial occlusion). Fig. 1b shows two new views of the VW car. These new images were not obtained from novel views of the car, but were generated by using linear combinations of the first three views. Fig. 1c shows two new views of the VW, obtained from new viewing positions. Fig. 1d superimposes these new views and the linear combinations obtained in Fig. 1c. It can be seen that the novel views are matched well by linear combinations of the three original views. For comparison, Fig. 1e shows the superposition of a different, but similar car (a Saab), with the best matching linear combinations of the VW images. As expected, the match is not as good. This illustrates that the linear combination method can be used to make fine distinctions between similar 3D objects in novel viewing directions. Although the two objects being compared have complex 3D shapes, and are quite similar, they were reliably discriminable by the view-combination method within the entire 60° rotation range. To represent the object from a wider range of viewing directions a number of different models of this type will be required. This notion is similar to the use of different object aspects suggested by Koenderink and Van Doorn (1979). It is worth noting that although the objects in this example are quite similar in shape, recognizing them reliably over a large range of viewing directions is a task mastered easily by human observers.

Fig. 2 shows another example of a view combination, applied to a gray-scale image. The two images in the top row are two input images of the same individual from different viewing directions. The bottom row shows two images produced by the view-combination method, depicting the same individual from different viewing directions. One is an intermediate view, between the two original viewing directions, the other is an extrapolation beyond the range spanned by the original views. The gray levels in the combined images were taken as the average of the corresponding points in the original views, for a detailed discussion of combining views containing gray-level information see Shashua (1992).

2.2. Using two views only

A novel object view was expressed in the scheme described above as the linear combination of three fixed views of the object. The three views are necessary if the transformations that the object is allowed to undergo are restricted to rigid transformations. In this case, the coefficients of the view combination are required to satisfy certain functional constraints that can be tested to verify whether the object trans-

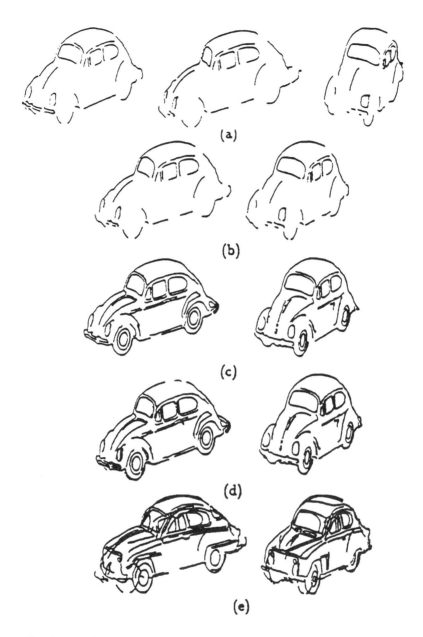

Fig. 1. Using view-combination to match a novel view. (a) Three model pictures of a VW car for ± 30° rotations around the vertical axis. Only a subset of the edges were used in the model. (b) Two linear combinations of the VW model. These are generated artificially by combinations of the first three views, rather than actual views. (c) Real novel images of the car. (d) Matching the linear combinations to the real images. The agreement is good within the entire range of ± 30°. (e) Matching the VW model to pictures of a similar car (Saab). (From Ullman and Basri, 1991; ©IEEE.)

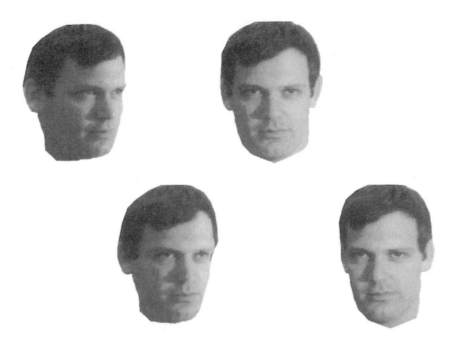

Fig. 2. A view-combination of gray level face images. On the top row are the two basic images. Bottom row: two view combinations, depicting the same person from new viewing directions. Left: an interpolated view. Right: an extrapolated view, beyond the range spanned by the original views.

formation was indeed rigid (Ullman and Basri, 1991). It is natural to consider also a more general case, in which objects are allowed to undergo more general distortions, for example, some stretch along one dimension. For general linear transformations of the object, it turns out that it becomes possible to use just two views of the object. (This observation was also made independently by T. Poggio.) Unlike the three-views formulation, this two-views formulation uses a mixture of x and y coordinates. This combination is somewhat less intuitive than the combination of three views, but the use of only two rather than three views is sometimes more convenient.

Mathematically, this combination has the following form. Let $\mathbf{x}_1$ be the vector of all the x coordinates of the points in the first view, $\mathbf{x}_2$ in the second, and $\hat{x}$ in the novel view; $\mathbf{y}_1$ is the vector of y coordinates in the first view. Then:

$$\hat{x} = a_1 x_1 + a_2 y_1 + a_3 x_2 \tag{1}$$

For any novel view of the same object (subject to the usual self-occlusion limitations), the set of new coordinates x is the linear combination of corresponding coordinates in the first two views. The y coordinates can be expressed in a similar manner:

$$\hat{y} = b_1 x_1 + b_2 y_1 + b_3 x_2 \tag{2}$$

In this version the basis vectors are the same for the x and y coordinates, and they are obtained from two rather than three views.

2.2.1. *A single view of a symmetric object*

In reducing the number of base images, it is possible under some conditions to take a further step, and perform image combination based on a single view. This extension was developed by Vetter et al. (1994) for the class of bilaterally symmetric objects. One intuitive way of looking at this special case of symmetric objects is by considering the two symmetric halves of the object as two distinct views of a single part. Under the assumptions discussed in the previous section (orthographic projections, affine object transformations), two views are sufficient to recognize the object in question.

Vetter et al. (1994) have shown that for human observers the recognition of symmetric 3D objects from a single training view is indeed better than for non-symmetric objects. For the symmetric objects, the experiments showed a broader generalization, that is, observers recognized the symmetric test objects correctly over a wider range of rotations.

2.3. *Using view-combinations for recognition*

A straightforward way of using the linear combination method in practice is to recover the coefficients of the combination, then use these coefficients to produce a new model image and compare it with the input image. One method of recovering the unknown coefficient is by using a small number of matching image and model features. For example, by using three corresponding features points in the image and the model, the coefficients can be recovered uniquely by solving linear equations (two simple systems of three unknowns each, for the x and y components). Mathematically, the procedure is the following. Let X be the matrix of the x-coordinates of the alignment points in the model. That is, x_{ij} is the x-coordinate of the jth point in the ith model picture. $\mathbf{p}x$ is the vector of x-coordinates of the alignment points in the image, and $\mathbf{a}$ is the vector of unknown combination parameters we wish to recover. The linear system to be solved is then simply $X\mathbf{a} = \mathbf{p}_x$. The combination parameters are given by $\mathbf{a} = X^{-1}\mathbf{p}x$ if an exact solution exists. We may use an overdetermined system (by using additional points), in which case $\mathbf{a} = X^{+}\mathbf{p}x$ (where X^{+} denotes the pseudo-inverse of X, (Albert, 1972)). A similar procedure is used to recover the coefficients in the Y direction. A convenient property of the scheme is that the matrix X^{+} used to derive the unknown coefficients does not depend on the image and can therefore be pre-computed and stored for a given model. Future recovery of the coefficients simply requires only a multiplication of $\mathbf{p}_x$ by the stored matrix. Using the recovered coefficients, an internal combined image will be generated and compared with the viewed object.

This scheme is simple and efficient for an artificial recognition system. However, for a biological system, it may not be straightforward to implement the required processes, such as the matching of corresponding features, solving for the coefficients, or using them for generating internal images. There are alternative ways in which the view-combination property can be used in the recognition process that I will mention here only briefly.

One possibility is to use an iterative method that starts with one of the stored images and successively refines it by combining it with additional images (Lipson, 1993). This method requires only approximate contour matches rather than precise pointwise matches between corresponding features.

An alternative approach is to use a 'correspondence-less' scheme that does not rely on matching image and model features. This can be done by performing a search in the space of possible coefficients. In this method, we first choose some initial values for the set of coefficients, and then apply a linear combination to the model using these values. We repeat this process using a different set of coefficients, and finally choose the coefficient values that produced the best match of the model to the image. The search can be guided by an optimization procedure, by measuring the residual discrepancy between the model and viewed image, and using minimization techniques to reduce this error. This procedure is similar to the approach taken by the deformable template method (Yuille and Hallinan, 1992). The advantage of the search approach is that it does not rely on the establishment of feature correspondence between the image and a stored model. The main disadvantage is that the search will typically require the generation and comparison of multiple internal patterns. In computational experiments with this scheme (Ullman and Zeira, 1997),a total of several hundred intermediate patterns were generated in the course of the recognition processes. For a biological system, performing in parallel multiple pattern comparisons may have an advantage over the explicit recovery of the transformation parameters. These considerations have discussed in more detail previously (Ullman, 1995, 1996).

2.4. Adding abstract descriptions

In the discussion so far we have treated object views in a simplified form. Object models consisted of image contours and similar features, without defining larger structures such as object parts, as used in the structural description approach to recognition (Biederman, 1985),or using abstract descriptions, as in the invariant properties approach (Ullman, 1989; Mundy and Zisserman, 1992). It is possible, however, to combine the main advantages of the part decomposition and invariant properties approaches with the view-combination approach. The resulting scheme is likely to be more suitable for recognizing objects that cannot be handled easily by the simpler method alone.

To illustrate how abstract descriptions might be used, suppose that one is trying to recognize a familiar person with characteristic curly hair. In matching the novel view with a previously stored model, the contours comprising the hair region are not expected to match in detail. However, the corresponding regions in the model and the image are expected to have similar textural properties. To compare the image and model at a more abstract level, one can imagine a region descriptor, or 'label', describing, for example, texture and color properties, being overlaid over the hair region. This description is abstract in the sense that it is less specific than the original image itself; many different images will map onto the single label ('curly' in this case). When the internal model is manipulated and compared with the viewed object, the detailed internal contours in the two will not be in close agreement, but they will both have the same label in corresponding locations. Abstractions of this type can describe properties of 2D contours, but may also be 3D in nature, such as convex or concave regions. It appears that the inclusion of multiple levels of abstraction is an important future direction, that will make view-based schemes more flexible and robust.

3. Class-based view combinations

In the discussion above we have seen how novel views of an object can be recognized by combinations of a number of representative views. Although the view-combination scheme allows a small number of stored views to deal with a large range of novel viewing directions, it still requires, for each individual object, a sufficient number of representative views. In contrast, it appears that the human visual system can obtain substantial generalization on the basis of a single view of a novel object. Single-view generalization can sometimes be based on the presence of a distinctive feature, such as a scar or birthmark on a face. It appears, however, that significant generalization from a single view can be obtained even in the absence of such distinctive features. For example, a study by Moses et al. (1996), examined the ability of human observers to generalize in face recognition to novel viewing directions and illumination conditions on the basis of a single example view. In this study, subjects were presented with a single image of each of a number (three or more) of individuals. They were later tested with additional images of the same individuals, but under novel viewing conditions. The results showed almost error-free recognition across wide changes in viewing direction (51°) and illumination conditions (e.g. left vs. right). Generalization was also tested for inverted face images. Recognition of inverted faces is known to be more difficult than of upright faces. In this study, however, the focus was not on the overall difficulty of the task, but on the ability to generalize from one view to another. It turned out that for inverted faces, even after training that made the training images easily recognizable and without error, generalization from a single view to novel conditions was limited.

Generalization from a single view was also examined in a study by Tarr and Gauthier (1998) using a set of artificial objects. Subjects were trained with multiple views of several similar objects. A novel object from the same general class was shown under a single viewing direction, but tested with different views. They found that the training objects, even a single similar object, could facilitate the recognition of the novel object under the new viewing directions.

At an intuitive level, the results are perhaps not surprising. For example, observers have seen in the past many different face images. Upon seeing a novel face image illuminated from the right, say, the visual system might be able to use its past experience to deal with the same face, only illuminated from the left. The question then arises as to how prior experience with different objects in the same general class might be used to facilitate the recognition of new individual members of the class.

Within the view-combination approach, such class-based generalization can be obtained by using views of different objects instead of different views of the same single object. Mathematically, the main process proceeds as follows (for a fuller description see Beymer and Poggio (1995) and Sali and Ullman (1998)).

Suppose that we have seen a number of objects, such as faces, where each of the objects is seen under two different viewing conditions, that we will call 'frontal' and 'non-frontal'. Let $V_1,...,V_k$ be the frontal views and $U_1,...,U_k$ the corresponding non-frontal views. We now have a single frontal view V' of a novel object, and we wish to predict U', the appearance of the novel object in the non-frontal view, based on its single view as well as the views of the other objects. We start by approximating the novel frontal view as a combination of the frontal views of the other k objects:

$$V' = \Sigma a_i V_i + \Delta \tag{3}$$

V_i are the k known views, a_i are the coefficients of the combination that are chosen to obtain the closest possible approximation to the novel view. The quantity Δ is the residual error that can be significant, especially if the number of examples used is small. To predict the new appearance U' we express it as a combination of the non-frontal views U_i with the same coefficients a_i (Beymer and Poggio, 1995) and the same residual Δ (Sali and Ullman, 1998):

$$U' = \Sigma a_i U_i + \Delta \tag{4}$$

This process can be used to obtain class-based generalization to changes in viewing direction as well as illumination changes. An example is shown in Fig. 3, depicting the result of this process applied to a novel face image on the basis of known face images. In this example, generalization to a new viewing direction is obtained from a single image of the novel object on the basis of three other objects in the same class.

In most approaches to recognition, generalization is obtained based on information associated with a single object. For example, in the view-combination approach, different views of the same object are combined to deal with novel views of the object in question. Similarly, in the structural descriptions approach, an object description is constructed for a given object, independent of the descriptions of similar objects. The discussion above illustrates that generalization in recognition can be class-based rather than object-based. Computationally, class-based schemes provide means for dealing with novel objects by using past experience with similar objects. Psychophysically, it appears that such processes play an important role in human object recognition. It seems, therefore, that class-based recognition is an important direction for further study in both the theoretical and the empirical studies of visual object recognition.

4. Extensions to the basic scheme

The image combination scheme outlined above is restricted in a number of ways, and it will be of interest to extend it in several directions. One attractive extension that will not be considered here is the use of object parts and partial views. The scheme discussed so far used views of the entire objects. It may be advantageous,

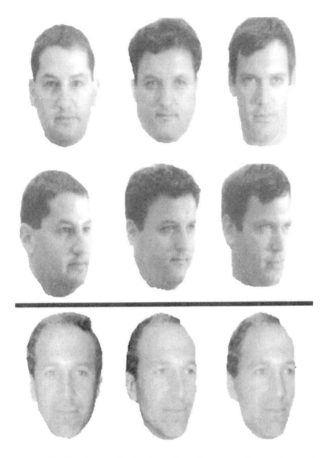

Fig. 3. Class-based generalization from a single view. Three face examples are shown above the horizontal line, in both frontal and side views. Below the line: a novel face, frontal view (left), a non-frontal view generated from the three examples and the frontal view (right). The view in the center is an actual side view, for comparison.

however, to use in a similar manner views covering only parts of the objects. Another important issue is the problem of model selection. The discussion so far has assumed that a candidate model has been selected, and the scheme evaluates the agreement between this selected model and the viewed object. If many object models are stored in memory, do we have to examine all of them in this manner, or can we somehow focus on a smaller number of potential models? Other issues include non-orthographic image views, non-linear image combinations, and dealing effectively with occlusion. This section contains a brief discussion of recent progress and future directions in these areas.

4.1. Perspective projections

The scheme as presented assumes rigid transformations and an orthographic projection. Under these conditions, all the views of a given object are embedded in a low-dimensional linear subspace of a much larger space. What happens if the projection is perspective rather than orthographic, or if the transformations are not entirely rigid?

The effect of perspectivity appears to be quite limited. Ullman and Basri (1991) applied the linear combination scheme to objects with a ratio of distance-to-camera to object-size down to 4:1, with only minor effects on the results. Instead of using the mathematically convenient approximation of orthographic projection it is also possible to perform image combination directly using perspective views. The view-combination scheme provides a method for predicting a new view of an object based on a model constructed from two or more corresponding views. Shashua (1995) developed a similar method for perspective views. The direct use of perspective views increases the accuracy of the reconstruction, but a larger set of corresponding features (seven or more) is required.

4.2. Non-linear image combinations

As for non-rigid transformations and other possible distortions, an interesting general extension to consider is where the set of views is no longer a linear subspace, but still occupies a low-dimensional manifold within a much higher-dimensional space. This manifold resembles locally a linear subspace, but it is no longer 'globally straight'. By analogy, one can visualize the simple linear combinations case in terms of a 3D space, in which all the orthographic views of a rigid object are restricted to some 2D plane. In the more general case, the plane will bend, to become a curved 2D surface within the 3D space.

This issue of dealing effectively with lower-dimensional subspaces appears to be a general case of interest for recognition as well as for other learning tasks. The general reason can be explained by the following consideration. For recognition to be feasible, the set of views {V} corresponding to a given object cannot be arbitrary, but must obey some constraints, that may be expressed in general in the form $F(V_i) = 0$. Under general conditions, these restrictions will define locally a manifold embedded in the larger space (as implied by the implicit function theorem). Algorithms that can learn to classify efficiently sets that form low-dimensional manifolds embedded in high-dimensional spaces will therefore be of general value.

An elegant approach that can use general, non-linear combination of images, is the radial basis functions (RBF) method, developed by Poggio and his collaborators (Poggio and Edelman, 1990; Poggio and Girosi, 1990). This method uses non-linear interpolation between 2D images for the purpose of recognizing 3D objects, as well as for other tasks that involve learning from examples.

4.3. Occlusion

The problem of occlusion is an important issue in any theory of visual recognition. The recognition process must be able to deal with incomplete data, and to distinguish between two sources of image-to-model mismatch: an incomplete match that results from occlusion, and mismatches that indicate the use of an inappropriate model.

In the view-combination scheme, combined views consist of object points that are visible in the generating views. Problems may arise, therefore, either because of self-occlusions (when object points are occluded from view by the object itself), or because of occlusion by other objects.

The problem of self-occlusion is handled in the view-combination approach by representing an object not by a single model, but by a number of models covering its different 'aspects' (Koenderink and Van Doorn, 1979). To cover the object completely, the main mathematical requirements are that each object point will be visible from at least two views, and, roughly, that each view will have at least four points in common (and with known correspondence) with two or more views. The overall number of required views is not fixed, but depends on the object. In practice, it was found that to distinguish between similar car models, for example, typically ten views or fewer were sufficient.

As for occlusion by other objects, the method is somewhat less sensitive to this problem than other methods such as the use of invariants or structural descriptions. In the simplest version of using view combinations, a small number of corresponding features are used to recover the coefficients of the combination. Occlusion will not present a major difficulty to this method, provided that the visible part of the object is sufficient for obtaining correspondence and thus for recovering the required coefficients. After performing the view combination, a good match will be obtained between the transformed model and the visible part of the object. The search method mentioned above is the least affected by occlusion. When the correct parameters are reached, a good match will be obtained between the model and the unoccluded part of the object.

To deal effectively with occlusion, the matching function used by the scheme must be able to distinguish between two different cases of a partial match between the image and the model. Occlusion results in a close match, restricted to a part of the object. The use of an inappropriate model can lead to some moderate agreement over a large portion of the object. A close agreement over a sufficient part of the object should therefore provide a stronger indication for the presence of an object than an inaccurate match spread over a larger region.

4.4. Multiple models and the role of classification

Objects can be recognized at different levels of specificity. Sometimes they are assigned to a general class, such as a 'house', 'dog', 'face' – classes that contain a variety of objects, of many different shapes. Objects can also be identified as unique individuals, such as someone's house, or a particular friend's face.

The scheme considered so far was aimed primarily at object identification. The image combination scheme can distinguish well between individual objects, such as two cars that have closely similar shapes. It will have a harder time, however, classifying a new car, whose shape is not yet represented in the system.

Classification is an important problem in its own right. It is clearly useful to be able to classify a novel object as a car, or a person, and so on, even if we have not seen the particular individual before. The ability to recognize objects at different levels of generality is therefore an important aspect of recognition.

From the point of view of individual identification, classification can also serve a useful role, particularly in dealing with large collections of stored objects. Classification can be used on the way to more specific identification in a number of ways. First, classification can reduce the number of candidate object models. The view-combination scheme discussed above assumed that a candidate object model has been selected, and the task of the recognition system is then to compare the internal model with a novel view of the object. When the number of object models is large, it becomes desirable to reduce the number of candidate models and allow the system to focus on the more likely object models. Classification can be useful in this process, by directing subsequent processing to a restricted class of models. If the image can be classified, for example, as representing a face, without identifying the individual face, then subsequent processing stages can be restricted to face models, ignoring models of other 3D objects.

Classification can also allow the recognition system to use class-specific information in the recognition process. Different classes of objects can undergo some characteristic transformations, for example, faces can be transformed by facial expressions, that are specific to this class of objects. Following classification, information regarding the relevant set of transformations can be used for the recognition of a specific individual within the class. Finally, as we have seen in the discussion of class-based view combinations, classification can help to generalize from limited object-specific information.

Classification is therefore a useful intermediate stage within a recognition system on the way to more specific identification. It restricts the set of candidate models, allows the use of class-specific information, and makes it possible to perform broader generalization by supplementing object-specific information with class-based information. It appears that the problems of general classification – how it is performed, and how it is related to more specific identification – will be important issues in the study of visual recognition in the future. It also remains to be seen whether classification can be performed by view-based methods, or whether more abstract approaches, such as the use of structural descriptions, are required for this task.

5. Psychophysical and physiological aspects

In this section I review briefly psychophysical and physiological findings that are relevant to view-based recognition. The psychological and biological study of object recognition is not an easy task, because recognition is likely to involve a range of different and interacting processes. In an empirical setting, one can bias the recognition process to use different routes, by using different recognition tasks. For example, if in a recognition test one of the objects has a unique distinctive feature, this feature will often be used to distinguish it from other objects (Eley, 1982; Murray et al., 1993). Similarly, the distinction between a small number of highly different objects will produce different results compared with the recognition of a larger number of generally similar objects. In other situations, recognition may involve reasoning about the object's function rather than the direct use of visual cues (Warrington and Taylor, 1978).

The findings listed in this section are not intended, therefore, to argue that view-based mechanisms are used exclusively in visual recognition, but that they play an important, perhaps a major part, particularly in the fast identification of individual objects. It should also be noted that, given the current state of knowledge, it would be premature to consider in detail specific mechanisms. The focus should therefore be on the main underlying principles, for example, that the system stores a number of different views of an object, and that these views are used collectively to compensate for the variability across views.

5.1. Psychophysical evidence

A large body of psychophysical evidence has been accumulated regarding the processes of visual object recognition. I will list here mainly recent findings that are directly related to view-based recognition.

5.1.1. New views are more difficult than trained ones

A number of different studies have examined the dependence of recognition performance on the viewing direction. In such studies an object is usually presented at a single orientation, and recognition is subsequently tested with the object presented at novel 3D orientations. In many studies of this type it was found that recognition performance decreased with the departure from the original, trained orientation: the error rates typically increased, as well as the response time for correct recognition (Jolicoeur, 1985, 1990; Rock and Di Vita, 1987; Corballis, 1988; Tarr and Pinker, 1989, 1991; Bülthoff and Edelman, 1992; Edelman and Bülthoff, 1992). In structural description as well as in variance-based schemes, the precise view has no particular importance, since it is replaced during the processing by a view-invariant description. As long as the new view gives rise to the same structural description, or has the same invariances, no significant effect of viewing direction is expected. The findings are more consistent, therefore, with theories, such as the image combination scheme, that use multiple 2D views directly in the recognition process. For example, the RBF method, as well as some implementations of the linear combination scheme, will exhibit this superiority of the training views.

It should be noted, however, that not all the studies in this area show the 3D orientation effect. For example, Biederman and Gerhardstein (1993) found complete invariance of their test objects to viewing position. The objects in this study were designed to have a clear decomposition into a small number of simple parts, and this design may have contributed to the difference between this and other studies. In any case, the exact nature of the viewing position dependency is still a matter of some controversy, and further studies will be required to clarify the issue.

5.1.2. The difficulty persists when strong 3D cues are available

The dependence on viewing direction is present even when the object is seen in both the training and subsequent testing under conditions that facilitate the recovery of 3D shape, using stereo, shading, and motion (Edelman and Bülthoff, 1992). Overall recognition performance is somewhat improved under these conditions, but the decrease in performance with departure from the trained conditions is not significantly affected. A study by Sinha (1995) manipulated systematically 2D and 3D similarities and compared their effects on generalization in recognition. A training object was viewed in this study under good 3D viewing conditions. Subsequent test objects were either similar to the training object in their 2D view, but with different 3D structure, or similar in 3D shape but with a different 2D view. The results indicated that generalization was determined primarily by similarity of views, rather than of object-centered structure. These findings provide evidence that the generalization process to novel conditions does not benefit significantly from the availability of rich 3D information. In the view-combination approach, generalization depends primarily on the availability of additional views. At the same time, as noted in the theoretical discussion, additional 3D information can be used by a view-based approach to improve the recognition of the trained views themselves.

5.1.3. Generalization improves with additional views

Recognition improves after training with additional object views (Tarr and Pinker, 1989; Poggio and Edelman, 1990). A similar finding was also observed in monkeys trained for object recognition (Logothetis et al., 1994). This is again expected in the view-based approach, where generalization depends primarily on the availability of a sufficient number of representative views. The fact that for bilaterally symmetric objects generalization requires fewer views, and that good generalization can be obtained on the basis of a single view (Vetter et al., 1994), is also consistent with this point of view.

5.1.4. Better generalization to same-axis rotation

In a study by Bülthoff and Edelman (1992) subjects were also presented with multiple views of the same object; however, the views were all obtained by rotations of the object about a fixed axis in the image plane, such as the horizontal or the vertical axis. The generalization to novel views proved to be better for views obtained by further rotations about the same axis, compared with rotations about the orthogonal axis. This effect appears unexpected, except for the image combination approach. In this approach, combination of images obtained from rotations about, say, the vertical axis, produce new images that are also constrained to rotations about the same axis.

5.1.5. Recognition is better than an 'ideal 2D observer'

The evidence listed above argues in favor of the direct use of object views in recognition, but does not address the issue of using the views independently or in some sort of view-combination scheme. A study by Liu et al. (1995) addressed this issue by comparing recognition performance of human observers with what they termed a '2D ideal observer'. The ideal observer compares a novel object view with all the previously seen views of the same object. The comparison is performed with each of the stored views separately, as opposed to the use of view combinations. They found that humans performed better than the ideal observer in generalizing to new views, demonstrating that independent comparisons to stored views are insufficient to account for human recognition performance.

5.2. Physiological aspects

The primate visual cortex contains multiple areas, but not all of them appear to be directly related to shape-based object recognition. A division has been suggested between two main processing streams, a ventral stream leading from V1 to the inferotemporal cortex (IT), where shape processing, leading to object recognition, seems to take place (Ungerleider and Mishkin, 1982), and a more dorsal stream, going to the parietal cortex, that may be related to object-directed action (Goodale and Humphrey, 1998).

The notion that IT cortex is involved with object recognition is supported by brain lesion studies, functional MRI (fMRI) studies, and by single cell recordings. Damage to IT cortex can cause deficits in object recognition. More restricted lesions usually affect mainly the precise identification of individual objects, and more extensive lesions can also affect the ability to perform broader classification (Damasio et al., 1990). Studies using fMRI techniques also indicate that these areas are involved in shape processing and object recognition (Tootel et al., 1996).

Single-cell recordings in IT showed that the stimuli required to drive these cells are often complex compared with those of lower-level visual areas. A particular population of such cells, mainly in the STS region of IT, responds selectively to face images (Perret et al., 1982, 1985; Rolls, 1984; Gross, 1992; Young and Yamane, 1992); other cells in a nearby region have been reported to respond to hand images. Some of the face-selective cells respond best to complete face images, others prefer face parts, such as the eye or mouth regions. In experiments performed by Logothetis et al. (1995), where monkeys viewed novel wireframe and ameboid objects for an extended training period, cells in IT developed specific responses to these novel objects. Similar findings were reported by Miyashita (1988) after training with fractal-like patterns. In addition to cells responding to complex and meaningful stimuli, other cells in IT, especially the posterior region, have been reported to respond to more elementary shapes and shapes that do not correspond to familiar objects (Tanaka, 1996).

In considering the response of IT units to specific objects, it is worth noting that shape-selective cells in IT often respond in a graded fashion, and will respond not only to a single shape, but to similar shapes as well. Some units also respond to a number of different shapes (Rolls et al., 1996). The shape of a specific object, such as a face, may still be represented by such cells in the population response of a number of cells. This may be a general principle of encoding of objects' shapes, that are represented by the combined activity of cells broadly tuned to different shapes, as well as units tuned to different parts of the entire shape.

5.2.1. Cells in IT are usually view-selective

Many IT cells show considerable selectivity in their responses when the stimulus changes in size, position, color, and sometimes orientation in the image plane. In terms of 3D viewing angle, most cells prefer a particular view of the objects. Some cells show a selective response to an individual face, or an artificial wireframe object, over a considerable range of viewing directions. At the same time, the response is usually not entirely object-centered. In face-selective cells, for instance, the selectivity does not cover the full range from frontal to profile view. The response is typically optimal for a particular orientation and decreases gradually for other orientations, but the decrease is sharper for some units and more gradual for others.

A possible interpretation of the increased tolerance to viewing direction is that a broadly-tuned cell receives converging input from a number of view-specific cells (Logothetis et al., 1995). This convergence of views belonging to the same object may be related to the view-combination approach; it may be a part of a biological implementation combining different views of the same object, leading to a broader generalization to novel views.

5.2.2. The response is determined by 2D similarity of views

The pattern of responses in IT to complex shapes appears to be consistent with the general notion of multiple pictorial representations. An object appears to be represented in IT by multiple units, tuned to different views of the object. The response of a face-selective unit, for example, to a given stimulus, appears to be governed by the overall similarity between the stimulus and the unit's preferred 2D pattern (Young and Yamane, 1992). Similarly, the units studied by Tanaka (1996) and his collaborators appear to be governed by 2D similarity of the test view to the view preferred by the unit. In these experiments, units were first tested using a large collection of different 3D objects. When a unit responded well to a particular object, additional attempts where made to characterize more precisely the effective stimulus for the unit. Units were typically driven by particular 2D patterns, rather than, for example, some preferred 3D shapes, regardless of their orientation in space.

5.2.3. Lesion evidence for the primacy of stored views

There is some evidence from animal lesion studies consistent with the notion that the system uses as a basic mechanism a direct comparison to stored views, augmented by mechanisms that are responsible for aspects of generalization to novel views.

For example, damage to area V4 and posterior IT (Weiskrantz, 1990; Schiller and Lee, 1991; Schiller, 1995) appears to affect especially the ability to compensate for transformations such as size, orientation, or illumination changes. The animal's ability to recognize the original views usually remains intact after the lesion. In the experiments carried out by Weiskrantz, monkeys were trained to recognize a set of test objects, under particular orientation and illumination conditions. They were then tested with the original objects as well as objects similar to the test objects except for changes in scale, orientation in the image plane, and illumination. Lesions to area AIT, the anterior part of IT, caused a general deterioration in recognition capacity. Lesions to the more posterior part of IT and some prestriate areas had a more specific effect on the ability to recognize the transformed views. Recognition of the original views were usually unaffected. Such results appear to support the notion that the most basic form of recognition relies on the direct comparison of stored views, as in the view-based approach, together with additional mechanisms that allow the undamaged system to also go beyond the stored views, and generalize to new ones.

6. Conclusions

A major problem in visual recognition comes from the fact that images of the same object are highly variable. To deal with this variability, one general approach has been to move away from the pictorial level and generate instead more abstract and view-independent representations. The view-based approach outlined here relies on the fact that the variability in the set of views belonging to a single object is still governed by regularities that can be captured at the pictorial level.

In the scheme presented above, an object is represented for the purpose of recognition by a number of its views, rather than, for instance, a single 3D object-centered representation. The views comprising the representation of a single object are not merely a collection of independent 2D object views. In the direct approach to recognition, objects are also represented by multiple views, but recognition is based simply on the best-matching individual view. In contrast, in the multiple views approach a number of object views are used collectively in the recognition process. The multiple views used to represent the object also include a known correspondence between individual views. As was discussed above, a set of corresponding 2D views provide a powerful and useful representation for the purpose of recognition. Without using explicit 3D information, this representation contains detailed information about the object's structure, and this information is stored in a convenient form for the purpose of the recognition process. The object views used in this approach are not limited to simple images of the object. The use of abstract descriptions allows the scheme to incorporate in addition more abstract pictorial representations.

The approach described above leaves several problems unanswered. Some of the major ones listed in the paper include the use of abstractions, class-based recognition, and the problem of classification. These and other problems will require considerably more research, both empirical and computational. In considering these problems, it should be emphasized that recognition is probably more than a single process; there may be many and quite different processes used by the visual system to classify and identify visual stimuli. Object recognition may be analogous in this respect to the perception of 3D space: the perception of depth and 3D shape is not a single module, but is mediated by a number of interacting processes that utilize various sources of information, such as binocular disparity, motion parallax, surface shading, contour shape, and texture variations. Similarly, visual object recognition is probably better viewed not as a single module, but as a collection of interacting processes.

Computational studies outlined in this paper show that significant aspects of object recognition can be approached by using combinations of a small number of object views. In examining the human recognition system it is worth keeping in mind, however, the distinction between the mathematical formulation of particular algorithms and the more general properties of the approach. The image combination computation described above illustrates the approach; however, variations and extensions of the scheme are possible. The general suggestion, based on the computational studies, is that recognition by multiple pictorial representations and their combinations may constitute a major component of 3D object recognition. According to this view, the brain will store for each object a small number of pictorial descriptions, and the recognition process will involve the manipulation and some combination of these views.

Acknowledgements

This work was supported by the Brain and Computation grant of the Israel Science Foundation and by the Israel Ministry of Science under the Integrated Visual Platform Project. I thank R. Basri, Y. Moses, A. Zeira and E. Sali for their contributions. The face images are from the Weizmann Institute Face Base. Thanks to IEEE PAMI for the reproduction of Fig. 1.

References

Abu-Mostafa, Y.S., Psaltis, D., 1987. Optical neural computing. Scientific American 256, 66–73.

Adini, Y., Moses, Y., Ullman, S., 1997. Face recognition: the problem of compensating for illumination changes. IEEE Transactions on Pattern Analysis and Machine Intelligence 19 (7), 721–732.

Albert, A., 1972. Regression and the Moore–Penrose Pseudoinverse. Academic Press, New York.

Beymer, D., Poggio, T., 1995. Face recognition from one example view. Proceedings of the International Conference on Computer Vision ICCV – 1995, 500–507.

Biederman, I., 1985. Human image understanding: recent research and theory. Computer Vision, Graphics, and Image Processing 32, 29–73.

Biederman, I., Gerhardstein, P.C., 1993. Recognition of depth-rotated objects: evidence and conditions for three-dimensional viewpoint invariance. Journal of Experimental Psychology: Human Perception and Performance 19, 1162–1182.

Bülthoff, H.H., Edelman, S., 1992. Psychophysical support for a two-dimensional view interpolation theory of object recognition. Proceedings of the National Academy of Science USA 89, 60–64.

Corballis, M.C., 1988. Recognition of disoriented shapes. Psychological Review 95, 115–123.

Daugman, J.G., 1989. Complete discrete 2-d Gabor transforms by neural networks for image analysis and compression. IEEE Transactions on Biomedical Engineering 36 (1), 107–114.

Damasio, A.R., Damasio, H., Tranel, D., 1990. Impairment of visual recognition as clues to the processing of memory. In: Edelman, G.M., Gall, W.E., Cowan, W.M. (Eds.), Signal and Sense: Local and Global Order in Perceptual Maps. John Wiley, New York.

Edelman, S., Bülthoff, H.H., 1992. Orientation dependence in the recognition of familiar and novel views of three-dimensional objects. Vision Research 32, 2385–2400.

Eley, M.G., 1982. Identifying rotated letter-like symbols. Memory and Cognition 10, 25–32.

Goodale, M.A., Humphrey, G.K., 1998. The objects of action and perception. Cognition 67, 181–207.

Gross, C.G., 1992. Representation of visual stimuli in inferiortemporal cortex. Philosophical Transactions of the Royal Society, London B 335, 3–10.

Hopfield, J.J., 1982. Neural networks and physical systems with emergent collective computational abilities. Proceedings of the National Academy of Science USA 79, 2554–2558.

Jolicoeur, P., 1985. The time to name disoriented natural objects. Memory and Cognition 13, 289–303.

Jolicoeur, P., 1990. Orientation congruency effects on the identification of disoriented shapes. Journal of Experimental Psychology: Human Perception and Performance 16, 351–364.

Koenderink, J.J., Van Doorn, A.J., 1979. The internal representation of solid shape with respect to vision. Biological Cybernetics 32, 211–216.

Koenderink, J.J., Van Doorn, A.J., 1990. Receptive field families. Biological Cybernetics 63, 291–297.

Kohonen, T., 1978. Associative Memories: a System Theoretic Approach. Springer, Berlin.

Lipson, P., 1993. Model Guided Correspondence. MSc Thesis, Computer Science, Massachusetts Institute of Technology.

Liu, Z., Knill, D.C., Kersten, D., 1995. Object classification for human and ideal observers. Vision Research 35 (4), 549–568.

Logothetis, N.K., Pauls, J., Bülthoff, H.H., Poggio, T., 1994. View-dependent object recognition in monkeys. Current Biology 4, 401–414.

Logothetis, N.K., Pauls, J., Bülthoff, H.H., Poggio, T., 1995. Shape representation in the inferior temporal cortex of monkeys. Current Biology 5, 552–563.

Lowe, D.G., 1985. Perceptual Organization and Visual Recognition. Kluwer Academic Publishing, Boston, MA.

Marr, D., Hildreth, E.C., 1980. Theory of edge detection. Proceedings of the Royal Society, London B 207, 187–217.

Miyashita, Y., 1988. Neuronal correlate of visual associative long-term memory in the primate temporal cortex. Nature 335, 817–820.

Moses, Y., 1993. Face Recognition: Generalization to Novel Images. PhD Thesis, Applied Mathematics and Computer Science, Weizmann Institute of Science, Israel.

Moses, Y., Ullman, S., Edelman, S., 1996. Generalization to novel images in upright and inverted faces. Perception 25, 443–461.

Mundy, J.L., Zisserman, A. (Eds.), 1992. Geometric Invariance in Computer Vision. MIT Press, Cambridge, MA.

Murray, J.E., Jolicoeur, P., McMullen, P.A., Ingleton, M., 1993. Orientation-invariant transfer of training in the identification of rotated natural object. Memory and Cognition 21, 604–610.

Perret, D.I., Rolls, E.T., Caan, W., 1982. Visual neurons responsive to faces in the monkey temporal cortex. Experimental Brain Research 47, 329–342.

Perret, D.I., Smith, P.A.J., Potter, D.D., Mistlin, A.J., Head, A.S., Milner, A.D., Reeves, M.A., 1985. Visual cells in the temporal cortex sensitive to face view and gaze direction. Proceedings of the Royal Society B 223, 293–317.

Poggio, T., Edelman, S., 1990. A network that learns to recognize three-dimensional objects. Nature 343, 263–266.

Poggio, T., Girosi, F., 1990. Regularization algorithms for learning that are equivalent to multilayer networks. Science 247, 978–982.

Rock, I., Di Vita, J., 1987. A case of viewer-centered object perception. Cognitive Psychology 19, 280–293.

Rolls, E.T., 1984. Neurons in the cortex of the temporal lobe and in the amygdala of the monkey with responses selective for faces. Human Neurobiology 3, 209–222.

Rolls, E.T., Booth, M.C.A., Treves, A., 1996. View-invariant representations of objects in the inferior temporal cortex. Society of Neurosci Abstracts 22, 1937.

Sali, E., Ullman, S., 1998. Recognizing novel 3-D objects under new illumination and viewing position using a small number of examples. Proceedings of the International Conference on Computer Vision ICCV – 1998, pp. 153–161.

Schiller, P.H., Lee, K., 1991. The role of the primate extrastriate area V4 in vision. Science 251, 1251–1253.

Schiller, P.H., 1995. Effect of lesion in visual cortical V4 on the recognition of transformed objects. Science 376, 342–344.

Shashua, A., 1992. Geometry and Phometry in 3-D Visual Recognition. PhD Thesis, Department of EECS, Massachusetts Institute of Technology.

Shashua, A., 1995. Algebraic function for recognition. IEEE Transactions on Pattern Analysis and Machine Intelligence 17 (8), 779–789.

Sinha, P., 1995. Perceiving and Recognizing Three-dimensional Forms. PhD Thesis, Electrical Engineering and Computer Science, Massachusetts Institute of Technology.

Tanaka, K., 1996. Inferotemporal cortex and object vision. Annual Review of Neuroscience 19, 109–139.

Tarr, M.J., Gauthier, I., 1998. Do viewpoint-dependent mechanisms generalize across members of a class? Cognition 67, 71–109.

Tarr, M.J., Pinker, S., 1989. Mental rotation and orientation dependence in shape recognition. Cognitive Psychology 21, 233–282.

Tarr, M.J., Pinker, S., 1991. Orientation-dependent mechanisms in shape recognition: further issues. Psychological Science 2, 207–209.

Tootel, R.B.H., Dale, A.M., Sereno, M.I., Malach, R., 1996. New images from the human visual cortex. Trends in Neurosciences 19 (11), 481–489.

Ullman, S., 1989. Aligning pictorial descriptions: an approach to object recognition. Cognition 32 (3), 193–254.

Ullman, S., 1995. Sequence seeking and counter streams: a model for bi-directional information flow in the visual cortex. Cerebral Cortex 5 (1), 1–11.

Ullman, S., 1996. High-level Vision: Object Recognition and Visual Cognition. MIT Press, Cambridge, MA.

Ullman, S., Basri, R., 1991. Recognition by linear combinations of models. IEEE Transactions on Pattern Analysis and Machine Intelligence 13 (10), 992–1006.

Ullman, S., Zeira, A., 1997. Object recognition using stochastic optimization. In: Pelillo, M., Hancock, E.R. (Eds.), Energy Minimization Methods in Computer Vision and Pattern Recognition, Lecture Notes in Computer Science. Springer, Berlin, pp. 329–344.

Ungerleider, L.G., Mishkin, M., 1982. Two cortical visual systems. In: Ingle, D.J., Goodale, M.A., Mansfield, R.J.W. (Eds.), Analysis of Visual Behavior. MIT Press, Cambridge, MA, pp. 549–586.

Vetter, T., Poggio, T., Bülthoff, H., 1994. The importance of symmetry and virtual views in three dimensional object recognition. Current Biology 4, 18–23.

Warrington, E.K., Taylor, A.M., 1978. Two categorical stages of object recognition. Perception 7, 152–164.

Weiskrantz, L., 1990. Visual prototypes, memory, and the inferotemporal lobe. In: Iwai, E., Mishkin, M. (Eds.), Vision, Memory and the Temporal Lobe. Elsevier, New York, pp. 13–28.

Willshaw, D.J., Buneman, O.P., Longuet-Higgins, H.C., 1969. Non-holographic associative memory. Nature 222, 960–962.

Young, M.P., Yamane, S., 1992. Sparse population coding of faces ininferotemporal cortex. Science 256, 1327–1331.

Yuille, A., Hallinan, P., 1992. Deformable templates. In: Blake, A., Yuille, A. (Eds.), Active Vision. MIT Press, Cambridge, MA.

3

Recovery of 3D volume from 2-tone images of novel objects

Cassandra Moore*, Patrick Cavanagh

Vision Sciences Laboratory, Harvard University, Cambridge, MA, USA

Abstract

In 2-tone images (e.g., Dallenbach's cow), only two levels of brightness are used to convey image structure – dark object regions and shadows are turned to black and light regions are turned white. Despite a lack of shading, hue and texture information, many 2-tone images of familiar objects and scenes are accurately interpreted, even by naive observers. Objects frequently appear fully volumetric and are distinct from their shadows. If perceptual interpretation of 2-tone images is accomplished via bottom-up processes on the basis of geometrical structure projected to the image (e.g., volumetric parts, contour and junction information) novel objects should appear volumetric as readily as their familiar counterparts. We demonstrate that accurate volumetric representations are rarely extracted from 2-tone images of novel objects, even when these objects are constructed from volumetric primitives such as generalized cones (Marr, D., Nishihara, H.K., 1978. Proceedings of the Royal Society London 200, 269–294; Biederman, I. 1985. Computer Vision, Graphics, and Image Processing 32, 29–73), or from the rearranged components of a familiar object which is itself recognizable as a 2-tone image. Even familiar volumes such as canonical bricks and cylinders require scenes with redundant structure (e.g., rows of cylinders) or explicit lighting (a lamp in the image) for recovery of global volumetric shape. We conclude that 2-tone image perception is not mediated by bottom-up extraction of geometrical features such as junctions or volumetric parts, but may rely on previously stored representations in memory and a model of the illumination of the scene. The success of this top-down strategy implies it is available for general object recognition in natural scenes. © 1998 Elsevier Science B.V. All rights reserved

Keywords: Two-tone images; Object recognition; Perceptual organization; Shadows

1. Introduction

Two-tone images are sparse, luminance-based representations which typically use

* Corresponding author. Present address: University of California, Los Angeles, Psychology Department, 128a Franz Hall, Los Angeles, CA 90095-1563, USA.

only black ink on a white background. Though scant in information, this form of depiction is highly representative of familiar scenes and objects (Fig. 1) and the perception of the 3D structure in these scenes is often immediate and effortless. However, not all such images are so easily interpreted. Several famous examples, such as the Dalmatian dog or Dallenbach's cow, are seen initially (for many of us) as scattered black islands on a flat white background. This interpretation may persist indefinitely but typically it reorganizes suddenly into a volumetric object (either by itself or following helpful hints from someone who already sees the object); thereafter, the image retains the volumetric interpretation, and the former percept is usually lost forever. To the human perceiver, seeing a 2-tone image as a 3D volumetric object can be a relatively effortless task, but computationally, it is a very powerful feat of perceptual organization and interpretation. Two-tone images have no exact counterpart in the natural world, yet many of these images are interpretable to human observers (and in some cases, monkeys as well; Perrett et al., 1984). Despite their non-ecological character, or perhaps because of it, 2-tone images offer numerous insights into the image features, mental representations, and perceptual processes underlying general object recognition.

The perceptual understanding of 2-tone images has typically focused only on *familiar* objects (e.g., Mooney, 1957; Galper, 1970; Phillips, 1972; Hayes, 1988; Cavanagh and Leclerc, 1989). It has been generally assumed that past experience enables interpretation (Rock, 1984), or more specifically, experience with familiar objects allows a partial match between 2-tone image contour and a stored memory representation; this partial match then influences organization of the rest of the image (Cavanagh, 1991). Object recovery from 2-tone images may require top-down guidance and thus be possible only when the image depicts familiar objects.

Fig. 1. Grayscale, line drawing and 2-tone image of a bullock. In the grayscale image most material changes (e.g., bridle to face) correspond to high contrast luminance contours; shadow contours tend to be softer. The drawing contains lines only for structural features (e.g., convexities and concavities at the ear and nostril, folds and creases in the rag on horns). Luminance contours in the 2-tone image occur at the occluding edges of objects (bridle strap), cast shadow edges (ear shadow on neck), and at attached shadow boundaries (right horn). These three contour types are physically undifferentiable in 2-tone images.

However, the recovery of *unfamiliar* objects from 2-tone images, and the bottom-up schemes which might enable such recovery, have never been directly tested. Object recovery from 2-tone images might use a bottom-up process in which essential features (e.g., contours, junctions, volumetric primitives) are first extracted from the image, then concatenated to form objects or object parts, which are only then compared to object representations in memory. If this were the case, a memory representation of the depicted object would not be necessary for the accurate recovery of at least the parts and structure of that object from a 2-tone image. However, 2-tone images present a daunting challenge to current models of bottom-up object shape recovery because the images do not appear to have any of the critical features on which these models rely, and yet they are recognizable. Using 2-tone images of novel objects, we test the explanatory power of three part-based approaches to object recovery.

We will demonstrate that accurate volumetric representations are rarely extracted from 2-tone images of novel objects, even when these objects are constructed from volumetric primitives such as generalized cones (Marr and Nishihara, 1978; Biederman, 1985), or from the rearranged components of a familiar object which is itself recognizable as a 2-tone image. This failure of volume recovery is not simply due to a lack of object contour and junction information. We will show that partially occluded line-drawings of the same objects, with exactly the same contour and junction features hidden, are readily seen as 3D. The failure appears to hinge on the interpretation of shadow areas. Shadow regions are typically mistaken for object surfaces, indicating observers do not have appropriate models of the lighting and shadow in the scene. Accordingly, we attempted to facilitate recovery of novel objects by making the nature of the lighting explicit in the 2-tone image. We placed the novel object beside a familiar, recognizable image where both had the same lighting; we presented several versions of the image with different light sources; we provided direct evidence of the location and direction of the lighting. None of these manipulations improved recovery. A prior memory representation is necessary for the recovery of volume from 2-tone images. Even then, only familiar objects of sufficient complexity were recovered in 2-tone images. Despite their high degree of familiarity, simple canonical volumes such as cubes or cylinders presented alone seldom appeared volumetric in 2-tone images. This failure of familiarity was perhaps not surprising given that the 2-tone images of cubes and cylinders offered so few cues and allowed so many alternative interpretations.

2. Characterization of the image and the problem

Two-tone images are created by thresholding a grayscale image; all pixels above a particular luminance level are set to white, and those below are set to black. Modeling (shading), texture and color information, features which commonly facilitate determination of 3D object shape and shadow identification, are absent in 2-tone images. There is no magic number (e.g., the average image luminance) for setting the threshold in an image. The point of maximum interpretability of each 2-tone image depends upon the lighting, the shape of the object surfaces, and the camera viewpoint.

Two-tone image interpretation presents a complex problem because the images conflate information about object structure and illumination. Luminance contour in a 2-tone image is a combination of: informative occluding object contour (Fig. 2a,b), potentially informative interior (e.g., attached shadow, pigment) contour (Fig. 2c), and potentially misleading cast shadow contour (Fig. 2d,e). The interior attached shadow contours, and the cast shadow contours, can vary dramatically with changes in illumination direction. The direction of illumination striking a curved object surface determines the contour along which the incident light is orthogonal to the surface normal (Fig. 2c). At this contour, the pictured surface in a 2-tone image turns from white (lit) to black (unlit), forming an attached shadow contour that does not correspond to the occluding contour of the object. If the direction of illumination is changed relative to the object surface, the location and shape of this contour also changes. In contrast, occluding object contours, and the attached shadow contours corresponding to occluding edges of the object (Fig. 2b), are relatively stable. Once the image has been thresholded, however, object and shadow contours are physically indistinguishable.

Surface segmentation in a 2-tone image is not simply a figure/ground differentiation in which the white region is exclusively ground and the black region is exclusively figure (or vice versa). In order to accurately recover the structure of an object, the perceiver must differentiate the contour types; mistaking shadow contour for object contour would lead to errors in calculating object structure. In addition, parts of the white region must be combined with parts of the black region to accurately recover a volumetric object from the image. Consider the 2-tone image in Fig. 2. The ends of the curved cylinder are white, but much of the rest of the object is black; these regions have to be united to form a volumetric cylinder.

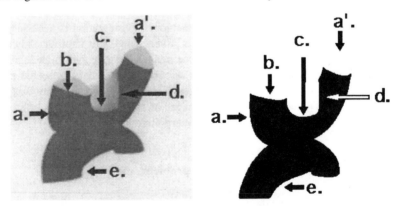

Fig. 2. Types of luminance contour: (a) external object boundary present in both the grayscale and 2-tone images, (a′) external object boundary absent in the 2-tone image, (b) attached shadow at object boundary, (c) attached shadow boundary not corresponding to object boundary, (d) self-shadow boundary, cast on the object by itself, and (e) cast shadow on ground plane. Contours (a,b) are relatively stable with changes in illumination, although (a′) illustrates that only part of the bounding contour of an object is present in a 2-tone image. Contours (c–e) vary dramatically with changes in the direction of illumination.

Although the computational problem of integrating black and white regions is complex, the human perceptual system is capable of deriving sufficient information from 2-tone images for naive observers to recognize faces and other familiar objects and scenes (Street, 1931; Mooney, 1957). Numerous researchers have shown that 2-tone images of faces are readily recognized by most observers (e.g., Mooney, 1957; Galper, 1970; Phillips, 1972; Hayes, 1988; Cavanagh and Leclerc, 1989). Even though 2-tone images contain none of the traditional depth cues, the observer does not simply see a 2D pattern that could be interpreted as a face, but rather sees the face with concave and convex regions, cast and attached shadows, much as full grayscale images are perceived. In 2-tone images of novel objects, which lack the guidance of familiarity cues, it may not be possible to differentiate contours arising from illumination effects (e.g., cast shadows, highlights) and those arising from object structure (e.g., occlusions, changes in material) and this could block the recovery of depicted object. Alternatively, stable contours which are relatively invariant to the effects of illumination (e.g., occluding object contours) might be sufficient for volume recovery via bottom-up methods that do not rely on familiarity.

The research reported in this paper is an attempt to assess the viability of bottom-up approaches for recovery of 3D structure from 2-tone images of novel objects. Two such approaches will be considered: the volumetric primitives approach (Binford, 1971; Marr and Nishihara, 1978; Biederman, 1985; Lowe, 1985) in which simple volumes are extracted from the image prior to derivation of global object structure, and the line labeling approach (Clowes, 1971; Huffman, 1971; Waltz, 1975; Malik, 1987) in which the unique interpretation of the lines constrains the formation of structural features such as corners, junctions and edges, theoretically allowing a single coherent 3D object to emerge.

The hypothesis to be tested is simple: if the perceived volumetric appearance of 2-tone images is attributable to the prior recovery of low-level structure such as corners, edges, volumetric primitives, or familiar parts, then novel single and multiple-part objects should appear volumetric as readily as familiar objects. Empirical support for this hypothesis would indicate that a part-based explanation of 2-tone image perception is sufficient. However, if images of novel objects appeared fragmented and 2D, or the volumes depicted could not be accurately recovered, an account of 2-tone image perception mediated by object familiarity, or top-down knowledge would gain support.

3. Experiment 1: single-part objects

3.1. Stimuli

To address this question we generated a set of 2-tone images of generalized cylinders after the primitives suggested by Marr and Nishihara (1978) and by Biederman (1985). These simple volumes were uniformly gray in color with a matte surface. They rested on an infinitely large white matte ground plane that was not visible in the image, but caught shadows cast by the objects. Illumination of the objects mimicked natural sunlight as nearly as possible. The objects were illuminated from above by a single point light source set at an infinite distance from the object. Placing the point light at an infinite distance insures that light rays are parallel and shadow shape is not distorted. The angle of the light relative to the surface normal of the ground plane was approximately 45°. This scheme produced fairly realistic grayscale images. Two-tone images were formed by setting the threshold in each image to a level at which all regions of the object not receiving direct illumination turned black, and all lit regions turned white (Fig. 2). This threshold level corresponded approximately to the average illumination of the image area encompassed by the smallest square that would fit around the depicted object. A total of 12 objects, each subtending 5° of visual angle, were included in the experiment.

3.2. Methods

The perceived organization of the 2-tone images was tested in 13 naive observers and several observers in our laboratory who were generally familiar with 2-tone images, but had not seen the experimental images. Observers were told they would be viewing a series of objects, some of which might appear flat or 2D, and some which might appear volumetric or 3D. They were further instructed that some objects might appear to have pieces missing, but they were to determine the shape of the object as best they could. The 2-tone images were presented individually on a computer monitor; the display was terminated by the observer's keypress response. The task of the observer was to decide whether a gray star placed on the image was, or was not, on the surface of the depicted object (Fig. 3). The star could appear in four different image areas: (1) the black region of the object surface, (2) the black region of the cast shadow, (3) the white region of the object surface, (4) the white region of the background or ground plane (these two were contiguous and undifferentiated). A correct decision about the location of the star required the observer to differentiate object regions, both black and white, from shadow and background regions. After performing the star task, the observers were asked to provide a qualitative description of the shape of the object in the image as it would appear if the object itself were before them.

To ensure the task could be performed with grayscale images, 10 subjects performed the 'star task' on the grayscale counterparts of the 2-tone images. Every object and every star location produced at least 90% accuracy with a 200 ms

Fig. 3. The observer's task was to decide whether the gray star was, or was not, on the object surface. The star appeared (left to right) on the black object region, black shadow region, white object region, white background region. The object is a cylinder illuminated from the upper left casting a shadow across the ground plane to the right.

exposure. Thus, any observed differences in the 2-tone images should be due to the information lost in converting the image to the 2-tone format.

3.3. Results and discussion

Our own observations, and those of several naive viewers revealed that the perceptual interpretation of 2-tone images of simple, isolated volumes, even common objects like cylinders and rectangular prisms, was rarely volumetric. Examples of the 2-tone objects appear in Fig. 4; readers should first view the images in Fig. 4, then compare their interpretations to the grayscale images in Fig. 15.

The most common impediment to the accurate recovery of the depicted object was misinterpretation of cast shadow areas as part of the object. The 13 naive observers tended to see all black areas as object regions and white areas as background. When the star was on the black object region, *all* observers correctly reported it to be on the object surface in *all* images. When the star was on the black *shadow* region, however, observers correctly reported that it was *not* on the object surface only 15% of the time. In signal detection terms, the observers' hit rate was 100%, whereas their correct rejection rate was only 15%. Integration of the white region into the object was marginally more successful. If the star was on the white background, observers correctly reported it was not on the object (correct rejection) in 81% of the trials; when it was on the white portion of the object, however, only 38% of the trials prompted a correct response (hit).

Signal detection analysis allows us to characterize the observer's performance in terms of the detectability of the object versus the background (d') and a response bias (beta). Although the detectability score for black regions, d' = 2.04, was higher than that of the white regions, d' = 0.57, this difference is probably exaggerated as a result of the 100% hit rate for black areas. More notable is the large difference in

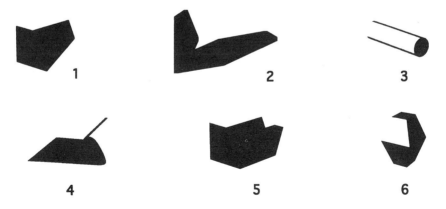

Fig. 4. Many observers fail to see volume in 2-tone images of generalized cones. Some of these single-part novel objects have cast and attached shadows (2, 4, 5), others have only attached shadows (1, 3, 6). The additional information provided by the cast shadows did not appear to be useful. For a volumetric view, see Fig. 15.

bias. The bias to see black regions as object (beta = 12.3) was far greater than the bias to see white regions as background (beta = 0.4). The first result clearly shows that observers were simply labeling black areas as figure (high bias). The second indicates that observers were willing to see white regions as part of the figure (low bias) but were doing so in a way that only weakly corresponded to the original figure areas (low d').

Observers described the objects as either substance on a surface (e.g., paint), or curved or folded sheets of material (e.g., paper). Occasionally the images were seen as silhouettes of 3D objects whose volume did not extend beyond the dark areas. For example, object 4 in Fig. 4 can be seen as a slug facing right with an extended antenna. Notice that only the black area is seen as the slug, whereas the *actual* object surface extends into the white area.

After providing their responses, a few observers were shown the grayscale versions of the objects and asked to reconsider their interpretation of the 2-tone images. Only with considerable effort could they see volumetric objects which encompass both dark and light regions of the image. Even then, identification of the volumes was frequently incorrect. Interestingly, the 2-tone representation of some objects appears more volumetric after viewing their grayscale versions but in others the perception of volume is effortful even after exposure to a grayscale version.

Even knowing the 2-tone images are pictures of objects with shadows does not necessarily enable the viewer to accurately distinguish surface from shadow regions of the image. In addition, the absence of volumetric junction information (due to thresholding) favors an image interpretation in which the entire black region is seen as a silhouette-like object against a white background. Incorporation of portions of the white area into the hypothesized object is necessary for accurate volume recovery, but this rarely occurred. Removal of cast shadows, so the black parts of the image correspond *only* to non-illuminated object surfaces, does not seem to increase the volumetric appearance of the depicted object, but rather reduces the perceived complexity of the percept (compare objects 1 and 5, or 2 and 6 in Fig. 4).

4. Experiment 2: multiple-part objects

Considering the complexity of objects that *are* recognizable in 2-tone images (e.g., faces) objects with multiple parts might be perceived as volumetric more readily than single-part objects. Shadows cast by some object parts fall on other parts (self-shadows), possibly revealing the shape of the shadow-receiving parts.

4.1. Stimuli and methods

To test this possibility we constructed 12 novel, multiple-part objects containing 3 or 4 of the generalized cones used in the previous 2-tone images (Fig. 5). The multiple-part objects were illuminated from above (the northern hemisphere of a viewing sphere) in each of the 4 quadrants. This lighting scheme caused some images of a particular object to contain many self-shadows, whereas shadows in

Fig. 5. The 2-tone images of objects constructed from generalized cylinders often appear to be complex paper cut-outs or silhouettes. Readers should compare their impression of volume in these images to grayscale versions of the images in Fig. 16.

other images were cast primarily on the ground plane. The task and instructions to the subjects were the same as those in the single-part object experiment.

4.2. Results and discussion

Once again, 13 naive observers displayed a bias to identify black regions as figure and white regions as ground. Black shadow regions were interpreted as non-object regions only 14% of the time; black object regions were identified as such on 91% of trials. White background regions were correctly identified as non-object regions 76% of the time, whereas white object regions were correctly identified as object surfaces in 36% of trials. Signal detection analysis again showed that observers were biased to see the black region as object (beta = 7.7) and the white region as non-object (beta = 0.43). In both cases responses were only weakly governed by the original figure and ground areas ($d' = 0.26$ for black and 0.35 for white image regions).

The objects with few self-shadows appeared to be complex paper cut-outs or folded or curved sheets of material. Perceived depth in the scene was less prevalent than in the single-part object images, and volumetric interpretations were partial at best. Some image regions were identified as shadow rather than surface regions (e.g., Fig. 5, rightmost part of the right object), but the differentiation was frequently incomplete (where does the object end and the shadow begin?) and the subsequent attempt to describe the shape of the depicted object was usually inaccurate. (Readers should compare their interpretation of the 2-tone images in Fig. 5 with the grayscale versions of the objects in Fig. 16). Self-shadows create luminance contours in the 2-

tone images that do not correspond to the edges of the object. These contours tended to obscure, rather than reveal, the shape of the object.

In general, the objects composed of several volumes did not appear more volumetric in 2-tone images than the single-part objects. That is, the ability of observers to differentiate the object from the background (as indicated by d') was equally poor in both experiments. The only exception was the moderate value of d' for the black regions of simple objects. But in this case, *all* black regions were labeled as 'on the object' and this 100% hit rate degrades the validity of the estimate of d'. Clearly, even with the single-part objects, observers were doing a poor job of distinguishing object from background as they always saw black regions as figure whether or not it corresponded to the original object or to its cast shadow.

4.3. General discussion

On the basis of the observations described above, the geometrical structure in 2-tone images of unfamiliar objects appears insufficient to produce the impression of 3D typical of 2-tone images of faces and other familiar objects. Object contour and shadow contour are not readily distinguished; neither simple volumes nor multiple-part novel objects are accurately recovered from 2-tone images. These results suggests that interpretable 2-tone images may require depiction of familiar objects, and that the interpretation may be mediated, top-down, by the perceiver's knowledge of specific objects.

Before accepting this explanation, however, two alternatives must be addressed.

First, the difference between comprehensible and incoherent 2-tone images might still be based upon the complexity of the object depicted, not its familiarity. Our multiple-part objects contained fewer parts, and were less compact than the typical 2-tone face. If only complex objects appear volumetric in 2-tone images, multiple-part novel objects made of 'face parts' should appear volumetric. If objects made of face parts do *not* appear volumetric, whereas the same parts in a face-like structure *do*, a familiarity explanation for 2-tone images would be supported.

Second, the amount of visible object contour in our images may have been too meager to allow recovery of 3D volume. It might be argued that a greater amount of object contour is available in traditional 2-tone images, e.g., in faces, than in our generalized cone objects, thus making recovery of volume in our objects problematic. If this were the case, line-drawings of the objects in which an equivalent amount of contour was deleted or occluded should appear as 2D as their corresponding 2-tone images. However, if partial line-drawings *did* appear volumetric, the misperception of the 2-tone images could not be attributed to lack of object contour or junction information.

We explore these two possibilities in turn in the following sections.

5. Object complexity – a demonstration

In an effort to create a novel object as 'face-like' as possible, we constructed a face (and several other objects, see Fig. 6) composed of several simple volumes, then rearranged those volumes. Both the face and the scrambled face were illuminated with the same lighting parameters, and submitted to a thresholding procedure to produce 2-tone images. As expected, the 2-tone image of the face looked quite volumetric, and was easily identified as a face. Although the 2-tone image of the scrambled face contained more luminance contour than the novel objects used earlier, it appeared either flat or silhouette-like, much as the single- and multiple-part objects.

From these observations we conclude that object complexity cannot explain why 2-tone images of faces and familiar objects are perceived veridically, whereas simple volumes are not. Furthermore, we conclude that recognition of familiar objects in 2-tone images cannot be mediated by bottom-up recovery of generalized

Fig. 6. The volumetric parts of the familiar object on the left were rearranged to create the novel object on the right. The surface of the face is mostly white, the espresso pot mostly black, but in both cases, the perceived volume incorporates both light and dark image regions. Most perceivers are unable to combine white and black regions in the objects on the left, resulting in non-volumetric or inaccurate representations. Grayscale versions of these images appear in Fig. 17.

cones, nor can the schemes that use them (Binford, 1971; Marr and Nishihara, 1978; Biederman, 1985; Lowe, 1985) be directly extended to explain the perception of volume in 2-tone images.

Although the familiar objects appeared appropriately volumetric, neither the objects made of their component parts, nor the isolated components, appeared volumetric. If generalized cones were the basic units of object recognition for 2-tone images, and were identified prior to their structural relations in the object as a whole (as hypothesized for line-drawings or full color images by Biederman, 1985), then we would expect the primitives to appear volumetric in isolation (Fig. 4), and in novel configurations (Fig. 6, right side), as well as in familiar objects (Fig. 6, left side). This was not the case. The perceptual interpretation of the generalized cones was dependent upon the familiarity of the configuration in which it appeared – the part itself was not 'primary'.

The ineffectiveness of volumetric primitives for 2-tone image interpretation seems to arise from a difficulty in image segmentation. Typically, luminance contour is used to derive the axis of the part (Blum, 1973), or deep concavities in the occluding contour of an object delineate its parts (Hoffman and Richards, 1985). Both part-recovery methods encounter problems in 2-tone images. Deriving part or object axes requires prior, successful discrimination of object and shadow regions of the image, otherwise axes are assigned to shadow regions as well as object regions. Concavities that could indicate appropriate part boundaries in line-drawings or grayscale images are obscured in 2-tone images and spurious concavities are introduced where luminance contours created by object edges meet contours created by shadows (Fig. 5b). The known means of volumetric part recovery do not seem applicable, without substantial modification, to 2-tone images.

6. Experiment 3: adequate object contour

It is possible that the object contour and junction information in 2-tone images of novel objects is either insufficient, or too ambiguous to produce a volumetric interpretation of the image. In line labeling schemes proposed by Waltz and others (Clowes, 1971; Huffman, 1971; Waltz, 1975; Malik, 1987) the constraint imposed by the unique interpretation of luminance edges, and subsequent structural features such as corners and junctions, allows only a single coherent 3D scene to emerge.

Thresholding a grayscale image to create a 2-tone obscures many of these key features for object recovery (Fig. 7b). Segments of occluding contour are missing or obscured by cast shadows; most interior edge and corner segments are eliminated as well. The loss of these contours and their defining labels changes the identity of the remaining visible edges, especially at intersections. There are no 'arrow', 'Y', or 'K' junctions to indicate corners in 2-tone images. All junctions consisting of three or more coterminating lines either become 'L' junctions in which only two contours coterminate, or become straight lines in which the contour of the object and that of the shadow are smoothly joined. Interposition information, mediated by T junctions in line-drawings, is lost in a 2-tone image. The alteration of junctions destroys what

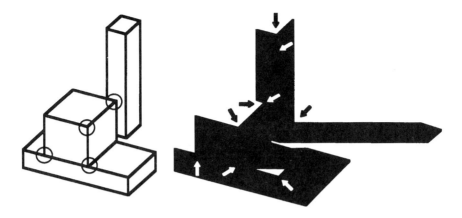

Fig. 7. Blocks world after Waltz (1975), (a) line-drawings with T, K, Y, and arrow junctions circled, (b) in a 2-tone image all 3-way junctions become L junctions or are obscured completely. The white arrows mark examples of obscured lines at junctions. Black arrows mark examples of spurious concavities which would irretrievably derail any attempt to accurately parse the image.

might have been a unique interpretation of the contours, rendering this type of representation intractable for Waltz-type line-labeling algorithms, and possibly interfering with volume recovery in human observers.

6.1. Stimuli

Testing the possibly deleterious effect of junction disruption required the dissociation of object contour and junction information from shadow or illumination information. This was accomplished by creating line-drawings of the single- and multiple-part objects used in the original 2-tone images. Segments of object contour corresponding to the segments obscured by thresholding the 2-tone images were deleted in one condition and occluded in the other. Thus the effects of contour and junction information were dissociated from illumination information.

6.2. Methods

Ten observers were shown five single-part and five multiple-part objects; each object was seen with contour occluded[1] and contour deleted (Figs. 9 and 10). Observer instruction began with the presentation of several examples of deleted and occluded line-drawings (Fig. 8). Observers were asked to form an impression of whether the drawings looked like a volume, a folded or curved sheet, or a wire. Examples of the drawings as volumes (line-drawings of whole objects), as wires

[1]The occluders were randomly shaped black blobs giving the appearance of paint on a transparent surface in front of the object. Many shapes of occluders were created with no observed difference in effectiveness. The properties of the various occluders (e.g., simplicity/complexity, symmetry/asymmetry, curvature/rectilinearity, filled/outline) did not seem to affect the perceived dimensionality of the occluded object, though unfilled occluders slowed the separability of occluder and object.

Fig. 8. Observers viewed line-drawings such as the occluded cylinder above, and were asked to state whether the depicted object looked more like a volume, a sheet of paper, or a wire. After making the decision, the observer was shown the three versions beneath the line and asked to indicate which of the three their impression was most like.

(contour deleted versions) and as surfaces (contours were closed by continuing each line end to its nearest neighbor) were then shown for comparison with observers' percepts.

During the test phase, single black line-drawings on white paper were sequentially presented to each observer. Objects were presented in a single random order with the stipulation that occluded and deleted versions of the same object were separated by at least two other objects presentations. Half the subjects received the random order, the other half saw the reverse order. The observer viewed each drawing, then indicated whether the sample drawing appeared more like a volume, a surface, or a wire. After a response was taken, observers were presented with the volumetric, surface, and wire versions of the object to ascertain how nearly their percepts corresponded to the depicted versions.

6.3. Results

When contour was *deleted* from line-drawings of single- and multiple-part novel objects leaving only those contours available in their 2-tone counterparts, the drawings did not appear volumetric (Fig. 9). Novel objects appeared volumetric in only 2% of trials, and as wires or surfaces in 98% of trials. The bare line terminations discouraged completion of the lines across missing sections, and the loss of a contour in Y or arrow junctions caused them to be interpreted as L junctions. Without these completions, the original volumetric shape was not recovered.

However, contour deletion in *familiar* objects, the cylinder and cube, was not nearly as deleterious. The cube and cylinder were interpreted as volumes in 56% of the deleted-contour trials, and as wires or surfaces in 44%. Contour completion in these familiar objects corroborates previous findings (Biederman, 1985; Biederman and Cooper, 1991; but see also Bregman, 1981). Our study of the *novel* objects suggests that completion of contour deleted volumes may require familiarity with the depicted object as well as local cues to contour relatedness.

Fig. 9. Line-drawings of single- and multiple-part objects isolate the contribution of contour information from illumination and surface information. Deleted contour segments correspond to obscured contour segments in the 2-tone counterparts of these objects. Like their 2-tone versions, these contour versions fail to appear volumetric.

When occluders covered the same lengths of contour that had been deleted (or obscured in the 2-tone images) 3D shape was accurately recovered in almost all instances. A 'volume' response was produced in 90% of all trials, whereas only 10% produced a 'surface' or 'wire' response. (Recall that *none* of these appeared volumetric in 2-tone images!) The strength of the volumetric appearance of the object seemed to depend upon the amount of contour occluded (Fig. 10) rather than the type of image feature hidden or revealed by the occluder. Single- and multiple-part objects did not differ in frequency of appearing volumetric, however, the simpler, more canonical objects (e.g., the cylinder) were usually perceived with greater accuracy than the more complex or unusual objects. The more unusual objects were seen as volumes, but the accuracy of the hypothesized structure is reduced for some observers. The volumes the observers described were consistent with the partially occluded or deleted drawings, but occasional simplification of the volumes did occur. For example, the leftmost object in Fig. 10 was usually described as having a flat top.

6.4. Discussion

Although one or more lines in every Y, K or arrow junction is occluded, the junctions complete spontaneously and perception of volume is immediate. The

Fig. 10. Line-drawings with occlusion of the segments deleted in Fig. 8 and obscured in the 2-tone images. Unlike the latter two versions, the occluded objects appear volumetric. Notice that occlusions occur at junctions, not in the middle of line segments.

completing junctions in the line-drawings contain the same contour as those that *did not* complete in the 2-tone images. The Y, K, or arrow junctions need not be explicit for the line-drawings to be interpreted as 3D objects; the lines appear to continue behind the occluder completing the implicit junction. These results imply that there *is* sufficient contour and junction information in 2-tone images to form a volumetric interpretation. Given the same contour and junction information appears in the different forms of representation, why would a volumetric interpretation succeed with the occluded line-drawings, but not with the 2-tone images?

This result exemplifies the 'generic' or 'non-accidental' nature of the world model used by the human visual system (e.g., Lowe and Binford, 1981; Witkin and Tenenbaum, 1983; Lowe, 1985; Koenderink, 1990; Freeman, 1994; Albert and Hoffman, 1995). Rather than assuming the image (either retinal or pictorial) resulted from unusual viewing conditions, the visual system assumes the image contains a generic or non-accidental, and therefore representative, view of objects in the world. Non-accidental interpretations are made on the basis of a few image features (e.g., T junctions, parallelism, symmetry) that are reliable indicators of the structure and location of objects in the 3D world. Their recovery may occur in the early stages of visual processing, suggesting the possibility of bottom-up image reconstruction.

In the case of the occluded objects, T junctions are formed at the intersection of the occluder and the bounding edge of the object, providing a simple (possibly bottom-up) mechanism for separating the occluder and the object (Fig. 10). The contour of the object appears to terminate extrinsically at the junction with the occluder (Nakayama et al., 1987). Even though the placement of the occluder itself is highly accidental, the resultant T junctions separate the occluder from the line drawing, implying that if the viewpoint of the observer were to change, more object contour might be revealed. Thus the presence of the T junctions provides an impetus for separating the object from the occluder, and the presence of the occluder provides support for postulating continuation of the object contour behind the occluder (Bregman, 1990; Fig. 11).

In contrast, the deleted-contour drawings provide no evidence that the object lines might continue into the solid white background, or that further information could be revealed by a change of viewpoint. Observers frequently see the lines of the object as

Fig. 11. The presence of the occluder suggests the object contour could continue on to form a volumetric object; the line terminates extrinsically at the junction with the occluder. In contrast, deleted line-drawings and 2-tone images provide no cues for continuation of their contours or surfaces into the white region. Consequently, no volumetric interpretation is formed.

intrinsically terminated (Nakayama et al., 1987) at the point of deletion. Similarly, the black regions in the 2-tone images are usually seen as surfaces which also appear to be intrinsically bounded. The image provides no obvious reason for postulating continuation of the surface beyond the luminance contour. The black regions occasionally appear as 3D silhouettes in which the entire black region (including the shadow) constitutes the object projecting the silhouette, but again the hypothesized object does not appear to encompass any of the white region. Since there are no differences between luminance contours caused by shadows and those caused by object edges, both are interpreted as surface edges, and both contribute to the perceived shape of the surface.

7. Illumination hypotheses

Although the available object contour is identical in the contour-occluded line-drawings and 2-tone images, the percept is very different. The compelling volume in the occluded line-drawings implies that ample contour is present, but contour alone is insufficient to enable a volumetric interpretation of novel objects in 2-tone images. What seems to be missing is a model of light and shadow in the scene. Since line-drawings do not contain illumination information, a lighting model is unnecessary, but it may be required to understand 2-tone images. If an object surface in a 2-tone image is to continue beyond a black region, across a luminance boundary, into a white region, there must be an external (non-object based) explanation of the black/white boundary. In the 2-tone images, shadows, caused by the particular illumination in the scene are the explanation.

The observer must generate a representation which includes a model of light and shadow for these borders to be attributed to illumination effects and not to object structure. If the object in the 2-tone image is a familiar one, a partial contour match may trigger, or even compel a lighting and shadow hypothesis. For example, some contours of the image may resemble contours of a face, but the whole image could only be a face if strong directional lighting and deep shadows were also present. If our conjecture is correct, then global familiarity is one means of triggering an appropriate lighting hypothesis. However, other means might be available; in the following sections we examine some alternative possibilities. Perhaps, if given the illumination direction, observers could complete surfaces in 2-tone images of novel objects just as they completed line-drawings behind the occluders.

7.1. Illumination information from recognizable objects

Previous research has shown that illumination direction is instrumental in determining the 3D shape of ambiguous *grayscale* objects that could be interpreted as bumps or dents (Yonas et al., 1979; Berbaum et al., 1983a; Berbaum et al., 1983b). Yonas et al. found that illumination direction determined perceived shape for adult observers. Berbaum et al. used the presence of a familiar object as implicit evidence of a particular illumination direction and found that observers incorporated this

Fig. 12. A multiple-part object illuminated from each of 4 quadrants of the northern hemisphere; the angle of the light is approximately 45°. The object contour *could* be computed from the information present, but it is unlikely to alter the how the observer perceives the object in the image.

information into their interpretations of the ambiguous objects. The illumination direction suggested by the unambiguous shading of the familiar object was extended to the ambiguous object, determining whether it will appear to be a bump or a dent.

A simple test of this effect in our 2-tone images is seen in Fig. 6 which contains both a familiar and an unfamiliar object. Unlike the results of Berbaum's grayscale studies the presence of a recognizable object beside a novel object did not provide a sufficiently strong cue to enable volume recovery in 2-tone images.

7.2. Illumination information from multiple views

We next considered whether multiple views of the same object, each illuminated from a different direction, could induce a volumetric interpretation. Illumination of the same object from different quadrants[2] of the northern hemisphere (Fig. 12) produced differently shaped shadows, but the external object contours remained fairly consistent from one lighting condition to another. In each image, some previously exposed segments, and some new segments of the object contour were exposed. By viewing four images of an object, each lit from a different quadrant, it is theoretically possible to extract and integrate consistent (object) contours while discounting the changing (shadow) contours, thus discriminating the object from its shadow. Previous studies have shown that observers can integrate partially deleted contours across multiple views of line-drawings well enough to enable object naming (e.g., Snodgrass and Feenan, 1990; Biederman and Cooper, 1991; Srinivas, 1993).

Observers who are knowledgeable about the creation of 2-tone images may be able to consciously extract and integrate the available contour for constructing an accurate object representation. However, these observers, the authors included, are unlikely to 'see' a volumetric interpretation of a novel object, such as occurred in the occluded line-drawings. The 'moment of insight' that accompanies the organization of a difficult 2-tone image of a familiar object (e.g., the famous Dalmatian) never arrives. The process seems more cognitive.

[2]When images of individual objects were shown in isolation, no particular illumination quadrant (in the northern hemisphere) revealed volume or improved shadow/object contour discrimination better than any other. Illumination from either the southern hemisphere or the equator of the viewing sphere produced nearly incomprehensible images.

7.3. Explicit illumination information

In previous images, lighting direction could (theoretically) be derived by locating the shadow in the image. However, deciding which image regions are shadows and which are object surfaces may depend upon knowing the direction and location of the light source. Perhaps the illumination and contour information in the 2-tone images is too interdependent to allow derivation of both simultaneously without the aid of cues like familiarity.

In an attempt to decouple the two, we made the direction, strength, and source of illumination explicit. Two-tone images of novel objects were placed in the context of a grayscale scene depicting a lamp with a very bright spotlight. When the object is truly novel (Fig. 13, left side) explicit information about the light striking the object does little to unite black and white regions or enable perception of volume (for a grayscale view, see Fig. 16). For several observers asked to describe the depicted shape, the explicit lighting depiction creates a volumetric appearance of familiar objects like the cylinder in the image on the right side of Fig. 13.

In previous 2-tone images of novel objects, neither familiar volumes like the cylinder nor more novel volumes like those depicted in Fig. 4 (all are generalized cylinders) appeared volumetric. When illumination was specified, familiar but simple objects such as the cylinder in Fig. 13 appeared reliably volumetric. If explicit lighting could create volume in the cylinder, why was it not also seen in other objects?

Cylinders are extremely common in the world, and it would be unlikely that perceivers would store representations of more complex namable objects (e.g., faces, espresso makers), but not cylinders. However, the match of such a simple shape may fail on some 2-tone images because it is not sufficiently complex to rule out other interpretations, or because more parsimonious interpretations are readily available. For example, adopting the folded sheet interpretation for the objects in

Fig. 13. Even though the illumination source is explicit, as are the lighting direction and strength, the novel object on the left (see grayscale version, Fig. 16) appears to be a folded sheet whereas the more familiar cylinder on the right appears volumetric to most observers.

Fig. 13 would allow the perceiver to ignore the illumination information in the image. Alternatively, a volumetric interpretation requires that the lamp generate a level of brightness uncharacteristic of the normal world. When an explicit lighting model is provided, the additional information may be sufficient to allow a volumetric match of the regular cylinder, but insufficient to enable a volumetric interpretation of an unfamiliar generalized cylinder. The interpretation of the novel generalized cylinder could be either a volumetric object with a complex lighting model, or a folded sheet with a generic lighting model. Both alternatives are compatible with the image information, but the latter may conform better to a generic model of the world, especially when a lighting model is not explicitly specified.

7.4. Illumination information from scenes

All the novel objects in the 2-tone images we have presented thus far appear in isolation. Although many interpretable 2-tone images contain only a single object (e.g., a face), the face may contain many redundant cues consistent with a memory-representation of a face and inconsistent other alternatives. In order to create 2-tone images with a multiplicity of cues to shadow location, we constructed scenes containing multiple novel objects, hoping the redundancy would facilitate differentiation of shadow from object surfaces.

Redundancy of shadow cues was facilitated by the spacing of the objects and the long, thin shadows from the vertical objects spanning the width of the horizontal object (and its shadow), and continuing on the ground plane. Although these shadow conditions may have enhanced the separation of the objects, the perception of a ground plane (Stevens, 1981), and the skewed symmetry relation between the object and shadow (Kennedy, 1974), they produced only a partial volumetric representation of the horizontal object on which the shadows were cast (Fig. 14, far left).

However, when familiar objects such as cylinders were depicted in the scene, they did appear to attain volume (Fig. 14, right). As with the explicit lighting model, the redundant cues in the scenes appeared sufficient to create volumetric interpretations of simple familiar objects, but less so with simple novel objects. The presence of several vertical objects in the scene, creating more redundancy, seems to enhance volume recovery. Some instances of cotermination of cast shadows created a modest

Fig. 14. Tall regular volumes, located far from one another, casting long shadows, produce a volumetric interpretation (center, right). Irregular volumes reduce the redundancy of segmentation cues and images appear less volumetric (left).

illusory contour coincident with the actual bounding contour of the horizontal object (Fig. 14, center), possibly facilitating segmentation of image regions into shadows and object surfaces, and encouraging continuation of object surfaces into the white area. Many of the organizing relations used in Fig. 14 also appear in 2-tone images of single objects (see especially Figs. 2 and 6), but in isolation they do not appear strong enough to differentiate shadow and object regions.

8. Conclusions

The observations reported here were an attempt to discover whether bottom-up, part-based approaches to object perception could be applied to the interpretation of 2-tone images of novel objects. It is well established that 2-tone images of familiar objects can be recognized, even by naive observers. We examined 2-tone images of novel objects to explore *how* objects might be recovered.

First, generalized cones were depicted in 2-tone images, both in isolation and in the context of multiple-part novel objects. If the volumetric primitives were the basic units of object recognition in 2-tone images, we would expect them to appear volumetric in isolation, in novel configurations, and in familiar objects. The parts did not appear reliably volumetric either alone or together. Next we created nonsense objects by rearranging parts that had appeared volumetric in 2-tone images of familiar objects. Only in the context of the familiar objects did the parts appear volumetric. From these results we conclude that recovery of volumetric parts does not precede, and thereby enable, object recognition in 2-tone images.

We next asked whether the amount of visible object contour in our images was sufficient to support a volumetric interpretation. To isolate the contribution of contour from that of illumination, we constructed line-drawings of each object, occluding segments of contour corresponding to segments obscured in the 2-tone images. Although both had identical contour exposed, the 2-tone images did not appear volumetric whereas the line-drawings with occluded segments did. The presence of the occluders enabled a perceptual hypothesis in which the object corners appeared to complete behind the occluders. The compelling appearance of volume in the occluded line-drawings indicated that the lack of volume in the 2-tone images cannot be attributed to insufficiency of local components such as junctions and contour.

Having established that bottom-up recovery of volumetric parts was not generally useful for 2-tone image interpretation, and that the images of novel objects did indeed contain ample object contour for volume recovery, we turned from the structural properties of objects to their illumination. When the objects were truly novel, even explicit lighting depiction did not produce volumetric representations. In a 2-tone image containing both a familiar object and a novel object, the unambiguous lighting of the familiar object failed to transfer to the novel object. The presentation of multiple 2-tone images of the same object, each illuminated from a different angle failed as well; even knowing the contour of the object did not make it look volumetric. Finally, we created a grayscale scene of a glaring spotlight shining on a 2-tone image of an object. The addition of an explicit lighting model enabled volume recovery of simple familiar objects, but neither simple nor complex novel objects. Even though the lighting strength, location and direction was explicit in the image, it did not induce a perception of volume in the novel objects.

We suggest that determination of illumination strength and direction is a necessary aspect of the perceptual understanding of 2-tone images. When a 2-tone image depicts a complex familiar object, a segment of identifiable contour can initiate the process of differentiating shadow from object regions and integrating an object surface that continues beyond a luminance boundary in the image. However, familiarity alone is not a sufficient condition for volume recovery from 2-tone images. Many of the generalized cones we used were simple, highly familiar objects, e.g., cubes and cylinders. In isolation, familiar volumes were interpreted as unusual bent or silhouetted shapes under generic lighting. The 2-tone images of these volumes are so sparse they allow multiple simple interpretations, many of which do not compel a complex lighting model with deep shadows. The possibility that the image depicts some unfamiliar object under generic lighting conditions appears preferable to the interpretation of a familiar volume with unusual lighting. Simple familiar shapes require explicit lighting or regular arrays with highly redundant shadow patterns to constrain possible interpretations and enable appropriate 3D recovery. These findings suggest that strictly bottom-up, or even part-based models are inadequate for explaining perceptual interpretation of 2-tone images.

We favor an approach in which recognition of familiar objects in 2-tone images (and perhaps natural scenes) is essentially top-down, requiring some hypothesis concerning the identity of the object depicted before the assignment of regions to figure and ground is made. This approach is similar to that of Peterson and Gibson (1994) who claim that object recognition precedes the assignments of figure and ground in simple black and white figures. We suggest that the first guess for the identity of the object is mediated by viewpoint-specific memory representations of familiar objects (Cavanagh, 1991; Poggio and Hurlbert, 1994; Tarr and Bulthoff, 1995; Shashua, 1997). This approach uses distinctive, perhaps deformable, templates (Yuille, 1991) at either the whole object level or the local part level. Recent work in computer vision (Belhumeur et al., 1996; Shashua, 1997) also demonstrates that only a few directions of illumination need to be stored in order to recognize an object illuminated from a novel direction. Although it is clear that canonical parts in our 2-tone images could not *initiate* the process of object recovery, evidence from line-drawings, explicit illumination and object redundancy in our studies suggests their presence may be beneficial once an illumination direction has been hypothesized. In natural scenes, which contain multiple segmentation cues such as T junctions, color and texture that could initiate object/shadow segmentation, part templates may play a more active role.

Object recognition in natural scenes may use a top-down match of characteristic views of familiar objects, or of familiar parts of unfamiliar objects, and image information. This template approach might be used to identify familiar parts (e.g., cylinders, bricks, or spheres) of unfamiliar objects (Dickinson et al., 1992) as well as whole namable objects. A hypothesis about a few simple volumes in probable orientations could provide a start for the structural analysis of the overall 3D shape. The end result of this recovery of familiar parts would be a set of volumetric parts and their orientations and locations very much like that provided by other part-based approaches. The difference is that the volumetric parts would be identified from stored 2D views and might be less vulnerable to the missing elements and ambiguous shadow regions which make 2-tone images so difficult. Observers may have mental models of familiar parts which, once triggered by other image cues, create expectations or predictions about where completing lines might be found, thus facilitating object recovery.

Clearly, parts are not interpretable in 2-tone images. Neither generalized cones, nor even familiar, canonical shapes like cylinders and cubes provided any reliable volumetric interpretation either in isolation or in complex groups. The recognition of sufficiently complex familiar objects appears to employ a more direct, holistic process that bypasses an initial part-based analysis.

Although our demonstrations reject part-based analyses in the interpretation of 2-tone images, they do not exclude part-based analyses in the interpretation of natural images with redundant cues to shadow and object edges. The critical message of 2-tone images is that familiar objects *can* be recognized without recourse to any known bottom-up schemes. The presence of this level of analysis for 2-tone images implies that it operates in natural scenes as well, for who would imagine that such a strategy would evolve for a style of image that did not exist before 1895. An holistic analysis for familiar objects would offer speed advantages in dealing with familiar items in the world, but undoubtedly would operate in concert with other more general, perhaps structural approaches to object recognition.

Appendix A. Figs. 15–17.

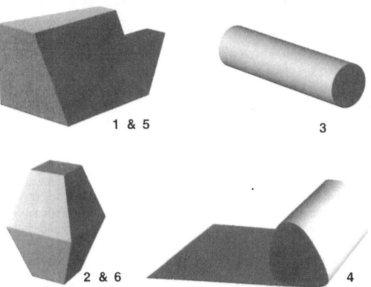

Fig. 15. Grayscale versions of 2-tone images in Fig. 4. Object numbers correspond to 2-tone versions with and without cast shadows.

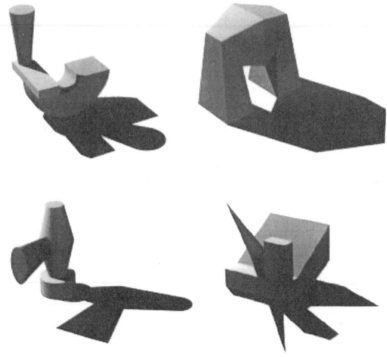

Fig. 16. Grayscale images of 2-tone objects in Fig. 5.

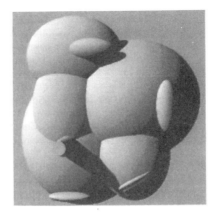

Fig. 17. Grayscale versions of 2-tone images in Fig. 6. Although the objects on the right are constructed from the rearranged parts of the objects on the left, the novel arrangements are rarely seen as volumetric.

References

Albert, M., Hoffman, D., 1995. Genericity in spatial vision. In: Luce R.D. (Ed.), Geometric Representations of Perceptual Phenomena: Papers in honor of Tarow Indow on his 70th birthday. Erlbaum, Mahwah, NJ, pp. 95–112.

Belhumeur, P.N., Yuille, A.L., Epstein, R., 1996. Learning and recognizing objects using illumination subspaces. Proceedings of the International Workshop on Object Representation for Computer Vision April, 1996.

Berbaum, K., Tharp, D., Mroczek, K., 1983a. Depth perception of surfaces in pictures: looking for conventions of depiction in Pandora's box. Perception 1–2, 5–20.

Berbaum, K., Bever, T., Chung, C.S., 1983b. Light source position in the perception of object shape. Perception 1–2, 411–416.

Biederman, I., 1985. Human image understanding: recent research and a theory. Computer Vision, Graphics, and Image Processing 32, 29–73.

Biederman, I., Cooper, E.E., 1991. Size invariance in visual object priming. Journal of Experimental Psychology: Human Perception and Performance 18, 121–133.

Binford, T., 1971. Visual perception by computer. Proceedings, IEEE Conference on Systems Science and Cybernetics. Miami, FL.

Blum, H., 1973. Biological shape and visual science, Part 1. Journal of Theoretical Biology 38, 205–287.

Bregman, A.S., 1981. Asking the 'What For' question in auditory perception. In: Kubovy, M., Pomerantz, J. (Eds.), Perceptual Organization. Lawrence Erlbaum, Hillsdale, NJ.

Bregman, A.S., 1990. Auditory Scene Analysis. MIT Press, Cambridge, MA.

Cavanagh, P., 1991. What's up in top-down processing? In: Gorea, A. (Ed.), Representations of Vision: Trends and Tacit Assumptions in Vision Research. Cambridge University Press, Cambridge, UK.

Cavanagh, P., Leclerc, Y.G., 1989. Shape from shadows. Journal of Experimental Psychology 15, 3–27.

Clowes, M.B., 1971. On seeing things. Artificial Intelligence 1, 79–116.

Dickinson, S.J., Pentland, A.P., Rosenfeld, A., 1992. From volumes to views: an approach to 3-D object recognition. CVGIP: Image Understanding 55 (2), 130–154.

Freeman, W.T., 1994. The generic viewpoint assumption in a framework for visual perception. Nature 368 (6471), 542–545.

Galper, R.E., 1970. Recognition of faces in photographic negative. Psychonomic Sciences 194, 207–208.

Hayes, A., 1988. Identification of two-tone images; some implications for high- and low-spatial-frequency processes in human vision. Perception 174, 429–436.

Hoffman, D.D., Richards, W.A., 1985. Parts of recognition. Cognition 18, 65–96.

Huffman, D.A., 1971. Impossible objects as nonsense sentences. Machine Intelligence 5, 295–323.

Kennedy, J.M., 1974. A Psychology of Picture Perception: Images and Information. Jossey-Bass, San Francisco, CA.

Koenderink, J.J., 1990. Solid Shape. MIT Press, Cambridge, MA.

Lowe, D.G., 1985. Perceptual Organization and Visual Recognition. Kluwer Academic, Boston, MA.

Lowe, D.G., Binford, T.O., 1981. The interpretation of three-dimensional structure from image curves. Proceedings of IJCAI-7 Vancouver, August, 613–618.

Malik, J., 1987. Interpreting line drawings of curved objects. International Journal of Computer Vision 1, 73–107.

Marr, D., Nishihara, H.K., 1978. Representation and recognition of the spatial organization of three-dimensional shapes. Proceedings of the Royal Society London 200, 269–294.

Mooney, C.M., 1957. Age in the development of closure ability in children. Canadian Journal of Psychology 114, 219–226.

Nakayama, K., Shimojo, S., Silverman, G.H., 1987. Stereoscopic occluding contours: a critical role in pattern recognition of background objects. Investigative Ophthalmology and Visual Science Supplement 28, 365.

Perrett, D.I., Smith, P.A., Potter, D.D., Mistlin, A.J., Head, A.S., Milner, A.D., 1984. Neurons responsive to faces in the temporal cortex: studies of functional organization, sensitivity to identity, and relation to perception. Human Neurobiology 3, 197–208.

Peterson, M.A., Gibson, B.S., 1994. Must figure-ground organization precede object recognition? An assumption in peril. Psychological Science 5, 253–259.

Phillips, R.J., 1972. Why are faces hard to recognise in photographic negative? Perception and Psychophysics 12, 425–426.

Poggio, T.A., Hurlbert, A., 1994. Observations on cortical mechanisms for object recognition and learning. In: Koch, C., Davis J.L. (Eds.), Large-Scale Neuronal Theories of the Brain. MIT Press, Cambridge, MA.

Rock, I., 1984. Perception. W.H. Freeman, New York.

Shashua, A., 1997. On photometric issues in 3D visual recognition from a single 2D image. International Journal on Computer Vision 21 (1–2), 99–122.

Snodgrass, J.G., Feenan, K., 1990. Priming effects in picture fragment completion: support for the perceptual closure hypothesis. Journal of Experimental Psychology: General 119 (3), 276–296.

Srinivas, K., 1993. Perceptual specificity in nonverbal priming. Journal of Experimental Psychology: Learning Memory and Cognition 19 (3), 582–602.

Stevens, K.A., 1981. The visual interpretation of surface contours. Artificial Intelligence 17, 47–74.

Street, R.F., 1931. A Gestalt completion test. PhD Thesis, Teachers College at Columbia University, New York.

Tarr, M.J., Bulthoff, H.H., 1995. Is human object recognition better described by geon structural descriptions or by multiple views? Comment on Biederman and Gerhardstein (1993). Journal of Experimental Psychology: Human Perception and Performance 6, 1494–1505.

Waltz, D., 1975. Understanding line drawings of scenes with shadows. In: Winston, P.H. (Ed.), The Psychology of Computer Vision. McGraw-Hill, New York.

Witkin, A.P., Tenenbaum, J.M., 1983. On the role of structure in vision. In: Beck, J., Hope, B., Rosenfeld, A. (Eds.), Human and Machine Vision. Academic Press, New York.

Yonas, A., Kuskowski, M.A., Sternfels, S., 1979. The role of frames of reference in the development of responsiveness to shading information. Child Development 50, 495–500.

Yuille, A.L., 1991. Deformable templates for face recognition. Journal of Cognitive Neuroscience 31, 59–70.

4

Do viewpoint-dependent mechanisms generalize across members of a class?

Michael J. Tarr[a],*, Isabel Gauthier[b]

[a]*Department of Cognitive and Linguistic Sciences, Brown University, P.O. Box 1978, Providence, RI 02912, USA*
[b]*Department of Psychology, Yale University, New Haven, CT 06520, USA*

Abstract

Evidence for viewpoint-specific image-based object representations have been collected almost entirely using exemplar-specific recognition tasks. Recent results, however, implicate image-based processes in more categorical tasks, for instance when objects contain qualitatively different 3D parts. Although such discriminations approximate class-level recognition, they do not establish whether image-based representations can support generalization across members of an object class. This issue is critical to any theory of recognition, in that one hallmark of human visual competence is the ability to recognize unfamiliar instances of a familiar class. The present study addresses this question by testing whether viewpoint-specific representations for some members of a class facilitate the recognition of other members of that class. Experiment 1 demonstrates that familiarity with several members of a class of novel 3D objects generalizes in a viewpoint-dependent manner to cohort objects from the same class. Experiment 2 demonstrates that this generalization is based on the degree of familiarity and the degree of geometrical distinctiveness for particular viewpoints. Experiment 3 demonstrates that this generalization is restricted to visually-similar objects rather than all objects learned in a given context. These results support the hypothesis that image-based representations are viewpoint dependent, but that these representations generalize across members of perceptually-defined classes. More generally, these results provide evidence for a new approach to image-based recognition in which object classes are represented as clusters of visually-similar viewpoint-specific representations. © 1998 Elsevier Science B.V. All rights reserved

Keywords: Class generalization; Image-based recognition; Viewpoint-specific representation

* Corresponding author. Tel.: +1 401 8631148; fax: +1 401 8632255; e-mail: Michael_Tarr@brown.edu

1. Introduction

A significant body of work on human object recognition has been concerned with the question of how observers recognize objects from unfamiliar viewpoints (Rock, 1973). Recent results suggest that there is no definitive answer to this question, rather there is a continuum ranging from extreme viewpoint dependence to almost complete viewpoint invariance. There is, however, a general principle underlying this continuum: The *degree* of viewpoint dependence is largely determined by the between-item similarity of objects that must be discriminated, with more homogeneity between objects leading to greater viewpoint dependence and less homogeneity leading to less viewpoint dependence (Tarr and Bülthoff, 1995; Schyns, 1998). This claim appears to hold across a wide range of stimuli and tasks, including studies using alphanumeric characters (Corballis et al., 1978), common objects (Bartram, 1974; Jolicoeur, 1985; Lawson et al., 1994), novel 2D (Tarr and Pinker, 1989) and 3D objects (Bülthoff and Edelman, 1992; Humphrey and Khan, 1992; Biederman and Gerhardstein, 1993; Tarr, 1995; Hayward and Tarr, 1997; Tarr et al., 1997), or faces (Yin, 1969; Troje and Bülthoff, 1996; Hill et al., 1997).

Given such mixed results, different theorists have drawn quite different conclusions regarding the mechanisms used for visual recognition (Biederman and Gerhardstein, 1995; Tarr and Bülthoff, 1995). On the one hand, relatively smaller effects of viewpoint (e.g. Corballis et al., 1978; Biederman and Gerhardstein, 1993) have typically been interpreted as evidence for a structural-description system in which objects are represented as assemblies of 3D parts that are stable over large changes in viewpoint (Marr and Nishihara, 1978; Biederman, 1987). On the other hand, relatively large effects of viewpoint (e.g. Bülthoff and Edelman, 1992; Tarr, 1995) have been interpreted as evidence for an image-based or view-based system in which objects are represented as sets of metrically-specific features that are unstable over changes in viewpoint (Poggio and Edelman, 1990; Bülthoff et al., 1995). While both types of theories offer parsimonious accounts for some subset of the data, there remains the larger question of the domain covered by each. One common reconciliation has been to assume only limited domains for each type of mechanism: basic- or entry-level recognition of object category being handled by a qualitative part-based system, while subordinate-level recognition of specific exemplars being handled by a quantitative image-based system (Jolicoeur, 1990).

By some views, this solution is less than satisfactory and inconsistent with at least some of the extant data. Consequently, theorists have begun to hypothesize that recognition is almost entirely part-based (Biederman and Gerhardstein, 1993, 1995) or almost entirely image-based (Edelman, 1995; Tarr and Bülthoff, 1995). What is still unclear is how each approach can be extended to accommodate recognition tasks that were not part of the original domain of explanation. Indeed, proponents of the part-based approach have explicitly criticized the generality of image-based theories on this basis, suggesting that such mechanisms are incapable of generalizing across unfamiliar instances of familiar classes, that is, entry-level recognition (Biederman and Gerhardstein, 1993, 1995). In contrast, proponents of the image-based approach have proposed schemes in which viewpoint-specific representations do generalize to new members of familiar classes (Poggio and Brunelli, 1992; Lando and Edelman, 1995; Vetter et al., 1995; Beymer and Poggio, 1996; Moses et al., 1996; Gauthier and Tarr, 1997b). Empirical evidence on this issue is, however, somewhat thin. Thus, the goal of this paper is to investigate the nature of image-based class generalization, asking: (1) Does such generalization occur? (2) What factors mediate generalization? (3) Is this generalization based on the same visual similarity that helps to define a visual class?

1.1. Evidence for generalization

Tests of viewpoint dependence in recognition have focused on whether subjects learn specific objects in specific views. In a typical experiment there is an initial viewpoint dependency that diminishes with extensive practice to near-equivalent performance at familiar views (Tarr and Pinker, 1989; Bülthoff and Edelman, 1992; Edelman and Bülthoff, 1992; Humphrey and Khan, 1992; Tarr, 1995). This near-invariance may be interpreted as evidence for either viewpoint-invariant or multiple viewpoint-specific object representations. Critically, Tarr and Pinker (1989) and since then Bülthoff and Edelman (1992) and Tarr (1995) found that performance for *unfamiliar* views remained viewpoint dependent and, moreover, was related to the distance from the nearest familiar view.

Interestingly, Jolicoeur and Milliken (1989) obtained diminished effects of viewpoint at unfamiliar viewpoints, reminiscent of those found after extensive practice, *without* the benefit of subjects actually viewing the specifically tested objects in the test viewpoints. Their subjects, however, did view *other* objects at the tested viewpoints, suggesting that viewpoint invariance may be produced by the context of the prior presentation of different objects – cohorts – at the same test viewpoints subsequently used to assess viewpoint invariance (Jolicoeur and Milliken, 1989). As with diminished effects of viewpoint due to practice, diminished effects due to context may be accounted for by either viewpoint-invariant or multiple viewpoint-specific representations. Largely because subjects never observed a given object (only its cohorts) at the viewpoints in question, Jolicoeur and Milliken interpreted their results as evidence for viewpoint-invariant mechanisms, as have subsequent transfer experiments (see Murray et al., 1993). An alternative interpretation of this result is that viewpoint-specific image-based representations formed for the objects actually seen at a given viewpoint may generalize to visually-similar objects seen only later at the same view, that is, image-based class generalization.

1.2. Image-based class generalization

A problem with image-based theories is that views are typically assumed to be specific to exact images features and attributes. For example, in the influential neural-network model by Poggio and Edelman (1990) (see also Weinshall et al., 1990; Edelman and Weinshall, 1991) objects were coded by the precise (x, y) coordinates of their vertices. Such a coding is both impractical and at odds with our intuitions regarding object recognition. Take for example, the typical real-world situation in which new exemplars of a familiar category are seen for the first time, e.g. a new model of car. Our intuitions tell us that our knowledge about cars we have seen in the past facilitates our recognition of this new car. In Poggio and Edelman's model, however, such generalization could not occur – the representation of one car would be specific to a given set of coordinates and, thus, would not match a new visually-similar car (although the Edelman and Weinshall model may be able to handle this case due to blurring of the input). In contrast, it seems that our knowledge about an entire category facilitates the recognition process. Thus, it may be possible to recognize a new exemplar of a known category from a novel view based on the knowledge of the class. Similar intuitions have led many proponents of the image-based approach to develop computational models for generalizing between members of a homogeneous class using viewpoint-specific representations (Poggio and Brunelli, 1992; Lando and Edelman, 1995; Vetter et al., 1995; Beymer and Poggio, 1996; Moses et al., 1996).

There is already considerable empirical evidence for image-based recognition mechanisms. What is unknown is whether the obvious strength of this approach, the coding of metric specificity that can support exemplar-specific recognition, can be retained while extending it to handle class-level recognition. One possible model for doing this, advocated by Gauthier and Tarr (1997b) (see also Edelman, 1995), involves pooling activation across a number of visually-similar image-based representations (for neural evidence for models of this sort, see Perrett et al., 1998). The idea is that classes may be represented as clusters of exemplar-specific and, crucially, viewpoint-specific image-based views that can support generalization from one exemplar to another. There are at least two sources of empirical support for this model. First, Moses et al. (1996) found that observers were good at generalizing from a single view of an unfamiliar upright face to new views of the same upright face, but were poor at generalizing from single views of inverted faces to new inverted views. This finding suggests that humans appear to have a class-general, viewpoint-specific, i.e. upright only, representation for faces. Second, Gauthier and Tarr (1997b) found that viewpoint-specific representations of visually-similar novel 2D shapes interacted to facilitate recognition. Specifically, we found evidence for *orientation priming* – better recognition of a shape at a particular orientation based on the prior presentation of other visually-similar shapes at the same orientation. In other words, given shapes from a homogeneous[1] class, e.g. S1, S2 and S3, learned at 0°, recognition of shapes S1 and S2 at 120° reduced the effect of viewpoint for the subsequent recognition of shape S3 at 120°. These results were limited, however, by the fact that the shapes were rotated only in the picture-plane and that orientation priming occurred quite early in testing – most likely before subjects could have acquired new object-specific representations at 120°. In research presented here we wished to explore 3D class generalization more directly, that is, in conditions where we were sure that subjects had learned object O1 at viewpoints α and θ and object O2 only at viewpoint α. We hypothesize that once a view has been learned for O1 at

---

[1]Throughout the paper, we use an informal definition of homogeneous and visually-similar. For purposes of the experiments presented here, we need only assume that the perceptual information that subjects rely on for object recognition overlaps across objects defined as similar.

θ, recognition performance for the visually-similar O2 will be enhanced at θ via image-based generalization.

In all three experiments the logic for testing this prediction is similar to that used for assessing whether diminished effects of viewpoint with practice are due to viewpoint-invariant or viewpoint-dependent mechanisms (Tarr and Pinker, 1989). The crucial difference here is that familiar test objects are now presented at viewpoints at which only their visually-similar cohorts have appeared previously (*cohort views*), as well as at unfamiliar viewpoints where neither the test objects nor their cohorts have appeared previously (*novel views*). Two outcomes are possible for performance at these test viewpoints.

(1) Response times are equivalent (and fast) at cohort and novel views. Such a result would support a viewpoint-invariant interpretation, suggesting that the appearance of only *some* members of a class at several viewpoints prompts subjects to acquire more general viewpoint-invariant representations. This is in contrast to earlier studies where *all* objects appeared at the same subset of viewpoints, apparently prompting subjects to acquire viewpoint-specific representations at each highly familiar viewpoint (Tarr and Pinker, 1989; Tarr, 1995).

(2) Response times for cohort views are fast, while response times for novel views are systematically related to the distance from the nearest familiar *or* cohort view. Such a result would support a viewpoint-dependent interpretation, suggesting that the appearance of only (*some*) members of a class at several viewpoints prompts subjects to acquire viewpoint-specific, but class-general, representations. Thus, as in earlier studies where highly familiar viewpoint-specific representations served as direct matches or targets for normalization processes, cohort views may serve similarly, but for objects never actually seen at those viewpoints.

2. Experiment 1

Experiment 1 examines whether learning viewpoint-specific information about novel objects generalizes to other visually-similar objects. Based on the earlier results of Jolicoeur and Milliken (1989) we know that naming familiar objects at a given orientation facilitates the naming of other familiar objects at the same orientation (see also Murray et al., 1993). However, because they failed to probe orientations that were unfamiliar for all of the objects, it is unclear whether the facilitation Jolicoeur and Milliken obtained is mediated by viewpoint-invariant or viewpoint-dependent mechanisms. We address this question by measuring recognition performance at familiar, cohort, and novel views, as well as extending Jolicoeur and Milliken's findings to novel 3D objects and rotations in depth.

2.1. Method

2.1.1. Subjects
Twelve subjects from the MIT community participated in the experiment for pay. All reported normal or corrected to normal vision.

2.1.2. Materials

The complete stimulus set of seven objects is illustrated in Fig. 1 at their arbitrarily designated canonical viewpoint of 10° around each of the three principle axes (Fig. 2); (see Tarr (1995) for details on how the objects were generated). As illustrated in Fig. 2 objects were rotated around either the X, Y, or Z axis with the other two axes held constant at 10° (the order of rotations was always X, Y, and Z). A complete set of 34 viewpoints (including the canonical viewpoint) was generated by rotating each object through eleven 30° intervals (40°, 70°, ... , 340°) around the X, Y, or Z axis.

Rotations were centered around the geometric midpoint of the object as defined by the furthest reaches of its arms. Stimuli were displayed centered on a color EGA monitor at a resolution of 512 × 512 pixels within a circle approximately 13 cm in diameter (19.4° of visual angle). The surfaces of the stimuli were colored a uniform light blue and the edges of the faces of each cube were colored red with hidden lines removed (for further details, see Tarr, 1995).

2.1.3. Design and procedure

In the *Training* phase subjects learned the names and 3D structure for a subset of four target objects at the canonical training viewpoint (Fig. 1). Subjects learned the objects by copying them and then building them from memory using a construction toy that allowed them to attach single units to the main axis fixed at the training

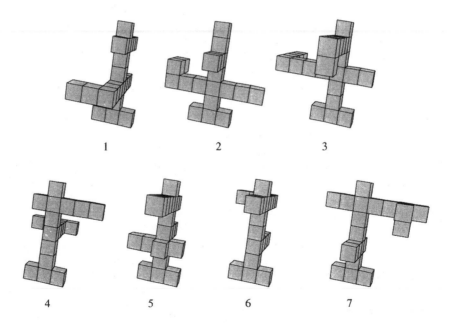

Fig. 1. The set of novel 3D objects used as stimuli in Experiments 1 and 2. The objects are shown at their near-upright training viewpoint (10°, 10°, 10°). Note that the set of objects form a somewhat homogeneous visual class in that they share common components (cubes) and a clearly marked bottom 'foot' and major vertical axis.

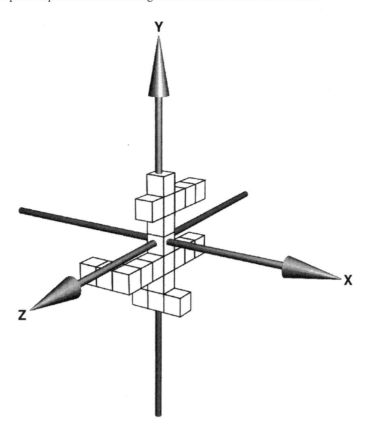

Fig. 2. Axes of rotation used to generate changes in viewpoint. For Experiments 1 and 2 each object was rotated around either the *X*, *Y* or *Z* axis with the other two axes held constant at 10°. For Experiment 3 each object was rotated only around the *Y* axis with the other two axes held constant at 0°. For all experiments rotations were centered around the geometric midpoint of the bounding box of a given object (as defined by the furthest reaches of the arms).

viewpoint (from their perspective). When subjects failed to correctly build an object they were given feedback as to where they made errors. Subjects were trained until they could twice successfully build all four of the objects from memory.

In the *Practice* phase subjects were shown the objects on the monitor at one of several select viewpoints and practiced naming each target object by pressing response keys labeled with their corresponding names. Other members of the complete stimulus set were presented as distractors and subjects responded by pressing a foot pedal. A subset of the objects, including two named targets and three unnamed distractors appeared at ten different viewpoints (the Rotated set), while the remaining two named targets appeared only at the training viewpoint (the Unrotated set). The viewpoints in which the Rotated set appeared, but the Unrotated set did not, were considered cohort views.

After extensive practice, in the *Surprise* phase, subjects were shown all of the objects, both targets and distractors from both the Rotated and Unrotated sets, in a much wider range of probe viewpoints (as well as the viewpoints used in the Practice phase). Otherwise the task remained unchanged, with subjects naming objects or identifying them as distractors.

Subjects were divided into three groups, each of which learned a different set of four target objects – this counterbalancing was done to guard against the idiosyncratic effects of any single object. In each block of trials in the Practice phase the two target objects and the three distractors in the Rotated set appeared at the training viewpoint and at separate rotations of 40°, 70°, and 190° around the X, Y, and Z axes (for a total of ten different viewpoints). The two target objects in the Unrotated set appeared at the training viewpoint only. The two target objects in the Rotated set appeared three times each at the training viewpoint and three times each at the other nine rotations. The two target objects in the Unrotated set appeared 30 times each at the training viewpoint. The three distractors appeared one time each at the same ten viewpoints as the Rotated target objects. A block in the Practice phase consisted of a total of 150 trials, preceded by six preliminary trials.

In each block of trials in the Surprise phase the target objects, whether from the Rotated or Unrotated set, appeared three times each at the training viewpoint and at the 33 viewpoints generated by rotation increments of 30° around the X, Y, or Z axis, while the distractor objects appeared one time each at the same 34 viewpoints. A block in the Surprise phase consisted of a total of 510 trials, preceded by six preliminary trials.

The experiment proceeded for 4 days as follows. On the first day subjects were trained to name the target objects and then ran in two blocks of the Practice phase. On the second and third days subjects ran in four blocks of the Practice phase on each day. On the fourth day, subjects ran in two blocks of the Practice phase and then one block of the Surprise phase. Both the Practice and Surprise phases also shared the following elements: feedback for incorrect responses was provided by a sharp beep; subjects were given a 5 s deadline and failure to respond within this deadline also resulted in a sharp beep; short rests were given to subjects every 50 trials; and, trials within each block were randomly ordered with a different random order for each subject on each block.

2.2. Results and discussion

Mean response times were computed from all correct naming responses collapsed over all stimulus subsets and objects within either the Rotated or Unrotated set; responses for distractors, preliminary trials, and trials where the subject did not respond within a 5 s time limit were discarded.

During the Practice phase naming times for objects in the Rotated set were initially dependent on the distance from the training viewpoint (mean response times were as follows in Block 1, training view: 3101 ms, X axis: 3785 ms, Y axis: 3428 ms, Z axis: 3537 ms; slopes, which measure the putative rate of normalization, were as follows in Block 1, X axis: 150°/s, Y axis: 343°/s, Z axis: 244°/s). With extensive practice, the effect of viewpoint diminished to near equivalent performance at all familiar viewpoints (mean response times in Block 12, training view: 1637 ms, X axis: 1714 ms, Y axis: 1639 ms, Z axis: 1643 ms; slopes in Block 12: X axis: 2385°/s, Y axis: 707°/s, Z axis: 2464°/s). These trends in response times were confirmed by a Block (1 vs. 12) × Viewpoint (40°, 70°, or 190°) ANOVA, where there were reliable main effects of Block, $F(1,11) = 179, P < 0.001$, Viewpoint, $F(2,22) = 12.4, P < 0.001$, and a reliable interaction, $F(2,22) = 4.31, P < 0.05$. Error rates for the Rotated set ranged from 23% in Block 1 to 5% in Block 12. For all blocks of Experiment 1, including Block 13, error rate patterns were consistent with response time patterns. Naming times for objects in the Unrotated set decreased with extensive practice (because these objects appeared at a single viewpoint, the effect of viewpoint could not be assessed during the Practice phase; the mean response times for the single view were 2512 ms in Block 1 and 1411 ms in Block 12). An ANOVA with Block (1 vs. 12) as the only factor revealed that this decrease in response times was reliable, $F(1,11) = 126, P < 0.001$. Error rates for the Unrotated set ranged from 4% in Block 1 to 1% in Block 12. Note that the lower error rates obtained for the Unrotated set as compared to the Rotated set are consistent with the fact objects in the Unrotated set appeared only at the canonical training view, while objects in the Rotated set appeared at unfamiliar views where recognition would be expected to be less accurate. Diminished viewpoint dependence with practice replicates Tarr and Pinker (1989) and Tarr (1995).

In the Surprise phase, naming times for the familiar objects in the Rotated set appearing at unfamiliar viewpoints were generally dependent on the distance from the nearest familiar viewpoint (Fig. 3). The two exceptions to this are the familiar viewpoints of 40° and 70° for X axis rotations where response times are slower than might be expected for familiar viewpoints; for a similar experiment using the same objects see Tarr (1995). However, naming times for the 40° and 70° Y and Z axis rotations were just as fast as those for the 10° view. Even given deviations from the predicted pattern, for the objects in the Rotated set regressing response times against distance from the nearest familiar viewpoint resulted in comparable slopes between Block 13 (Fig. 3), where objects were familiar in several views, and Block 1, where objects were familiar in only one view.

Overall, the pattern of viewpoint dependence was systematically related to the distance from the nearest familiar view in both Blocks 1 and 13 and the pattern of response times for the Rotated set again replicates Tarr and Pinker (1989) and Tarr (1995). This result lends credence to the conclusion that extensive practice led subjects to encode viewpoint-specific representations at each practiced viewpoint.

The question is, how did these learned views for the Rotated set influence the recognition of the Unrotated set in these same views? As shown in Fig. 3 both qualitative appearance and quantitative measures indicate that the pattern for the Unrotated set is similar to that obtained for the Rotated set. The similarity between the patterns of response times observed for the two sets may be assessed by correlating response times at each viewpoint for the Rotated set with response times at each viewpoint for the Unrotated set. This analysis revealed reliable correlations for all three axes of rotation: X axis: $r(10) = 0.65, P < 0.05$, Y axis: $r(10) = 0.77, P <$

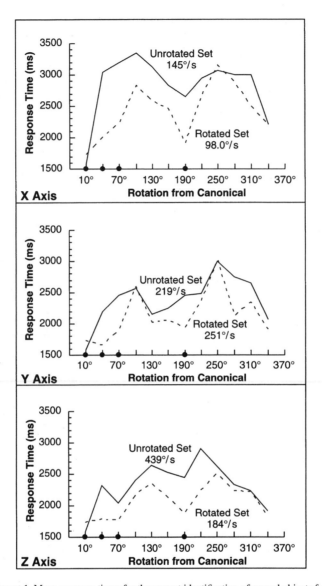

Fig. 3. Experiment 1. Mean response times for the correct identification of named objects for the Rotated and the Unrotated sets as a function of viewpoint and axis of rotation for the Surprise phase. Because rates of rotation vary with axis of rotation (Parsons, 1987) and because subjects appear to rotate through approximately the shortest 3D path (Tarr, 1995), each set of viewpoints around a given axis is displayed separately. Familiar practiced viewpoints (for the Rotated set) are marked with filled circles along the abscissa. The 10° rotation is the canonical training viewpoint and is the same across all three axes. Reported slopes were computed for Block 13 by averaging over all response times for unfamiliar viewpoints equidistant from a familiar viewpoint and then regressing these averaged response times against the distance to the *nearest* familiar viewpoint. For the Rotated sets the familiar viewpoints were defined as those viewpoints actually seen during the Practice phase. For the Unrotated sets the familiar viewpoints were defined as all cohort views.

0.01, Z axis: $r(10) = 0.73$, $P < 0.01$. Examining Fig. 3, however, it is also apparent that two patterns emerge depending on which cohort views are considered.

First, for the cohort views of 40° and 70° the predicted transfer from practice with the Rotated set to the Unrotated set does not seem to occur. In other words, response times for the Unrotated set at 40° and 70° are consistent with the pattern expected if only the training view was familiar (e.g. the pattern obtained by Tarr, 1995) – systematically increasing response times with increasing distance from this single familiar view. Why might this be the case? One possibility is that image-based views do not generalize to visually-similar objects. Although this explanation cannot be ruled out, it becomes less plausible when we consider the results for the 190° cohort view and for Experiments 2 and 3. An alternative possibility is that the 10° training view is highly canonical, and as such, subjects never learned (i.e. X axis rotations) or transferred (i.e. Y and Z axis rotations) viewpoint-specific representations for the practiced viewpoints of 40° and 70°. Why might the canonicality of the 10° view produce reduced transfer effects at adjacent viewpoints? It is known that canonical views are often weighted more heavily in determining the most effective match for objects appearing at nearby, albeit familiar, viewpoints (Palmer et al., 1981). There are several reasons for this to be true in Experiment 1. Subjects were taught the names of the target objects by repeatedly seeing only the 10° view. Thus, this view was presented first and more frequently than other views at the beginning of the experiment. Moreover, as illustrated in Fig. 4, this view displays the same surfaces as in the 40° and 70° views. Thus, the additional views provided little new information regarding the appearance of each object and distinct new views would be less likely to be encoded (Tarr, 1995).

Second, for the cohort view of 190° the predicted transfer from practice with the Rotated set to the Unrotated set does occur (Fig. 3). Specifically, when objects in the Unrotated set appeared at or near at the unfamiliar viewpoint of 190°, response times were generally dependent on this viewpoint – one at which objects in the Rotated set were familiar (this is confirmed by the similarity of slopes measured for the Rotated and Unrotated sets). In particular, diminished effects of viewpoint are apparent at 190° for all three axes of rotation – the familiar cohort view furthest from the familiar training viewpoint. If we consider only performance at 190°, the apparent transfer from the Rotated set to the Unrotated set replicates the pattern of viewpoint generalization obtained by Jolicoeur and Milliken (1989) and Murray et al. (1993). As stated earlier, however, these studies failed to probe viewpoints surrounding the cohort views to ascertain whether this transfer was mediated by viewpoint-dependent or viewpoint-invariant object representations (the latter being the usual interpretation). Thus, the pattern of recognition performance at viewpoints where neither objects from the Rotated or the Unrotated sets had previously appeared is particularly diagnostic. As shown in Fig. 3 response times at these viewpoints systematically increased with increasing distance from 190° and the training viewpoints. This increase in response times is not predicted by a viewpoint-invariant account, but is consistent with a viewpoint-dependent image-based account (Bülthoff et al., 1995). The fact that this pattern was obtained for the Unrotated set extends earlier findings of viewpoint dependence, e.g. (Tarr, 1995), indicating that viewpoint-spe-

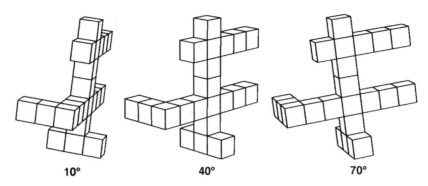

Fig. 4. The 10°, 40° and 70° views for one of the target objects used in Experiment 1. The 10° view was used for teaching subjects the name for each target object and therefore was presented both first and more frequently. Enhancing the canonicality of this view, the 40° and 70° views display the same visible surfaces as the 10° view.

cific representations may generalize to visually-similar objects never actually seen at the familiar views.

One question that arises is why we obtained generalization for the cohort view of 190°, but not for 40° or 70°. We have already discussed reasons why the canonicality of the 10° training view may have ameliorated the influence of adjacent views. Beyond this there may be other factors that facilitated generalization at the 190° view. In particular, geometric and structural similarity between this cohort view and the training view may have allowed better perceptual inferences regarding the appearance of objects in the Unrotated set at this viewpoint. First, consider that the silhouette of the 190° view is almost an exact mirror image of the 10° view (Hayward, 1998). It is well known that observers often show invariance across mirror reflection (Biederman and Cooper, 1991; Cooper et al., 1992). Note that this silhouette similarity did more than simply facilitate recognition of the 190° view – the roughly linear increase in response times with distance from this view indicates that a viewpoint-specific representation was instantiated and served as a target for recognition of adjacent viewpoints. Second, given that some objects actually appeared in the 190° view, subjects had reliable information regarding the orientation of surfaces for objects never seen at that view (since all objects shared the same components). Third, subjects might have been able to use symmetries and other structural regularities within objects to extrapolate or project so-called virtual views at unseen viewpoints. One possible mechanism for the creation of virtual views has been proposed by Poggio and Vetter (Poggio and Vetter, 1992; Vetter et al., 1994). Importantly, all of the objects used in Experiment 1 contained many symmetries
and a highly regular structure. Thus, it may be that image-based generalization between visually-similar objects is only possible or at least more likely when there is supporting geometric and structural information regarding the potential appearance of objects from new viewpoints – a hypothesis we explore in Experiment 2.

Finally, before accepting the proposal the image-based views can generalize between members of a visually-similar class, we should consider an alternative – that subjects learned a common shape-independent viewpoint-specific reference frame for each cohort view. The use of such abstract reference frames would serve equally well for objects in both the Rotated and Unrotated sets and would allow subjects to bypass some of the typically viewpoint-dependent mechanisms required for locating the top, bottom, and major axes of objects prior to recognition (Tarr and Pinker, 1991; Hummel and Biederman, 1992). Indeed, because all of the objects used in Experiment 1 shared a common foot and main axis, we may have made it relatively easy for subjects to learn an abstract reference frame at each practiced viewpoint. Although this explanation cannot be ruled out, there are two points suggesting that subjects did not learn abstract reference frames. First, in Experiment 1 the putative rates of normalization in Block 13 were much slower than those usually associated with top-bottom and axis finding procedures, but were in the range of rates found in other studies where normalization has been the preferred explanation (Parsons, 1987; Tarr and Pinker, 1991; Cohen and Kubovy, 1993; Tarr, 1995). Thus, the recognition of the objects in the Unrotated set is consistent with a dramatic change in performance specifically predicted by normalization to cohort views, rather than the slight diminution in viewpoint dependency related only to specifically-learned views that might result from bypassing relatively fast axis-finding procedures. Second, Gauthier and Tarr (1997b) found that orientation priming was shape dependent, in that, within a single homogeneous class, orientation priming was larger for those objects that were judged by subjects to be most similar. These results suggest that the representations at cohort views are specific to familiar objects rather than shape-independent reference frames. Finally, Experiments 2 and 3 address this alternative directly, providing evidence for image-based class generalization under conditions where a shape-independent reference frame account cannot hold.

3. Experiment 2

Experiment 1 establishes that viewpoint-specific knowledge about the appearance of objects may transfer to visually-similar cohort objects. This finding provides evidence that frequency of appearance, not just of a given exemplar, but of all members of a perceptually-defined object class, plays an important role in structuring view-based object representations – that is, determining which views are represented in visual memory. In Experiment 1, however, there were frequently-appearing viewpoints where subjects did not appear to learn viewpoint-specific representations – at viewpoints near to the canonical training view (40° and 70°), response times for objects in the Unrotated set increased with distance from the training view. Why might this be the case?

One possibility is that frequency, either of objects or their cohorts, is not the sole factor in determining whether representations are instantiated at particular viewpoints (otherwise diminished effects of viewpoint should occur at all cohort views). In particular, changes in image structure, as determined by the geometry of an object, may account for the presence of a view at 190° and the absence of views at 40° and 70°. Consider that the image structure of objects appearing at these latter two viewpoints will be quite similar to the image structure at the training view (Fig. 4). In contrast, the overall image structure of the same objects appearing at 190° will be quite different as compared to the training view. Thus, views may be stored preferentially in those instances where there are significant qualitative changes in image structure – a hypothesis reminiscent of aspect graph theory (Koenderink, 1987; Effelterre, 1994). Note, however, that the aspect graph approach assumes that views are defined only by qualitative transitions in image structure – here we are suggesting that qualitative variation is simply one factor taken into account in defining views within the representation. Again consider the pattern of results obtained in Experiment 1. The frequent appearance of objects at 40° and 70° was not reason enough to learn representations at these viewpoints given a qualitatively-similar preexisting view at 10° (which was presumably sufficient for recognition of objects appearing at 40° and 70°, albeit only through normalization processes). Consequently cohort views were learned only when the appearance of cohorts coincided with viewpoints that produced drastic changes in image structure, i.e. the 190° view.

Given the above argument, one might expect a difference between depth rotations that produce changes in image structure (rotations around the X axis or Y axis in Experiment 1) and image-plane rotations that do not produce changes in image structure (rotations around the Z axis). Experiment 1, however, does not offer any strong evidence for a difference between these two cases in terms of the particular views that were learned by subjects (nor does Tarr (1995)). In Experiment 2, we wish to consider the possibility that two distinct processes operated in Experiment 1.

First, for any viewpoint of an object, the more often a cohort of visually-similar objects appears at a given viewpoint, the greater the likelihood that this view will be represented in visual memory and will transfer to new exemplars of the class. This is simply an extension of the frequency of appearance principle offered by many researchers (Tarr and Pinker, 1989; Bülthoff and Edelman, 1992; Tarr, 1995) and apparently at work in Experiment 1. Crucially, this type of process is equally applicable to both depth and image-plane rotations. Second, exclusively across rotations in depth, the greater the qualitative dissimilarity between cohort views and actually-seen views, the greater the likelihood that a qualitatively-distinct view-point will be represented in visual memory and will transfer to new exemplars of the class. This process is based on the principle that views are organized into subregions (aspects) where the image structure remains relatively stable.

In Experiment 1 it appeared that the first principle was responsible for the transfer observed at the cohort view of 190° and the second principle was respon-sible for the failure of transfer at other cohort views. This, however, is an admittedly post hoc explanation and for most cases it is difficult to differentiate between these principles in that both may typically facilitate generalization across exemplars. In Experiment 2 we used a design similar to that used in Experi-ment 1, but we attempted to tease these two factors apart by reducing the effec-tiveness of the first principle (frequency of appearance) by presenting each exemplar at a different set of viewpoints. This manipulation had the effect of reducing the frequency of any specific viewpoint for the class as a whole. At the same time we hoped to specifically engage the second principle by presenting a large range of viewpoints. In such a case, transfer would be predicted for rotations in depth but not for rotations in the image-plane. Thus, for Experiment 2 we expected that cohort views generated by rotations around either the X axis or Y axis would transfer to objects in the Unrotated set, but that cohort views generated by rotations around the Z axis would not transfer.

3.1. Method

3.1.1. Subjects
Seventeen subjects from the MIT community participated in the experiment for pay. Two subjects were removed from the study because their performance was consistently at chance. All reported normal or corrected to normal vision. None of the subjects who participated in Experiment 2 served as subjects in any other experiment reported in this paper.

3.1.2. Materials
The stimuli used in Experiment 2 were identical to those used in Experiment 1 (see Fig. 1).

3.1.3. Design and procedure
Experiment 2 was quite similar to Experiment 1 with the exception of the specific viewpoints used during the Practice phase and the number of trials in the Surprise phase. The Training phase was identical to that used in Experiment 1. In each block of trials in the Practice phase one target object (A) in the Rotated set appeared at the training viewpoint and at separate rotations of 70° and 190° around the X, Y and Z axes (for a total of seven different viewpoints), while a second target object (B) in the Rotated set appeared at the training viewpoint and at separate rotations of 130° and 250° around the X, Y and Z axes (for a total of seven different viewpoints). The two target objects in the Unrotated set appeared at the training viewpoint only. The two target objects in the Rotated set appeared four times each at the training viewpoint and four times each at the other six rotations, while the two target objects in the Unrotated set appeared 28 times each at the training viewpoint. The two rotated distractors appeared two times at the same seven viewpoints as the rotated targets – one distractor object appearing at each subset of six target viewpoints – while the remaining distractor appeared 14 times at the training viewpoint only. A block in the Practice phase consisted of a total of 154 trials, preceded by six preliminary trials.

In each block of trials in the Surprise phase the target objects, whether from the Rotated or Unrotated set, appeared 12 times each at the training viewpoint and four times each at the 33 viewpoints generated by rotation increments of 30° around the X, Y or Z axis, while the distractor objects appeared six times each at the training viewpoint and two times each at the same 33 viewpoints. A block in the Surprise phase consisted of a total of 792 trials, preceded by six preliminary trials.

3.2. Results and discussion

As in Experiment 1 mean response times were computed from all correct naming responses collapsed over all stimulus subsets and objects within either the Rotated or Unrotated set; responses for distractors, preliminary trials, and trials where the subject did not respond within a 5 s time limit were discarded.

During the Practice phase naming times for objects in the Rotated set were initially dependent on the distance from the training viewpoint (mean response times were as follows in Block 1, for Object A: training view: 2073 ms, X axis: 2670 ms, Y axis: 2405 ms, Z axis: 2474 ms; slopes, which measure the putative rate of normalization, were as follows in Block 1: X axis: 683°/s, Y axis: 800°/s, Z axis: 306°/s; for Object B: training view: 2559 ms, X axis: 3125 ms, Y axis: 2648 ms, Z axis: 2756 ms; slopes: X axis: 203°/s, Y axis: 1853°/s, Z axis: 550°/s. With extensive practice, the effect of viewpoint diminished to near equivalent performance at all familiar viewpoints (mean response times in Block 12, for Object A: training view: 983 ms, X axis: 1030 ms, Y axis: 1012 ms, Z axis: 938 ms; slopes in Block 12: X axis: 5043°/s, Y axis: 13 569°/s, Z axis: −4386°/s; for Object B: training view: 1026 ms, X axis: 1048 ms, Y axis: 1000 ms, Z axis: 1000 ms; slopes: X axis: 53 476°/s, Y axis: 15 129°/s, Z axis: −58 140°/s − such incredibly fast slopes indicate that recognition performance became equivalent at all practiced, familiar views). These trends in response times were confirmed by Block (1 vs. 12) × Viewpoint (Object A: 10°, 70°, or 190°; Object B: 10°, 130°, or 250°) ANOVAs, where for Object A[2] there were reliable main effects of Block, $F(1,13) = 121$, $P < 0.001$, Viewpoint, $F(2,26) = 10.1$, $P < 0.001$, and a reliable interaction, $F(2,26) = 7.52$, $P < 0.005$, and for Object B[3] there was a reliable main effect of Block, $F(1,14) = 289$, $P < 0.001$, a nearly reliable effect of Viewpoint, $F(2,28) = 2.96$, $P = 0.07$, and a marginally reliable interaction, $F(2,28) = 2.36$, $P = 0.11$. Error rates for the Rotated set ranged from 40% for Object A and 43% for Object B in Block 1 to 4.0% for Object A and 5.0% for Object B in Block 12. For all blocks of Experiment 2, including Block 13, error rate patterns were consistent with response time patterns. Naming times for objects in the Unrotated set decreased with extensive practice (because these objects appeared at a single viewpoint, the effect of viewpoint could not be assessed during the Practice phase; the mean response times for the single view were 1880 ms in Block 1 and 855 ms in Block 12). An ANOVA with Block (1 vs. 12) as the only factor revealed that this decrease in response times was reliable, $F(1,14) = 132$, $P < 0.001$. Error rates for the Unrotated set ranged from 9.6% in Block 1 to 2.5% in Block 12. Again, such patterns, particularly diminished viewpoint dependence with practice, replicate the findings of Tarr and Pinker (1989) and Tarr (1995).

In the Surprise phase, naming times for the familiar objects in the Rotated set appearing at unfamiliar viewpoints were generally dependent on the distance from the nearest familiar viewpoint (Fig. 5, left panels). Several results stand out in this

---

[2]One subject was omitted from the analysis for Object A due to low accuracy rates in Block 1.

[3]Note that for Object B the practice viewpoints were located at 110° (250°) and 130°. As these two viewpoints were almost equidistant from the training viewpoint, practice would not be expected to dramatically change the relationship between response times at these two views.

regard. First, unlike most earlier studies of viewpoint dependence (e.g. Tarr, 1995), different objects were practiced at *different* viewpoints. According to view-based accounts of recognition, this should lead to the instantiation of viewpoint- *and* exemplar-specific representations. Thus, the view-based prediction is that only viewpoints in which a given object was actually seen should show diminished effects of viewpoint and a pattern for nearby viewpoints indicating that the familiar viewpoint was used as a target for normalization. For objects in the Rotated set, this strong prediction holds true. In the Surprise phase, Object A clearly shows systematic viewpoint dependency related to the distance from 10°, 70°, and 190° – the three familiar viewpoints (see Fig. 5). A similar pattern is observed for Object B. There is systematic viewpoint dependency related to the distance from 10°, 130° and 250° – again the three familiar viewpoints. Second, the putative rates of normalization measured by the slopes and the patterns of response times observed in Fig. 5 (left panels) are consistent with results where subjects have learned multiple views of familiar objects. In contrast to Experiment 1, the number of viewpoints per an object and the reasonably wide spacing between practice viewpoints apparently led subjects to instantiate views at every familiar viewpoint. Third, the fact that the slopes for Block 13, where objects were familiar in several views, are comparable to the slopes for Block 1, where objects were familiar in only one view, suggests that similar processes of normalization to a familiar view are operating in both the Practice and the Surprise phases. Overall, the results for the Rotated set again replicate the findings of Tarr and Pinker (1989) and Tarr (1995) regarding the recognition of familiar objects in unfamiliar viewpoints. Thus, we can once more conclude that extensive practice led subjects to encode viewpoint-specific representations at each practiced viewpoint.

As in Experiment 1, the crucial question is how did these learned views for the Rotated set influence the recognition of the Unrotated set in these same views? Inspecting Fig. 5 (right panels) it seems clear that, in contrast to the pattern obtained in Experiment 1, the pattern of response times for the Unrotated set was *not* similar to that obtained for the Rotated set. This was true in terms of the patterns for either of the objects in the Rotated set separately and the pattern expected if all of the cohort views were used as targets for the Unrotated set. In particular, response times for the Unrotated set were not dependent on the distance from the nearest cohort view (when that same view showed evidence of being a learned view for the Rotated set). Notably, the degree to which cohort views had *any* effect on the recognition of the objects in the Unrotated set varied with the axis of rotation. For depth rotations around the X axis or Y axis, there was little evidence for a specific influence of cohort views, but evidence for a general influence of cohort views. Thus, response times for the Unrotated set for depth rotations followed a pattern suggesting the presence of a single view for which cohort generalization was obtained. In contrast, for image-plane rotations around the Z axis, there was *no* evidence for any influence of any cohort views. Thus, response times for the Unrotated set for image-plane rotations followed a pattern suggesting that only the actually-seen canonical training view was used as a target for recognition. These inferences are supported by the correlations between response times at each viewpoint for the Rotated set (both Objects A

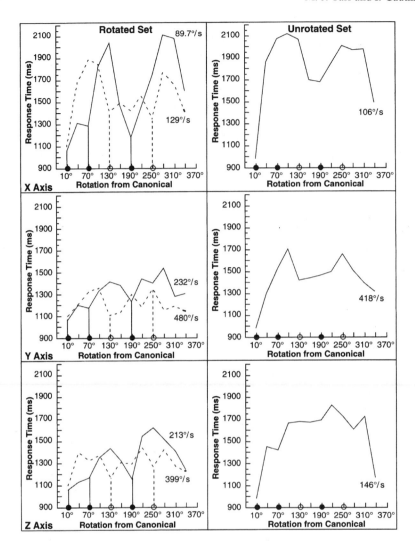

Fig. 5. Experiment 2. Mean response times for the correct identification of named objects for the Rotated and the Unrotated sets as a function of viewpoint and axis of rotation for the Surprise phase. Viewpoints around a given axis were again plotted separately. The left panels show the data for the two named objects in the Rotated set as filled and unfilled circles with the corresponding familiar practice viewpoints marked along the abscissa. The right panels show the data for the named objects in the Unrotated set with the cohort views marked along the abscissa. The 10° rotation is the canonical training viewpoint and is the same across all three axes.

and B) with response times at each viewpoint for the Unrotated set: Object A: X axis: $r(10) = 0.42$, n.s., Y axis: $r(10) = 0.41$, n.s., Z axis: $r(10) = 0.78$, $P < 0.01$; Object B: X axis: $r(10) = 0.65$, $P < 0.05$, Y axis: $r(10) = 0.77$, $P < 0.01$, Z axis: $r(10) = 0.07$, n.s.

We introduced Experiment 2 by suggesting that there are at least two principles that govern when a viewpoint is stored in visual memory. First, frequency of appearance for specific viewpoints has often been shown to prompt the creation of views for the exact exemplars seen in those viewpoints (Bülthoff and Edelman, 1992; Tarr, 1995). Experiment 1 demonstrated that this same principle applies more generally to visually-similar object classes. Second, we hypothesized that differences in image structure that arise with rotations in depth may also prompt the creation of views for both specific exemplars and visually-similar object classes. In Experiment 2 we tested for the existence of this latter principle by making the frequency of appearance principle less potent for the overall object class (by varying the viewpoints in which each exemplar appeared). The results of Experiment 2 suggest that this manipulation was successful. While each exemplar seen at several viewpoints was apparently represented as a set of views located at familiar viewpoints (Fig. 5) left panels, these same cohort views did not transfer to visually-similar objects in either the Rotated or Unrotated sets. This interpretation is supported by the finding that individual objects in the Rotated set showed performance patterns that were viewpoint dependent specifically to the viewpoints in which each object was actually seen – familiar viewpoints for the other member of the Rotated set had little effect. Second, objects in the Unrotated set showed performance patterns that were viewpoint dependent only to the canonical training view or to this view plus a single view approximately 180° from this view – even though, unlike Experiment 1, some of these cohort views were quite far from the training view. Thus, reducing the frequency of any specific viewpoint for the entire class of objects had the effect of disengaging frequency of appearance as a class-general principle for the creation of views in visual memory.

At the same time, this manipulation also had the desired effect of engaging object geometry as the basis for instantiating distinct views in visual memory. This is evidenced by the differences in the patterns obtained for depth rotations and for image-plane rotations for the Unrotated set (Fig. 5) – right panels. Indeed, the strong prediction we made was that familiarity with cohort views would transfer for rotations in depth, but not transfer for rotations in the image plane. Qualitatively, this is the case. For depth rotations there is a clear shift in the pattern of viewpoint dependence relative to the pattern expected if no cohort views were present (that is, performance related only to the distance from the single familiar canonical viewpoint). In contrast, for image-plane rotations there is little shift in the pattern of viewpoint dependence relative to the pattern expected in the absence of cohort views. The most obvious explanation for this set of results is that changes in the image structure influenced the instantiation of views. Specifically, while there were an equal number of cohort views for each axis of rotation, only for depth rotations were the consequent changes in image structure significant enough to warrant the instantiation of new views in visual memory.

Why might the apparent geometric effects for depth rotations manifest themselves only as a single view rather than at each cohort view? Put another way, why did the effects of the cohort views not transfer to each of the specific viewpoints where such a view occurred? As suggested earlier, one possible explanation is that the degree of visual similarity in the image structure at adjacent viewpoints led subjects to ignore some cohort views (Fig. 4). Effectively, the visual system may have computed the qualitative or aspect graph structure for each object or class and then only instantiated views where new aspects were apparent (Koenderink, 1987). This explanation is supported by the observation that some of the cohort views are sufficiently different from the canonical training view to prompt the instantiation of at least one new view. For depth rotations, the presence of the single view where transfer occurred suggests that observers were sensitive only to dramatic changes in qualitative image structure. It should be noted that this result does not support the notion of aspect graphs per se. In particular, current models of how aspect graphs are computed (Freeman and Chakravarty, 1980; Koenderink, 1987) rely on features that are so unstable as to produce intractable numbers of qualitatively-distinct views – many more for the objects used here than is evidenced by the behavioral data.

How then should the specific viewpoint of such a geometrically-defined view be determined? On the one hand, it might be sufficient to store the viewpoint maximally dissimilar from the canonical view; on the other hand, such a view might also be dissimilar from some of the already-seen familiar cohort views. One compromise might be to select a view that is qualitatively distinct from the canonical view, but also easily extrapolated from the canonical views and observed cohort views. Indeed, this latter explanation was suggested in Experiment 1 to account for the finding of cohort generalization for the 190° view, but not for the 40° or 70° views. The same factors that allowed generalization for the 190° case in Experiment 1 are true for the views that show the best transfer in Experiment 2. Adding to these factors, these particular views were intermediate between views at which a subset of the objects were actually seen. Thus, further facilitation may have arisen through view interpolation (Poggio and Edelman, 1990; Bülthoff and Edelman, 1992) or linear combinations of surrounding views (Ullman and Basri, 1991; Ullman, 1998).

In summary, the results of Experiment 2 provide further evidence for viewpoint-specific generalization from some members of a perceptually-defined object class to other members of that same class. Again there is some evidence that familiarity with specific viewpoints transfers to objects never actually seen in those viewpoints. In contrast to Experiment 1, however, generalization in Experiment 2 was also based on how the visible image structure of the objects varied with changes in viewpoint. Thus, there appear to be at least two principles governing how views are created in visual memory: the familiarity of a given viewpoint and the distinctiveness of the image structure for a given viewpoint.

4. Experiment 3

The stimulus set used in Experiments 1 and 2 may be thought of as a homogeneous object class analogous to a set of exemplars drawn from a single basic-level perceptual category (Brown, 1958; Rosch et al., 1976). While Experiment 2 demonstrated that not all familiar viewpoints for such a class generalize to all members of that class, we were also interested in viewpoint-specific generalization in the context of multiple object classes. That is, how would viewpoint-specific familiarity with one exemplar generalize to a second exemplar of the same class under conditions where subjects learned several distinct object categories? The idea that class generalization is mediated by viewpoint-specific image-based views would be supported if familiar views transfer only to objects of the same) perceptual category, thereby indicating that transfer is a function of visual similarity rather than a generic or strategic effect (Gauthier and Tarr, 1997b). Moreover, this transfer effect would be even more striking if it occurred when subjects were discriminating *between* exemplars of a single category. As mentioned earlier, a similar argument has already been made for orientation priming of 2D novel objects (Gauthier and Tarr, 1997b): blocking identification trials by orientation led to significant orientation priming of different objects within the same class but alternating objects between two distinct classes (i.e. qualitatively-different objects) rendered the blocking manipulation ineffective. Note, however, that the orientation priming in Gauthier and Tarr's study was transient in that generalization was tested only over a small number of consecutive trials. Experiment 3 tests whether the same type of class-specific transfer is present for the long-term generalization effects found in Experiments 1 and 2.

A second goal of Experiment 3 was to better measure the variation that is likely to be produced by changes in image structure associated with rotations in depth. As discussed in Experiment 2, the manner in which the visible geometry of an object or class changes is one principle that is likely to govern which views should be represented in visual memory (Freeman and Chakravarty, 1980; Koenderink, 1987; Tarr, 1995). However, to guard against idiosyncratic geometric effects for single objects, Experiments 1 and 2 counterbalanced sets of target objects across subjects. This counterbalancing manipulation meant that results were necessarily averaged over the different sets and, as a consequence, the geometric variation that might arise from specific viewpoints of specific objects would be lost. Thus, an object-specific baseline in the absence of any transfer effects could not be established. Because evidence for transfer between objects is best interpreted in terms of such a baseline, determination of more subtle generalization effects at cohort views was not possible in Experiments 1 and 2. For this reason, Experiment 3 used the same set of objects as targets for all subjects and limited the number of objects in each category to two (one Rotated set object and one Unrotated set object). In this way, the function relating response time to viewpoint in the Transfer condition will reflect more directly the factors of familiarity and object geometry.

We also introduced a second Baseline condition run on a separate group of subjects. In this latter condition, the same objects were trained and practiced only in the canonical training viewpoint and then tested in the same larger set of viewpoints used in the Surprise phase of the Transfer condition. This manipulation afforded us a measure of the variation in response times present when familiar objects were recognized for the first time in unfamiliar viewpoints where there were no familiar or cohort views other than the training view – that is, a condition in which deviations from linearity must be due to object geometry and not familiarity. Note that while this control would be useful in any study that assesses viewpoint dependence across multiple trained viewpoints (e.g. Bülthoff and Edelman,

1992; Humphrey and Khan, 1992), in the present study we omitted it from Experiments 1 and 2 because Tarr (1995) had already collected extensive data on the recognition of the same stimuli across viewpoints under various training conditions. In contrast, the stimuli used in Experiment 3 had not previously been used in any such experiment.

4.1. Method

4.1.1. Subjects

Thirty-four undergraduate students enrolled in Introduction to Psychology at Yale University were given course credit in return for their participation – because of extremely high error rates and excessive variation across different viewpoints in the final test phase of each condition, six subjects were excluded from excluded from the study, leaving twenty-eight subjects. All reported normal or corrected to normal vision. Fourteen of the subjects were run in the Transfer condition and 14 of the subjects were run in the Baseline condition. None of the subjects who participated in Experiment 3 served as subjects in any other experiment reported in this paper.

4.1.2. Materials

Twelve computer-generated 3D objects were created on a Macintosh computer using 3D modeling software (Alias Research, Toronto, Canada). The objects are shown in Fig. 6 in their arbitrarily designated canonical view (0° – leftmost column). There were six targets and six distractors, each group including three pairs of objects sharing the same central part, but with a slightly different arrangement of the smaller attached parts – it was assumed that subjects would treat objects sharing similarly-shaped central parts as members of the same distinct perceptual category (Tversky and Hemenway, 1984; Gauthier and Tarr, 1997a). The targets were given arbitrary names such as 'Kip', 'Kal', or 'Mar'. Images of targets and distractors were generated from 12 viewpoints (every 30° around the vertical/Y axis). Photo-realistic rendering of these images was done with 24-bit color and then each image was reduced to a common 8-bit palette using Debabilizer (Equilibrium, CA, USA). All objects were colored the same orange-ocher hue. They were presented centered on the screen against a white background. Stimuli were approximately 6.5 cm × 6.5 cm and subjects sat about 60 cm from the screen, yielding a display area subtending approximately 6.2° × 6.2° of visual angle. The experiment was run on an Apple Macintosh LC 475 equipped with a Trinitron 13 inch color monitor with a resolution of 640 × 480 pixels (72 dpi).

4.1.3. Design and procedure

Experiment 3 used the same Training-Practice-Surprise phase sequence used in Experiments 1 and 2. As before, the experiment was spread over 4 days, with the Training phase and two blocks of the Practice phase on day 1, four blocks of the Practice phase on days 2 and 3, and two blocks of the Practice phase and one block of the Surprise phase on day 4. In terms of presentation times, response deadlines, feedback and randomization of trials, Experiment 3 used the same procedures as used in Experiments 1 and 2.

The Training phase consisted of three parts and was identical for the Transfer and Baseline conditions. First, each target object was presented on the screen in its canonical training viewpoint (0°, Fig. 6) for 5 s with its associated name. Subjects were instructed to simply study each object and learn its name. Second, the six target objects were shown four times each with their names, for 5 s each, and subjects were required to press the key labeled with the appropriate name for each object. An incorrect key press resulted in a beep. Third, subjects ran in 36 randomly ordered naming trials with each target being shown a total of six times without its name. Again subjects were required to press the correct key within 5 s or a beep would result.

In the Practice phase subjects practiced recognizing the objects from a small number of viewpoints generated by rotations in depth around the vertical axis (Fig. 6). In the Transfer condition the Rotated set named target objects (one of each pair – $A_2 \rightarrow C_2$) were presented at 10° and at one other viewpoint, either 60°, 150° or 240°. The Unrotated set named target objects ($A_1 \rightarrow C_1$) appeared as

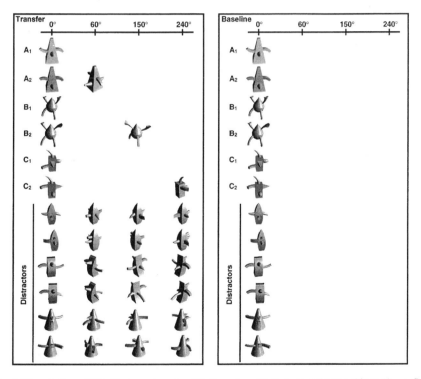

Fig. 6. The set of novel 3D objects used as stimuli in Experiment 3. Both named target objects ($A_1 \rightarrow C_1$, $A_2 \rightarrow C_2$) and unnamed distractor objects are shown in their arbitrarily defined canonical viewpoint (0°). Objects are also shown in the other viewpoints used during the practice phase. The left panel shows the viewpoints used for the Transfer condition and the right panel shows the viewpoints used for the Baseline condition.

frequently as the Rotated set, but only at the canonical training viewpoint of 10°. All six of the distractor objects appeared in all practiced viewpoints. The three target objects in the Rotated set appeared six times each at the training viewpoint and six times each at the other viewpoint. The three target objects in the Unrotated set appeared 12 times each at the training viewpoint. The six distractors appeared once each at the four viewpoints used individually for the objects in the Rotated set. A block in the Practice phase consisted of a total of 96 trials (75% targets/25% distractors). In the Baseline condition all of the named target objects and the distractors appeared only at the canonical training viewpoint (0°). Target objects were shown 12 times each and distractors were shown four times each. Note that the objects in the Unrotated set of the Transfer condition ($A_1 \rightarrow C_1$) appeared in the identical) set of viewpoints repeated the same number of times in the Baseline condition. Thus, the only difference for these objects (and between the Transfer and Baseline conditions) was whether or not their cohorts ($A_2 \rightarrow C_2$) appeared at other viewpoints.

In each block of trials in the Surprise phase for both the Transfer and Baseline conditions the target objects, regardless of the viewpoints shown during the Practice phase, appeared six times each at the training viewpoint and the 11 viewpoints generated by rotation increments of 30° around the Y axis. The distractor objects appeared two times each at the same 12 viewpoints. A block in the Surprise phase consisted of a total of 576 trials (75% targets/25% distractors). Note that the Surprise phase for the Transfer and Baseline conditions were identical). Thus, any differences in the pattern observed for target objects must be attributed to either direct or cohort familiarity with viewpoints seen during the Practice phase.

4.2. Results and discussion

Mean response times were computed from all correct naming responses collapsed over subjects; responses for distractors and trials where the subject did not respond within a 5 s time limit were discarded.

During the Practice phase in the Transfer condition naming times for objects in the Rotated set were initially dependent on the distance from the training viewpoint for two of the three objects (mean response times were as follows in Block 1, Object A_2: 1866 ms, Object B_2: 1691 ms, Object C_2: 2291 ms; slopes were as follows in Block 1, Object A_2: 71.6°/s, Object B_2: 641°/s, Object C_2: 157°/s). Note that an exception to the typical pattern of viewpoint dependence was obtained for Object B_2 – response times reflected much greater viewpoint invariance. Object B_2 was highly dissimilar from the other objects and showed the same parts attached to its top regardless of any rotation around the vertical axis – apparently this allowed subjects to use distinctive features to recognize the object (Tarr and Bülthoff, 1995). Given this immediate invariance it was not possible to obtain any evidence for class generalization for Object B_2 (in that no effects of viewpoint were expected for the Surprise phase).

With extensive practice, the effect of viewpoint diminished to near equivalent performance at both familiar viewpoints for Objects A_2 and C_2 (mean response times in Block 12, Object A_2: 750 ms, Object B_2: 743 ms, Object C_2: 774 ms; slopes in Block 12, Object A_2: $-1795°/s$, Object B_2: $-15\,267°/s$, Object C_2: $-11\,779°/s$). These trends in response times were confirmed by a Block (1 vs. 12) × Viewpoint (60°, 150° or 240°, depending on the object) ANOVAs. For Object A_2 there was a reliable main effect of Block, $F(1,11) = 39.2$, $P < 0.001$, Viewpoint, $F(1,11) = 9.72$, $P < 0.01$, and a reliable interaction, $F(1,11) = 14.6$, $P < 0.005$ (two subjects were excluded from this analysis because they had no correct responses in the Block $1 \times 60°$ cell). For Object B_2 there was a reliable main effect of Block, $F(1,13) = 47.2$, $P < 0.001$, but no reliable main effect of Viewpoint, $F(1,13) = 2.63$, n.s., or interaction, $F(1,13) = 1.70$, n.s. For Object C_2 there was a reliable main effect of Block, $F(1,12) = 52.0$, $P < 0.001$, Viewpoint, $F(1,12) = 4.62$, $P < 0.05$, and a near-reliable interaction, $F(1,12) = 4.07$, $P = 0.07$ (one subject was excluded from this analysis because they had no correct responses in the Block $1 \times 240°$ cell). Error rates for the Rotated set ranged from 24.4% for Object A_2, 17.3% for Object B_2, and 25.6% for Object C_2 in Block 1 to 0.60% for Object A_2, 1.79% for Object B_2, and 2.38% for Object C_2 in Block 12. For all blocks of Experiment 3, including Block 13, error rate patterns were consistent with response time patterns. Naming times for objects in the Unrotated set decreased with extensive practice (because these objects appeared at a single viewpoint, the effect of viewpoint could not be assessed during the Practice phase; the mean response times for the single view were 1300 ms for Object A_1, 1, 448 ms for Object B_1, and 1548 ms for Object C_1 in Block 1 and 748 ms for Object A_1, 741 ms for Object B_1, and 758 ms for Object C_1 in Block 12). ANOVAs with Block (1 vs. 12) as the only factor revealed that this decrease in response times was reliable for all three objects, $F(1,13) = 11.5$, $P < 0.005$, for Object A_1, $F(1,13) = 49.7$, $P < 0.001$, for Object B_1, and $F(1,13) = 52.2$, $P < 0.001$, for Object C_1. Error rates for the Unrotated set ranged from 11.9% for Object A_1, 14.9% for Object B_1, and 7.74% for Object C_1 in Block 1 to 0.60% for Object A_1, 1.19% for Object B_1, and 3.57% for Object C_1 in Block 12. Error rate patterns were always consistent with response time patterns.

During the Practice phase in the Baseline condition naming times for objects decreased with extensive practice. For individual objects response times and errors were quite similar to those obtained in the Transfer condition. Overall, for objects that were members of the Rotated set in the Transfer condition, in the Baseline condition[4] mean response times were 1758 ms for Block 1 and 1098 ms for Block 12 and error rates were 24.6% for Block 1 and 1.98% for Block 12. For objects that were members of the Unrotated set in the Transfer condition, in the Baseline condition mean response times were 1528 ms for Block 1 and 1198 ms for Block 12 and error rates were 17.1% for Block 1 and 2.98% for Block 12.

In the Transfer condition of the Surprise phase, naming times for the familiar objects in the Rotated set appearing at unfamiliar viewpoints were generally dependent on the distance from the nearest familiar viewpoint (Fig. 7). However, an inspection of the response times graphs makes it clear that there were also instances where viewpoint dependency occurred independently of viewpoint familiarity. This

---

[4]Due to a computer error one subject was not included in the analysis for the Practice phase of the Baseline condition.

can be seen for Object A_2 – there is a unexpected dimunition in response times around the 180° viewpoint. The possible reasons for this pattern may be assessed by comparing the results of the Transfer condition to those of the Baseline condition. For the objects in the Rotated set, the difference between these conditions is that the objects were actually practiced in the cohort view in the Transfer condition, therefore subjects had direct familiarity with these viewpoints. Thus, any apparent viewpoint dependency related to familiarity would be expected to be absent for the Baseline condition.

The fact that familiarity did alter performance at familiar viewpoints may be verified statistically by comparing the response time for a practiced familiar viewpoint for a given object to the response time for that same viewpoint when it is unfamiliar for the same object. This amounts to a t-test between the Transfer and Baseline conditions for each object in the Rotated set for its unique familiar viewpoint. These analyses revealed reliable differences for Object A_2, $t(26) = 3.51, P < 0.005$, and Object C_2, $t(26) = 2.62, P < 0.01$, as well as a near-reliable difference for Object B_2, $t(26) = 1.82, P = 0.08$ (suggesting that some viewpoint-specific learning was occurring despite the relative lack of viewpoint dependence during the Practice phase). Alternatively, viewpoint dependency related to properties intrinsic to the stimuli, e.g. object geometry, would be expected to be present for the Baseline condition. Such is the case for the patterns obtained for Object A_2 (and to a lesser extent, Object C_2) – there is a clear parallel between the response times for the Transfer and Baseline conditions for this object. Notably, this unexpected viewpoint dependency was centered around 180° – the most obvious virtual view in terms of both a simple mirror-reflection in the silhouette (Hayward, 1998) and the symmetries present in each object. As discussed earlier, Poggio and Vetter (1992) have proposed a mechanism by which such views may be inferred for symmetrical objects (for related work see Vetter et al., 1994; Logothetis and Pauls, 1995). Our results seem to indicate that this effect is not limited to perfectly symmetrical objects. These observations are reflected by the fact that the slopes measured for Block 13 do not capture the pattern of viewpoint dependence seen in the response time graphs shown in Fig. 7.

As in the previous experiments, the crucial question is how did the learned views for Objects A_2 and C_2 of the Rotated set influence the recognition of Objects A_1 and C_1 of the Unrotated set in these same views? Inspecting Fig. 8 it appears that the pattern of response times for the Unrotated set was sometimes similar to that obtained for the Rotated set. As stated earlier, the exception is Object B_1 – the post hoc explanation for this being the near immediate viewpoint invariance observed in Block 1 for its cohort, Object B_2, and now observed for Object B_1. Given the absence of any significant viewpoint dependency, it is impossible to assess whether transfer occurred between the Rotated and Unrotated sets. Indeed, there was no reliable difference between the Transfer and Baseline conditions for Object B_1 at the cohort view, $t(26) < 1$. Given this result, Objects B_1 and B_2 will not be included in any further analyses or discussion. For the remaining two objects in the Unrotated set, there does appear to be a shift in the pattern of response times at the cohort view and viewpoints nearby this view. This can be clearly seen in Fig. 8

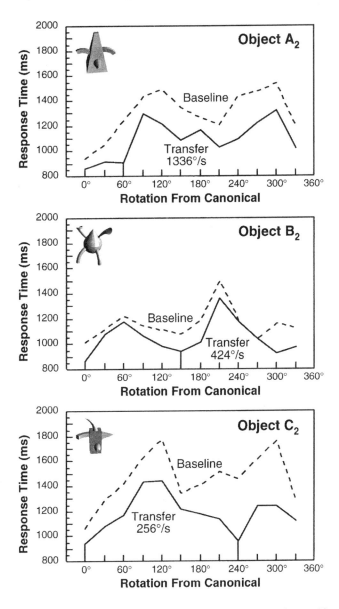

Fig. 7. Experiment 3, Rotated set. Mean response times for correct identification of target objects that were familiar at two viewpoints ($A_2 \rightarrow C_2$) in the Transfer condition as a function of viewpoint for the Surprise phase. The solid line plots the results from the Transfer condition and the dashed line plots the results from the Baseline condition for the same objects. Note that vertical lines mark the viewpoints at which the objects in the Rotated set were *actually* studied during the Practice phase of the Transfer condition; only the 0° viewpoint was used in the Baseline condition. Slopes were not computed for the Baseline condition because of the clear influence of virtual views – an effect not predicted prior to the experiment. Thus, any computation of the putative rates of normalization would be based on post hoc assumptions about the targets of normalization.

by comparing the functions for the Unrotated set objects in the Transfer and Baseline conditions.

It should be emphasized that there is no difference in the *direct* experience subjects received with the objects in the Unrotated set between these two conditions. Therefore, any difference in the response time patterns must be attributable to contextual differences – that is, the cohort views at which objects in the Rotated set appeared. For Object A_1 this shift can be observed in three ways: the lower response time at the cohort view between the Transfer and Baseline conditions, $t(26) = 2.79$, $P < 0.01$; the lower response times at viewpoints adjacent to the cohort view; and, crucially, the shift in the location of the peak denoting the midpoint between views used as targets of normalization. For Object A_1 the peak moves to between 60° and 180° for the Transfer condition. For Object C_1 this shift can be similarly observed: there is a lower response time at the cohort view between the Transfer and Baseline conditions, $t(26) = 1.88$, $P = 0.07$; the dramatically lower response times at viewpoints adjacent to the cohort view; and, crucially, the absence of a peak denoting the midpoint between views used as targets of normalization. For Object C_1 the peak shifts from being between 180° (the mirror-image silhouette and the geometrically-defined virtual view) and 360° for the Baseline condition to being entirely absent for the Transfer condition.

To summarize, Experiment 3 had two goals. First, we were interested in viewpoint-specific generalization in the context of multiple object classes. Here we found that viewpoint-specific familiarity with one exemplar of a perceptually-defined class generalized *only* to other exemplars of that same class and not to exemplars of other classes. Indeed, this class generalization occurred despite the fact that subjects were discriminating between members of a class. This is evidenced by the patterns of performance obtained for Objects A_1 and C_1 in the Transfer condition relative to the patterns obtained for the same objects in the Baseline condition (the only difference between conditions being the viewpoints in which *other* members of each class appeared). Second, we were interested in comparing object- and class-specific familiarity effects to class-general geometric effects as caused by variations in image structure. We found that there were class-general viewpoint dependencies – in particular, for the silhouette mirror-image and at virtual views where symmetry relationships in the bounding contours provided information about the appearance of objects not actually seen at those viewpoints (Hayward, 1998). This is evidenced by the similarity in the patterns of performance between the same objects in the Transfer and Baseline conditions at non-familiar/cohort views (specifically at viewpoints where previous studies suggest that there should be much larger costs for recognition, (Tarr, 1995). Overall, such results lend further support to the hypothesis that image-based representations may support generalization across members of a class. These results, however, also indicate that transfer effects may be relatively subtle and expressed differently depending on the geometry of an object as well as the specific image structure at familiar views. Thus, some of the evidence garnered in Experiment 3 would most probably have been undetectable were results averaged over several different target objects as in Experiments 1 and 2.

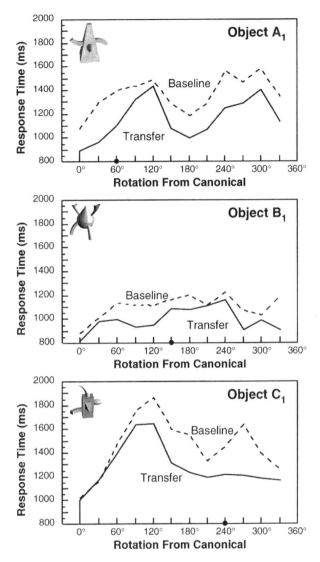

Fig. 8. Experiment 3, Unrotated set. Mean response times for correct identification of target objects that were familiar at only one viewpoint ($A_1 \rightarrow C_1$) in the Transfer and the Baseline conditions as a function of viewpoint for the Surprise phase. The solid line plots the results from the Transfer condition and the dashed line plots the results from the Baseline condition for the same objects. Note that vertical lines mark the viewpoint at which the objects were *actually* studied during the Practice phase of both conditions; the black dots mark the viewpoints at which objects in the Rotated set were studied during the Transfer condition. Note that there was no difference between the Transfer and Baseline conditions for the objects in the Unrotated set – any differences must be attributed to differences in familiarity for views of the Rotated set. Slopes were not computed for the Unrotated set and the Baseline condition because of the clear influence of virtual views – an effect not predicted prior to the experiment. Thus, any computation of the putative rates of normalization would be based on post hoc assumptions about the targets of normalization.

5. General discussion

We began this paper by asking whether image-based recognition mechanisms are capable of generalizing from known instances of a class to unknown instances of that same class. Because earlier image-based mechanisms such as those proposed by Poggio and Edelman (1990) have been associated with rigid templates (Biederman and Gerhardstein, 1995) it has often been assumed that they are incapable of such class generalization. Given that basic-level or categorical recognition is an important element of everyday object recognition, it is critical that any theory of visual recognition exhibit some stability across object classes (Marr and Nishihara, 1978). Indeed, several computational models of image-based recognition tacitly acknowledge this fact in their attempts to develop object representations that generalize across members of a given class. For example, the model proposed by Edelman and Weinshall (1991) used blurred template matching – a process that presumably would allow for greater generalization across members of a class (although with a some concomitant loss of sensitivity). More recently, Edelman (1995) (see also Edelman et al., 1996) has proposed an approach to visual representation in which objects are stored in terms of their relative similarity in a high-dimensional space. Importantly, this representation allows for dynamic access to task-relevant features, thereby supporting both categorical and exemplar-specific recognition within a single system. Some experimental implications of this approach for class-based generalization in face recognition have been explored by O'Toole et al. (1998). Finally, also in the domain of face recognition, Beymer and Poggio (1996) describe a model that uses a vector representation of images and computes a dense correspondence, e.g. visual similarity, between each image in the database. They suggest that this process allows the learning of a *flexible* exemplar-based model for a class of objects. Moreover, this flexible model specifically allows the generation of new virtual views for an object from a single example view, represented as a 2D shape vector, if appropriate prototypical views of other objects in the same class are available (Beymer and Poggio, 1996). Here we investigated whether a similar class-generalization mechanism is used in human object recognition. The results of three experiments indicate that viewpoint-specific representations are *sensitive* enough to support discrimination between visually-similar exemplars, yet *stable* enough to generalize to visually-similar exemplars (transfer views). More specifically, we found that:

- Experience with an object at a given viewpoint transfers to visually-similar objects, albeit in a viewpoint-dependent manner. Thus, the representations or virtual views instantiated for new objects appear to share a status similar to that of viewpoint-specific image-based representations arising from extensive practice (Experiment 1).
- Viewpoint-specific image-based representations are encoded according to at least two principles: the frequency with which objects of a given class are seen at specific viewpoints and the distinctiveness of these views in terms of their geometrical image structure (Experiment 2).

- Transfer between image-based views is class specific (as defined by the visual similarity for a set of objects) in the sense that generalization across viewpoint-specific representations occurs only between objects of a visually homogeneous class (Experiment 3).

Overall, these results are consistent with the hypothesis that human perceivers learn viewpoint-specific representations based on: the frequency with which a specific object appears at different viewpoints; the frequency with which visually-similar objects appear at different viewpoints; and, the distinctiveness of the image structure of different viewpoints relative to other known viewpoints. In total, these findings represent a significant extension to the image-based approach to object recognition.

Although both viewpoint-dependent performance (Jolicoeur, 1985) and diminished viewpoint dependency with increasing familiarity (Tarr and Pinker, 1989; Bülthoff and Edelman, 1992; Tarr, 1995) have been reported previously, the present experiments provide a demonstration that experience with an object's visually-similar cohorts can facilitate its recognition at novel viewpoints – presumably through the instantiation of image-based views. Moreover, by probing recognition performance at unfamiliar viewpoints adjacent to such views, our results demonstrate that this class generalization is mediated by viewpoint-specific representations.

Earlier evidence for class transfer between objects seen at a given view and objects not seen at that view (Jolicoeur and Milliken, 1989; Murray et al., 1993) can be reinterpreted based on our present results. Specifically, such findings were typically taken as support for the existence of viewpoint-invariant object representations. Our results, however, suggest that class transfer can occur when subjects learn *viewpoint-specific* representations that have some visual similarity or visual feature overlap with new objects subsequently presented at the familiar viewpoints. One caveat worth mentioning regarding our interpretation of these earlier results is that both studies found transfer between familiar objects that, for the most part, were members of different basic-level classes. Thus, the visual similarity between objects actually seen at a given orientation and the transfer objects was presumably somewhat less than that between the novel objects used in the present experiments. On the other hand, several factors may have contributed to obtaining viewpoint-specific transfer even with low object similarity. First, all of the familiar objects used in these studies had a canonical upright orientation relative to gravity. Second, a constant test orientation was used for all of the objects. Third, rotations were always in the picture plane. As a consequence of these factors, the intrinsic axes of the objects were similar across classes, the relative change in the tops and bottoms of the objects was consistent across the experiment, and the image structure of objects from familiar to unfamiliar orientations remained unchanged. Taken together, these conditions may have resulted in transfer orientations in which the appearance of unfamiliar objects was highly predictable. Unfortunately, in these earlier studies (Jolicoeur and Milliken, 1989; Murray et al., 1993) the possibility that transfer was mediated by viewpoint-specific representations was never considered and, as a consequence, the view specificity of the facilitation obtained for objects seen for the first time at new viewpoints was not tested. Obviously, further investigation is necessary to establish whether our account of image-based transfer holds for the experimental conditions used by other researchers.

Interestingly, our results also allow us to reinterpret a classic finding of Bartram (1974). Bartram tested naming performance across blocks of trials in which pictures of objects could be the same, pictures of objects could vary in viewpoint, or pictures of objects could be different objects with the same names as previously named objects. He found strong practice effects in all three conditions, including instances where subjects used the same names for new pictures. Bartram also investigated what happened when subjects were switched from one condition to another. Here he found that there was good transfer from named objects in one view to the same objects in new views, but little transfer from named objects to new objects with the same names. His interpretation of these results was that memory for pictures includes both visual 2D (stimulus) and visual 3D (object) codes. Interestingly, Bartram observed that his results were consistent with an exclusively 2D code if transfer was a function of the extent to which physical features present in one picture overlap with features in other views of the same object. Moreover, he presented some data supporting this hypothesis, pointing out that naming latencies for new viewpoints were more variable than for familiar viewpoints and that this difference may have been related to the fact that the degree of overlap between different spatial viewpoints was varied from almost complete (45° rotation) to minimal (180° rotation). Thus, Bartram's results are consistent with modern theories of view normalization (Tarr and Pinker, 1989; Poggio and Edelman, 1990; Bülthoff and Edelman, 1992).

Regarding same-name/different-picture manipulations, Bartram concludes that the fact that subjects showed practice effects for continuously naming new objects with the same names as previously named objects, but did not show transfer from naming the same objects several times to new objects with the same names is evidence for the presence of a semantic code. He argues that any practice advantage obtained for *repeatedly* applying the same name to different objects must be semantically mediated because the visual codes that would produce such practice effects would, according to his reasoning, also result in transfer when the same object is named for only one or two *presentations* and a new object with the same name is then shown. Based, however, on the recent results of Gauthier and Tarr (1997b), class transfer between different exemplars of an object class may require many exposures (in order to build up sufficient activation in the recognition network – see the discussion below) and may be highly viewpoint specific (Bartram is not clear about whether different same-name objects are shown at the same viewpoints used for earlier exemplars of the class). Thus, Bartram may have obtained practice effects when subjects continuously named new exemplars of a class because class-general activation accumulated over many trials, but failed to obtain transfer effects when subjects named new exemplars after only a few trials because of insufficient activation and because the viewpoints for different objects were not held constant. Indeed, the class transfer reported in this paper is the end-result of many repetitions of the same objects in the same viewpoints. By this account, Bartram's experimental findings are consistent with a model of object recognition in which viewpoint-specific representations mediate both view and class generalization based on visual similarity.

5.1. An image-based network for class recognition

In Section 1 we proposed that a network of linked image-based viewpoint-specific representations could support both subordinate-level discriminations *and* basic-level generalizations. Fig. 9 illustrates a simple conceptualization of such a network that is composed of units (possibly ensembles of neurons) that represent particular exemplars of objects at familiar viewpoints. The key idea of this model is that averaging across different subpools of these units could yield descriptions that would be well suited for basic-level or for subordinate-level recognition tasks. Upon presentation of a stimulus, viewpoint-specific units coding for all visually-similar objects would be activated in proportion to the degree of image-based similarity or feature overlap (for specific models of how such high-dimensional feature spaces might be created see Edelman, 1995; Edelman et al., 1996). For example, when shown a front view of a Victorian chair, the unit coding for the front view of that chair *and* the units coding for other views of the same chair would be activated. Activation related to the degree of view similarity is similar to the neural model of viewpoint-dependent recognition proposed by Perrett et al. (1998). Additionally, because objects of the same class share a configuration of features, units coding for the front view of *other exemplars* of the class of chairs would also be activated. With a large number of exemplars of the same class stored in such a network, clusters of visual similarity would result in a coarse description of the object class, in other words, a visual representation of the basic level (Edelman (1995) proposes a similar population response for representing the basic level). Note that this model may also help to account for the fact that visually atypical members of a class are often named with greater specificity or at what is sometimes referred to as the entry level (Jolicoeur et al., 1984). For example, penguins are typically first identified as penguins rather than birds (the putative basic-level category). Due to the relatively low visual similarity between most birds and penguins, exemplars of penguins will not be included within the cluster of units that defines the category 'birds'. Moreover, when an image of a penguin is encountered it will almost exclusively activate units coding for views of penguins – thus, access to the category penguin (rather than bird) is immediate. In contrast, when subordinate-level or exemplar-specific discrimination is required, a cluster of visually-similar views could eventually arrive at a state in which the most appropriate view reaches a threshold and 'wins' over the other exemplar-specific representations. Thus, a subordinate-level task would set a relatively high threshold of pooled activation as compared to a basic-level task.

5.2. Neural correlates

In this special issue, Perrett et al. (1998) present an elegant model of how cumulative evidence from cells tuned to image-based features can provide the information necessary for recognition *and* account for behavioral effects such as viewpoint dependency. They propose an approach in which the neural response to the presentation of a complete object can lead to faster accumulation of evidence as compared to the accumulation of evidence for individual parts of the same object. This behavior holds even if there are more cells tuned to individual parts than the whole: presentation of the complete object leads to the activation of more cells that contribute to the recognition of the object. Importantly, the model presented by Perrett et al. makes use of the broad tuning across viewpoints, typical of neurons responsive to body parts or other objects (Logothetis et al., 1995), to explain how a population of neurons can respond, albeit with a cost in time, to novel views of familiar objects. There is evidence that visual neurons in the temporal cortex are also broadly tuned to overall object similarity, that is, cells tend to prefer visually-similar pictures (Miyashita et al., 1993). Therefore, Perrett et al.'s model might be extended to account for transfer across different exemplars of a homogeneous class. What is required is that neurons coding for an object's visually-similar cohorts also contribute to the recognition of that object (as suggested in Fig. 9). Consistent with Perrett et al.'s account, we propose that the greater the number of visually-similar exemplars encoded at a given viewpoint the greater the class transfer expected for that particular view (although here we were able to obtain this transfer with only two known exemplars per class – perhaps because of the clearly restricted nature of the class in the context of the experiment). We also suggest that increased variation in the views experienced for a particular class will facilitate transfer by geometrical interpolation (Bülthoff and Edelman, 1992; Librande, 1992; Poggio and Vetter, 1992) by virtue of a large diversity of neurons coding for different visual attributes. Given a large set of geometric information regarding the appearance of an object or class, there may

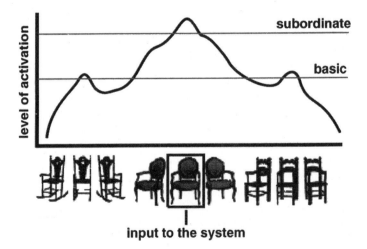

Fig. 9. An exemplar-based mechanism for view and class generalization. Upon presentation of an object, units coding for similar views of the same object and similar views of similar objects are activated. Depending on the specificity of the judgment required, the system can derive either a coarse or a progressively finer match by varying the threshold of pooled activation (see also Edelman, 1995).

exist sufficient complementary information for inferring the virtual appearance an object at novel viewpoints in depth. Thus, views may sometimes be based on the geometric overlap among visible features rather than absolute differences in viewpoint – an interpretation also consistent with the findings of Perrett et al.

5.3. Conclusions

To summarize our results, we find evidence that viewpoint-specific object representations are apparently learned according to three distinct principles:

1. How frequently a given object appears at a given viewpoint.
2. How frequently visually-similar objects appear at a given viewpoint.
3. How dramatically the geometric image structure of objects changes at different viewpoints.

Earlier models of image-based recognition assumed that viewpoint invariance was a consequence of practice with specific viewpoints and that viewpoint-dependent performance at unfamiliar viewpoints was best explained by normalization to familiar viewpoint-specific representations (Bülthoff and Edelman, 1992; Tarr, 1995). The inherent view-specificity of this account seemed to associate, at least implicitly, the mechanisms used for view generalization with inflexible templates, a point reinforced by related computational models of the time (Poggio and Edelman, 1990; Weinshall et al., 1990). Motivated by the well-known limitations of standard template models, proponents of alternative approaches claimed that image-based models were incapable of generalizing across class (Biederman and Gerhardstein, 1993, 1995), a problem at least as challenging as generalizing across viewpoint. To the extent that no specific image-based model proposed a mechanism for achieving class generalization, this criticism remained valid. Recent computational work, however, indicates that this limitation does not apply to more sophisticated image-based approaches (Poggio and Brunelli, 1992; Lando and Edelman, 1995; Vetter et al., 1995; Beymer and Poggio, 1996; Edelman et al., 1996). Here we demonstrate that this limitation does not apply to viewpoint-dependent recognition mechanisms in humans either. We found that viewpoint-specific information learned for some members of a homogeneous class generalized to other members of that class. Such results indicate that shape representations in humans are indeed viewpoint-specific, depicting the appearance of an object from distinct views, but that these representations are flexible enough to support a range of recognition tasks, including both fine exemplar-specific discriminations and coarse categorical judgments.

Acknowledgements

The authors wish to thank Laurie Heller, Shimon Edelman, and Tommy Poggio for their comments, William Milberg and Sheila Blumstein for their help in interpreting the data, Scott Yu for creating the objects used in Experiment 3, and Carmita

Signes and Tom Andrus for help in running some of the experiments. This work was supported by NSF grant BNS 8518774 to Steven Pinker, MIT, and grants from the Yale University Social Science Faculty Research Fund and the Air Force Office of Scientific Research, contract number F49620-91-J-0169 to MJT.

References

Bartram, D.J., 1974. The role of visual and semantic codes in object naming. Cognitive Psychology 6, 325–356.

Beymer, D., Poggio, T., 1996. Image representations for visual learning. Science 272, 1905–1909.

Biederman, I., 1987. Recognition-by-components: a theory of human image understanding. Psychological Review 94, 115–147.

Biederman, I., Cooper, E.E., 1991. Evidence for complete translational and reflectional invariance in visual object priming. Perception 20, 585–593.

Biederman, I., Gerhardstein, P.C., 1993. Recognizing depth-rotated objects: evidence and conditions for three-dimensional viewpoint invariance. Journal of Experimental Psychology: Human Perception and Performance 19 (6), 1162–1182.

Biederman, I., Gerhardstein, P.C., 1995. Viewpoint-dependent mechanisms in visual object recognition. Journal of Experimental Psychology: Human Perception and Performance 21 (6), 1506–1514.

Brown, R., 1958. How shall a thing be called?. Psychological Review 65, 14–21.

Bülthoff, H.H., Edelman, S., 1992. Psychophysical support for a two-dimensional view interpolation theory of object recognition. Proceedings of the National Academy of Science USA 89, 60–64.

Bülthoff, H.H., Edelman, S.Y., Tarr, M.J., 1995. How are three-dimensional objects represented in the brain?. Cerebral Cortex 5 (3), 247–260.

Cohen, D., Kubovy, M., 1993. Mental rotation, mental representation, and flat slopes. Cognitive Psychology 25 (3), 351–382.

Cooper, L.A., Schacter, D.L., Ballesteros, S., Moore, C., 1992. Priming and recognition of transformed three-dimensional objects: effects of size and reflection. Journal of Experimental Psychology: Learning. Memory and Cognition 18, 43–57.

Corballis, M.C., Zbrodoff, N.J., Shetzer, L.I., Butler, P.B., 1978. Decisions about identity and orientation of rotated letters and digits. Memory and Cognition 6, 98–107.

Edelman, S., 1995. Representation, similarity, and the chorus of prototypes. Minds and Machines 5 (1), 45–68.

Edelman, S., Bülthoff, H.H., 1992. Orientation dependence in the recognition of familiar and novel views of three-dimensional objects. Vision Research 32 (12), 2385–2400.

Edelman, S., Cutzu F., Duvdevani-Bar, S., 1996. Similarity to reference shapes as a basis for shape representation. In: Cottrell, G.W. (Ed.), Proceedings of 18th Annual Conference of the Cognitive Science Society. San Diego, CA, pp. 260–265.

Edelman, S., Weinshall, D., 1991. A self-organizing multiple-view representation of 3D objects. Biological Cybernetics 64, 209–219.

Effelterre, T.V., 1994. Aspect graphs for visual recognition of three-dimensional objects. Perception 23, 563–582.

Freeman, H., Chakravarty, I., 1980. The use of characteristic views in the recognition of three-dimensional objects. In: Gelsema, E.S., Kanal, L.N. (Eds.), Pattern Recognition in Practice. New York: North-Holland Publishing Company, pp. 277–288.

Gauthier, I., Tarr, M.J., 1997a. Becoming a 'Greeble' expert: exploring the face recognition mechanism. Vision Research 37 (12), 1673–1682.

Gauthier, I., Tarr, M.J., 1997b. Orientation priming of novel shapes in the context of viewpoint-dependent recognition. Perception 26, 51–73.

Hayward, W.G., 1998. Effects of outline shape in object recognition. Journal of Experimental Psychology: Human Perception and Performance, 24 (2) 427–440.

Hayward, W.G., Tarr, M.J., 1997. Testing conditions for viewpoint invariance in object recognition. Journal of Experimental Psychology: Human Perception and Performance 23 (5), 1511–1521.

Hill, H., Schyns, P.G., Akamatsu, S., 1997. Information and viewpoint dependence in face recognition. Cognition 62 (2), 201–222.

Hummel, J.E., Biederman, I., 1992. Dynamic binding in a neural network for shape recognition. Psychological Review 99 (3), 480–517.

Humphrey, G.K., Khan, S.C., 1992. Recognizing novel views of three-dimensional objects. Canadian Journal of Psychology 46, 170–190.

Jolicoeur, P., 1985. The time to name disoriented natural objects. Memory and Cognition 13, 289–303.

Jolicoeur, P., 1990. Identification of disoriented objects: a dual-systems theory. Mind and Language 5 (4), 387–410.

Jolicoeur, P., Gluck, M., Kosslyn, S.M., 1984. Pictures and names: making the connection. Cognitive Psychology 16, 243–275.

Jolicoeur, P., Milliken, B., 1989. Identification of disoriented objects: effects of context of prior presentation. Journal of Experimental Psychology: Learning. Memory and Cognition 15, 200–210.

Koenderink, J.J., 1987. An internal representation for solid shape based on the topological properties of the apparent contour. In: Richards, W., Ullman, S. (Eds.), Image Understanding 1985–86. Norwood, NJ: Ablex Publishing Corporation, pp. 257–285.

Lando, M., Edelman, S., 1995. Receptive field spaces and class-based generalization from a single view in face recognition. Network 6, 551–576.

Lawson, R., Humphreys, G.W., Watson, D.G., 1994. Object recognition under sequential viewing conditions: evidence for viewpoint-specific recognition procedures. Perception 23 (5), 595–614.

Librande, S., 1992. Example-based character drawing. Unpublished Master's thesis, School of Architecture and Planning, Massachusetts Institute of Technology, Cambridge, MA.

Logothetis, N.K., Pauls, J., 1995. Psychophysical and physiological evidence for viewer-centered object representation in the primate. Cerebral Cortex 3, 270–288.

Logothetis, N.K., Pauls, J., Poggio, T., 1995. Shape representation in the inferior temporal cortex of monkeys. Current Biology 5 (5), 552–563.

Marr, D., Nishihara, H.K., 1978. Representation and recognition of the spatial organization of three-dimensional shapes. Proceeding of the Royal Society of London B 200, 269–294.

Miyashita, Y., Date, A., Okuno, H., 1993. Configurational encoding of visual forms by single neurons of monkey temporal cortex. Neuropsychologia 31, 1119–1132.

Moses, Y., Ullman, S., Edelman, S., 1996. Generalization to novel images in upright and inverted faces. Perception 25, 443–462.

Murray, J.E., Jolicoeur, P., McMullen, P.A., Ingleton, M., 1993. Orientation-invariant transfer of training in the identification of rotated natural objects. Memory and Cognition 21 (5), 604–610.

O'Toole, A., Edelman, S., Bülthoff, H.H., 1998. Stimulus-specific effects in face recognition over changes in viewpoint. Vision Research, in press.

Palmer, S., Rosch, E., Chase, P., 1981. Canonical perspective and the perception of objects. In: Long, J., Baddeley, A. (Eds.), Attention and Performance IX. Hillsdale, NJ: Lawrence Erlbaum, pp. 135–151.

Parsons, L.M., 1987. Visual discrimination of abstract mirror-reflected three-dimensional objects at many orientations. Perception and Psychophysics 42 (1), 49–59.

Perrett, D.I., Oram, M.W., Wachsmuth, E., 1998. Evidence accumulation in cell populations responsive to faces: an account of generalisation of recognition without mental transformations. Cognition, in press.

Poggio, T., Brunelli, R., 1992. A novel approach to graphics (Technical Report No. 1354). Massachusetts Institute of Technology, USA.

Poggio, T., Edelman, S., 1990. A network that learns to recognize three-dimensional objects. Nature 343, 263–266.

Poggio, T., Vetter, T., 1992. Recognition and structure from one 2D model view: observations on prototypes, object classes and symmetries (Technical Report No. 1347). Massachusetts Institute of Technology, USA.

Rock, I., 1973. Orientation and Form. New York: Academic Press.

Rosch, E., Mervis, C.B., Gray, W.D., Johnson, D.M., Boyes-Braem, P., 1976. Basic objects in natural categories. Cognitive Psychology 8, 382–439.

Schyns, P.G., 1998. Diagnostic recognition: task constraints, object information, and their interactions. Cognition, in press.

Tarr, M.J., 1995. Rotating objects to recognize them: a case study of the role of viewpoint dependency in the recognition of three-dimensional objects. Psychonomic Bulletin and Review 2 (1), 55–82.

Tarr, M.J., Bülthoff, H.H., 1995. Is human object recognition better described by geon-structural-descriptions or by multiple-views?. Journal of Experimental Psychology: Human Perception and Performance 21 (6), 1494–1505.

Tarr, M.J., Bülthoff, H.H., Zabinski, M., Blanz, V., 1997. To what extent do unique parts influence recognition across changes in viewpoint?. Psychological Science 8 (4), 282–289.

Tarr, M.J., Pinker, S., 1989. Mental rotation and orientation-dependence in shape recognition. Cognitive Psychology 21 (28), 233–282.

Tarr, M.J., Pinker, S., 1991. Orientation-dependent mechanisms in shape recognition: further issues. Psychological Science 2 (32), 207–209.

Troje, N., Bülthoff, H.H., 1996. Face recognition under varying pose: The role of texture and shape. Vision Research 36 (12), 1761–1771.

Tversky, B., Hemenway, K., 1984. Objects, parts, and categories. Journal of Experimental Psychology: General 113, 169–193.

Ullman, S., 1998. Three-dimensional object recognition based on the combination of views. Cognition 67, 21–44.

Ullman, S., Basri, R., 1991. Recognition by linear combinations of models. IEEE Transactions on Pattern Analysis and Machine Intelligence 13 (10), 992–1006.

Vetter, T., Hurlbert, A.M., Poggio, T., 1995. View-based models of 3D object recognition: invariance to imaging transformations. Cerebral Cortex 2 (3), 261–269.

Vetter, T., Poggio, T., Bülthoff, H.H., 1994. The importance of symmetry and virtual views in three-dimensional object recognition. Current Biology 4 (1), 18–23.

Weinshall, D., Edelman, S., Bülthoff, H.H., 1990. A self-organizing multiple-view representation of 3D objects. In: Touretzky, D.S. (Ed.), Advances in neural information processing systems 2. California: Morgan Kaufmann, pp. 274–281.

Yin, R.K., 1969. Looking at upside-down faces. Journal of Experimental Psychology 81 (1), 141–145.

5

Evidence accumulation in cell populations responsive to faces: an account of generalisation of recognition without mental transformations

D.I. Perrett*, M.W. Oram, E. Ashbridge

Psychological Laboratory, St Andrews University, St Andrews, KY16 9JU, UK

Abstract

In this paper we analyse the time course of neuronal activity in temporal cortex to the sight of the head and body. Previous studies have already demonstrated the impact of view, orientation and part occlusion on individual cells. We consider the cells as a population providing evidence in the form of neuronal activity for perceptual decisions related to recognition. The time course of neural responses to stimuli provides an explanation of the variation in speed of recognition across different viewing circumstances that is seen in behavioural experiments. A simple unifying explanation of the behavioural effects is that the speed of recognition of an object depends on the rate of accumulation of activity from neurones selective for the object, evoked by a particular viewing circumstance. This in turn depends on the extent that the object has been seen previously under the particular circumstance. For any familiar object, more cells will be tuned to the configuration of the object's features present in the view or views most frequently experienced. Therefore, activity amongst the population of cells selective for the object's appearance will accumulate more slowly when the object is seen in an unusual view, orientation or size. This accounts for the increased time to recognise rotated views without the need to postulate 'mental rotation' or 'transformations' of novel views to align with neural representations of familiar views. © 1998 Elsevier Science B.V. All rights reserved

Keywords: Mental rotation; Face recognition; Cell populations

1. Introduction

One phenomenon that has featured heavily in accounts of the way object recogni-

* Coresponding author. Fax: +44 1334 463042; e-mail: dp@st-andrew.ac.uk

tion processes cope with changes in view and orientation is that of 'mental rotation'. The basic finding is that the time to match two views of an unfamiliar object differing by a rotation in depth or orientation in the picture plane is linearly related to the 3-D angular difference between the views (Shepard and Metzler, 1971). Introspectively, subjects feel that they are mentally rotating one version of the object and then checking whether the rotated image matches the other. A consciously-driven process has been envisaged whereby an internal representation of one object is subjected to a continuous, analogue transformation until it matches the image of the second object. The increasing reaction times (RT) with larger angular differences between views is taken as reflecting the greater degree of internal rotation subjects need to perform to achieve a match.

An effect which appears analogous is the extra time taken to recognise familiar or recently learnt objects when they are rotated in the picture plane from their usually experienced orientation (Cooper and Shepard, 1973; Jolicœur, 1985, 1990; Tarr and Pinker, 1989, 1991). Here again the amount of extra time required for recognition is related to the angular rotation from upright. The increase in reaction time with orientation is not necessarily linear as with the original experiments on matching of Shepard and Metzler (1971). Indeed the function relating RT to orientation is usually monotonic but can have anomalous inflections (e.g. for inverted images; see Tarr, 1995). However the similarity in the dependence of RT on orientation has led to the assumption that one mechanism (mental rotation) underlies both phenomena.

Similar accounts have been suggested for the effect of perspective view on the recognition of familiar objects. Palmer et al. (1981) found that subjects could most easily bring to mind one 'prototypical' or 'canonical' view of everyday objects (e.g. a model car, shoe or house). Photographs taken from this same view were matched to a category name (e.g. 'car') more quickly than photographs taken from different perspective views. Reaction time to match names with pictures depended on how much the objects were rotated in perspective from the canonical orientation. These findings are often interpreted as suggesting that, for each object, a single canonical view is represented in memory and that all other views and orientations of objects are mentally rotated to bring them into alignment with the single stored view in its normal orientation.

Analogous effects are present when subjects learn the appearance of a novel object from one perspective view and then are tested with views of the same object rotated in perspective. The time required for recognition increases as the angular difference between trained and test views increases up to a maximum of 180° (Tarr and Pinker, 1989; Humphreys and Kahn, 1992; Edelman and Bülthoff, 1992) or to a 'virtual' view (Vetter et al., 1994; Logothetis et al., 1994, 1995). Several authors account for the monotonic increase in processing time by postulating a process which is engaged to 'align', 'normalise', 'transform' or 'mentally rotate' the image of the novel test view of the object so that it matches the representation of the view previously experienced.

The effect of image size on simultaneous and successive matching of stimuli follows a similar pattern, with subjects taking progressively longer the greater the difference in size between stimuli (Bundesen and Larsen, 1975; Besner, 1983; Jolicœur, 1987; Jolicœur and Besner, 1987; Ellis et al., 1989). To account for these findings, a process referred to as 'mental adjustment of size' or 'size normalisation' (Shepard and Metzler, 1971; Bundesen and Larsen, 1975; Besner, 1983; Larsen, 1985) has been suggested in which the internal representation of a stimulus is size specific and any image of the same stimulus in a non-standard size must first be size transformed to match the internal representation. The greater the size difference between image and internal representation, the greater the degree of mental size change before a match can be successful and recognition accomplished.

More recent theoretical accounts of recognition suggest that multiple views are represented in memory for each familiar object (Koenderink and van Doorn, 1979; Perrett et al., 1984, 1991; Poggio and Edelman, 1990; Edelman and Weinshall, 1991; Logothetis et al., 1994, 1995). Most models postulate that novel viewpoints of familiar objects are recognised by transformation, or alignment to the nearest stored view or by matching the input view to a view constructed as an interpolation between stored views (Tarr and Pinker, 1989, 1990, 1991; Ullman, 1989; Bülthoff and Edelman, 1992; Tarr, 1995; Edelman, 1997). Such models extend to generalisation across unusual orientations and sizes.

1.1. Problems with the mental rotation account

The main evidence for an involvement of 'mental rotation' or 'mental size change' in recognition is circumstantial. It is assumed that a monotonic increase in the time required to process images that are rotated in the picture plane or in 3-D perspective, or changed in size from a training stimulus, is a reflection of the operation of continuous transformation processes which are executed until completion. The increase in reaction times is not in itself evidence for mental rotation since it is also consistent with any process that takes more time the greater with greater differences between the test stimulus and the training stimulus.

There are several findings that make mental rotation implausible in accounting for object recognition. The rate of mental rotation reported in matching experiments of Shepard and Metzler (1971) was between 60 and 460°/s. This appears too slow to account for the recognition of misoriented objects. With this speed of mental rotation, an inverted object would take an extra 0.4 to 3 s to recognise compared to an upright object. Yet in some experiments, the extra time taken to process misoriented objects is only a few milliseconds and thus rotation speeds of 12 000°/s would be necessary to account for the identification (Humphreys and Quinlan, 1987). In such experiments subjects may employ recognition strategies that do not involve mental rotation but still give rise to a dependency of RT on orientation. This dependency is, however, the hallmark of mental rotation. Explaining different RT-orientation slopes with different mechanisms lacks consistency.

When researchers use the same objects for both recognition tasks and for left-right comparisons (equivalent to the Shepard and Metzler original mental rotation tasks) then RT orientation functions are comparable across tasks (Tarr and Pinker, 1989; Tarr, 1995). However, such consistency does not explain the radically different speeds of mental rotation that are supposed to underlie recognition of rotated objects in different circumstances.

More problematic is the finding that the extra time required for recognising rotated objects depends on the task and decreases with practice (Jolicœur, 1985; Tarr and Pinker, 1989; Perrett et al., 1988b). One might assume that practice increased the efficiency of the transformational process and hence the speed of mental rotation but the practice effect is selective for the training pattern and the training orientation. Training at a particular novel orientation or view speeds up recognition selectively at that view and orientation (Perrett et al., 1988b; Tarr and Pinker, 1989; Tarr, 1995; Logothetis et al., 1994). If more efficient mental transformation to the canonical view accounted for the improvement with practice, then one would expect an improvement for all orientations and views between trained and canonical conditions.

Models postulating multiple stored representations account for practice effects by assuming that new representations are formed as a result of experience (Bülthoff and Edelman, 1992; Tarr and Pinker, 1989). Subjects, frequently exposed to an object in an inverted orientation, will form a representation of the object in the inverted orientation. Such subjects will no longer need to transform the inverted orientation to upright but horizontal orientations will still need transforming to match either the canonical upright representation or the new inverted representation.

Problems with the mental rotation account of recognition are not restricted to recognition by normal subjects. Mental rotation does not provide a parsimonious account of the impact of brain lesions on object recognition. Farah and Hammond (1988) describe a patient who was able to recognise objects presented in various orientations but yet was impaired in the mental rotation tasks of Shepard and Metzler (1971). Perrett et al. (1988a) described a patient who was able to discriminate face configuration at any orientation yet (unlike normal subjects) showed no increase in reaction time with rotation of stimuli from upright. Thus orientation invariant object recognition can occur in individuals who do not show signs of mental rotation processes.

Similarly, a patient (L.G.) described by Turnbull et al. (1995) could recognise line drawn objects without being able to indicate the canonical orientation of the drawings. Turnbull et al. (1995) suggest that there are two pathways in normal object recognition, one displaying object-centred (view-independent) properties and a second displaying view-dependent properties. The second pathway would be selectively damaged in patient L.G. Such an explanation follows the account of Goodale and Milner (1992) of two streams of cortical visual processing. They suggest that the dorsal (parietal) pathway employs view-dependent visual descriptions to guide motor reactions and that the ventral (temporal) pathway employs view-independent descriptions to support recognition of what an object is. Such accounts overlook the extensive view-dependent processes within the temporal cortex (for review see Perrett and Oram, 1993). The patient described by Turnbull et al. (1995) could also be interpreted as having intact orientation-dependent descriptions in the ventral system. These descriptions may access limbic structures containing view-independent descriptions and semantic associations but for the patient the descriptions may have no access to the parietal systems necessary for defining orientation with respect to egocentric or gravitational axes.

1.2. A physiological explanation

The thesis advanced here is that mental rotation is not necessary to account for the effect of view or orientation on recognition of familiar objects. An alternative explanation relies on two assumptions. First, one stage in the processing leading to recognition involves neurones tuned to the appearance of objects in an orientation, view and size-specific manner and, second, the number of neurones tuned to an object at a given orientation, view and size depends on the amount of experience for the object in that circumstance. It follows that evidence for the presence of an object (in terms of neuronal activity) will accumulate more slowly when the object is presented at an unusual orientation, view or size.

If an object's appearance is learned in a view-specific manner, then more cells will become tuned to the view or views of the object that are commonly experienced. Fewer cells will respond to the object the more it is rotated from the experienced view(s). If we assume that any 'decision making' neural process guiding behavioural output acts on the basis of evidence in the form of input neuronal activity, then behavioural output will take longer and longer for progressively more unusual views. This will be the case simply because visual neuronal populations weakly activated by unusual views will take longer to provide sufficient input for the neurones in the 'decision apparatus' to act upon. Physiological data support this account of the generalisation across unusual viewing conditions with respect to perspective view, orientation, size and part occlusion. Manipulations of perspective view will be considered in the next section.

Explanations in which signals of different strengths require different durations for detection are familiar to Experimental Psychology and follow from information theory. Weak signals can give rise to longer reaction times compared with strong signals because, in a noisy background, sampling of weak signals takes longer to achieve a given level of evidence. Previous studies have presented such an account for sensory processing and for the way reaction time relates to simple stimulus parameters such as visual intensity (e.g. Vaughan et al., 1966; Lennie, 1981). We argue that the same applies to higher stages of visual processing and can account for what has been assumed to be a cognitive operation within visual recognition. We show that the responses of populations of neurones processing faces collectively exhibit the properties equivalent to those assumed in previous models of signal processing.

2. View

In the mental rotation tasks of Shepard and Metzler, the effects of change in view and change in orientation were comparable. The psychological impact of view and orientation change on recognition was also noted to be similar in the introduction.

Stimulus rotation in depth, however, changes the visibility of features while rotation in the picture plane changes orientation with respect to gravity but does not change feature visibility. In principal, the mechanisms by which the nervous system cope with the two types of rotation may be fundamentally distinct. Therefore, the physiological impact of the effect of view and orientation are considered separately in Sections 1 and 2. Section 4 also addresses changes in view that affect feature visibility.

From the studies so far, the vast majority of cells in temporal cortex that respond selectively to complex objects are sensitive to perspective view (Perrett et al., 1985, 1991; Logothetis et al., 1995). Different cells are maximally responsive to different views. View sensitivity is apparent for cells processing the appearance of socially significant stimuli such as the face and body and for cells processing arbitrary objects (amoeboid or angled wire frame shapes) that have acquired significance in the context of behavioural tasks. For cells responsive to the head and body, the distribution of view coding is uneven; more cells are tuned to particular characteristic views (full face, profiles and back) and more cells are tuned to the frontal views than to the back views (Perrett et al., 1991, 1994). There are probable behavioural consequences of these anisotropies (Harries et al., 1991; Perrett et al., 1994). The prevalence of cells tuned to frontal views presumably reflects greater experience and attention to these views and might mean that front views are detected more efficiently than back views. Stronger predictions for behavioural data can be made on the basis of cell tuning for view.

Most cells show a gradual decline of activity for views progressively more rotated from one (the cells preferred) view. The sharpness of the tuning function varies from cell to cell. For cells selectively responsive to the head, a rotation of 60° from optimal views reduces cell responses by approximately 1/2 and a rotation of 180° from optimal generally elicits responses barely different from background activity or the responses to other classes of control object. This type of tuning function characterises 83% of all cells responsive to the head (Perrett et al., 1991).

Tuning curves are usually calculated on the basis of the neural activity over extended periods of time, 250–500 ms (Hasselmo et al., 1989; Perrett et al., 1991; Logothetis et al., 1995). Responses of individual cells are assessed over these time periods because fixation of the stimulus is constant for the initial 250 ms and therefore one can consider cell responses as reflecting processing of the same stimulus. To make predictions for behavioural reaction times during recognition it is appropriate to look in detail at how the neuronal responses develop over time. After cells in temporal cortex have commenced firing they provide continuous output to other brain systems. Control of behaviour can be generated in such systems as soon as sufficient sensory evidence is available. This may occur well before temporal cortex cells have been firing for 250–500 ms. The view tuning of cells responsive to the sight of the face and other views of the head have been well characterised and the methods of study detailed extensively elsewhere (Perrett et al., 1985, 1991; Oram and Perrett, 1992, 1994; Wachsmuth et al., 1994). Here we present an analysis of the time course of cells' responses recorded in area STPa of the temporal cortex and characterised in these other studies.

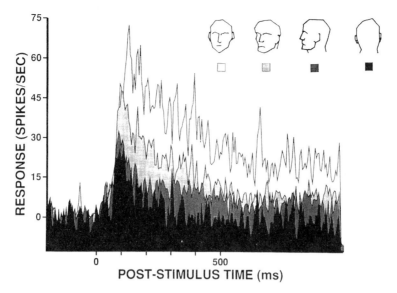

Fig. 1. Post-stimulus time histogram of responses showing effect of rotation from face view. Average response of a population of 20 cells selective for the face view of the head plotted as a function of time relative to stimulus presentation (0 ms) in successive 5 ms bins. View is expressed as the angle of rotation (45, 90 and 180°) away from the face (optimal) view. Data from views (5–10 trials per cell per view) rotated clockwise and anticlockwise by an equal angle from the face view have been pooled. At the population level, responses to views rotated an equal amount from face view were statistically indistinguishable (protected least significant difference post-hoc testing: $P>0.5$ each comparison; overall effect of condition: $F_{(9,171)} = 35, P < 0.0005$). The angle of rotation from face view is symbolised by schematic head views. S.A., spontaneous activity.

Fig. 1 displays the average responses of a population of 20 cells to different views of the head (Perrett et al., 1991; Oram and Perrett, 1992, 1994). The population is comprised of cells that were selective for the face view with a declining response function for views rotated from the face.

Fig. 1 gives the total number of spikes recorded in successive 5 ms time bins before and after presentation of different views of the head. Non-face control stimuli (not shown in Fig. 1) produced responses equivalent to the view rotated by 180° from best view. This peri-stimulus time histogram (PSTH) format is a conventional way for neurophysiologists to display the time course of neuronal activity. Most visually responsive neurones are spontaneously active even in the absence of visual stimuli. For cells in the temporal cortex this spontaneous activity occurs at a rate of about 10 spikes/s. During the presentation of an optimal stimulus the firing rate rises to approximately 50–250 spikes per second (the exact magnitude of response and spontaneous firing rate varies from cell to cell).

To compare activity of cells across a population all firing rates can be expressed as a % of the difference between the cell's maximum rate (set to 100%) and the cell's spontaneous activity (set to 0%). This normalisation allows each cell to make an equivalent contribution to the estimate of the population activity displayed in Fig. 1 (Oram and Perrett, 1992, 1994). Since results of analysis with and without normalisation were equivalent, data from different cells have been combined without normalisation in subsequent analysis (Figs. 2–4).

For the cells tested in Fig. 1, all visual stimuli were presented at time 0 ms after a 0.5 s signal tone and continued to be visible for the following one second. Cells in the temporal cortex commence stimulus related activity some 70–150 ms after the presentation of a visual stimulus (time 0 ms on the abscissa). It is apparent in the figure that the population activity rises after 70 ms for all stimuli; firing rate increases to peak levels over the following 100–300 ms and then declines to lower rates. In Fig. 1 it is evident that the overall activity declines as the head is rotated from the face view. Cell responses to clockwise and anticlockwise rotations of the head from the face view have been combined because the population responses to rotations through an equivalent angle (clockwise or anticlockwise) were statistically indistinguishable ($P > 0.5$ each comparison). The precise nature of the relationship between firing rate and view is, however, difficult to visualise because of the moment by moment fluctuations in spike frequency due to the fine time resolution of the data collection, the stochastic way neurones fire and because of the relatively limited sample of cells and test trials.

Neural activity in conventional PSTHs is illustrated as the average firing rate at each instant prior to and after stimulus onset. An alternative mode of display of the same data is one in which the spike activity that has occurred recently has a cumulative impact on the response assessed at any instant. Fig. 2 (upper) displays this cumulative difference between firing rate for each stimulus type and spontaneous activity. This cumulative analysis is like a statistical procedure in which a statistician does not want to base judgements on input occurring in a limited time window but prefers to assess activity over the entire time period from sample onset up until the present moment; this includes the current activity level and any evidence of activity that has occurred previously. The cumulative neural response, in this analogy, becomes equivalent to the level of certainty or weight of evidence for the presence of the cells' preferred stimulus in the visual scene.

Such evidence accumulation is biologically plausible in that it is equivalent to temporal summation by neurones receiving multiple synaptic inputs at different times. The postsynaptic membrane acts like a capacitor; the depolarisation caused by input excitatory postsynaptic potentials therefore accumulates over time. Fig. 2 (upper) would be equivalent to the membrane potential of a cell receiving the input activity displayed in Fig. 1. For simplicity, it is assumed here that the cells have a long memory (>1.0 s) and that membranes act like perfect capacitors. In reality membranes act like leaky capacitors and lose charge slowly over time. The time constant for this loss varies though for pyramidal cells the effect of synaptic activity at the site of spike generation can persist for 200 ms (Stratford et al., 1989). For clarity, cumulative analysis is presented in the following sections without modelling information loss. Analysis incorporating a rate of 'forgetting' caused by membranes discharging with an appropriate time constant, however, produces qualitatively similar results.

In Fig. 2 (upper), prior to stimulus presentation, the firing rate fluctuates around the level of spontaneous activity so there is on average, zero cumulative difference from spontaneous activity. When responses to stimuli commence, the cumulative response curves show a positive deflection. The evidence for each view being present in the image rises over time and this rise is fastest for the face view. The rate of accumulation of response decreases in proportion to the angular rotation of the head from the face. This difference occurs despite the onset of responses to the different views occurring at the same latency (see also Oram and Perrett, 1992).

Neural populations upstream (i.e. those receiving output from populations equivalent to those whose activity is displayed) will begin their own responses when the

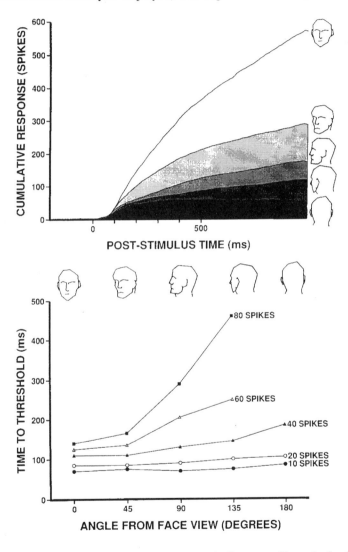

Fig. 2. Effect of rotation from face view on the time course of cell responses. Upper: the data from Fig. 1 plotted as cumulative neuronal activity (spikes) above spontaneous activity. Lower: the time for cumulative responses to exceed different threshold levels.

cumulated input activity exceeds a certain level above background. This is equivalent to input excitatory post-synaptic potentials exceeding the threshold voltage for action potential generation in the post-synaptic elements. Responses upstream will be triggered fastest for the face view, and progressively slower for views rotated in depth 45, 90, 135, 180° away form the face.

Another way of looking at the situation is to think of the differences between activity in cell populations. If two types of object are to be discriminated (e.g. face 1 vs. face 2 or view 1 vs. view 2 of the same object) then a decision can only be reached when the cumulative difference between the activity in two populations exceeds a threshold. At the cellular level, this may correspond to excitatory post-synaptic inputs from one population and inhibitory post-synaptic inputs from a second population. Note for such a comparison speed of output or decision depends not on the absolute rate of firing but on the difference between activity rates. Again if the difference in activity accumulates rapidly then reaction can be quick. In general, detecting a weak signal in noise takes longer detecting a strong signal imbedded in the same noise.

With the assumption that learning about an object from one view leads to cells optimally tuned to that view, then these results can be used to account for the impact of view on recognition. If a previously unfamiliar object is experienced extensively at a 'training' view, then it is assumed here that the visual appearance of the object will be 'stored in memory', in the sense that the experience will establish neural populations that are selective for the feature configuration of the object at the training view, orientation and image size. In subsequent recognition testing, the order in which individual test views produce a supra-threshold level of accumulated activity will depend on the angle of rotation between test and training views. This level will be exceeded fastest when the test view exactly matches the trained view and progressively larger angles of rotations will exceed the threshold criterion at longer and longer intervals after stimulus presentation.

While data are presented here for cells responsive to the sight of the head, view tuning has been found for other classes of cell in the temporal cortex responsive to other types of object. Logothetis et al. (1994) trained monkeys to discriminate 3-D wire frame and amoeboid objects similar to the stimuli used in psychophysical studies of humans (Bülthoff and Edelman, 1992; Edelman and Bülthoff, 1992; Rock and DiVita, 1987). Like humans, the monkeys displayed view sensitivity at the behavioural level with efficiency of recognition declining as the test stimuli were rotated in perspective away from the trained views (Logothetis et al., 1994). Neurophysiological studies of the trained monkey subjects revealed cells in the temporal cortex that were tuned to particular familiar wire frame stimuli (Logothetis et al., 1995). These cells displayed view sensitivity comparable to those selective for the sight of the head and body. Thus the results presented in Figs. 1 and 2 will apply equally to wire frame or amoeboid objects and presumably most other classes of 3-D object.

The notion that the cumulative response rate must exceed a threshold level is equivalent to a test of statistical significance or a decision criterion being applied at a cognitive level such that behavioural output is made only when sufficient sensory evidence has accumulated. A statistical or decision criterion can be set at various levels of evidence. The account provides no indication of what that level should be but it should be apparent that the results are qualitatively similar over a range of thresholds. This is confirmed in Fig. 2 lower which shows that the time for cumulative responses to different views to exceed different threshold levels. Over a range of arbitrarily defined threshold values (between 10 and 80 spike above spontaneous activity), the time to threshold increases monotonically and approximately linearly as the view is rotated from the best view. Highly rotated views (e.g. 180°) do not evoke sufficient response to exceed thresholds greater than 40 spikes above spontaneous activity. The ordering effects may well be qualitatively similar for very low thresholds (<10 spikes) but limitation in the sample size and time resolution of sampling (5 ms time bins) prevent the rank ordering from being apparent for small angles of rotation. Indeed, when responses are calculated for cells with the same response latency, then the rank order of response to views is the same during the first 5 ms of response as it is several hundred milliseconds after response onset (Oram and Perrett, 1992). This analysis implies that the rank ordering of effectiveness is not dependent on integration over large time scales but is present at response onset.

At the stage of processing studied here, responses to unusual views exhibit slower rise times do not have longer latencies compared to typical views. At subsequent stages of processing, differences between typical and unusual views may amplify and slower rise times for unusual views will translate into increased response latencies. Cells receiving outputs from the visual representations in temporal cortex will act as described, pooling information (input excitatory post-synaptic potentials) over time until their threshold level for firing is reached. This will be slower for weak inputs from the temporal cortex. By the time stages controlling behavioural output are reached, neuronal responses (related to muscle contraction and limb motion) will commence later for unusual views than for typical views since differences in the latency of muscle operation will underlie RT differences.

The nature of generalisation (and the function relating RTs to view) will depend on the recognition task and the view tuning functions of cell responses. These functions could be steeper or more shallow depending on the degree of familiarity with the object class and the discriminability of pattern features that differentiate exemplars within the class. Cells tuned to wire frame objects show tighter view tuning functions (Logothetis et al., 1995); behavioural performance in generalising recognition from one trained view of such objects also shows a steeper decline with perspective rotation (Logothetis et al., 1994).

Note that there is no need to postulate that an image of a novel view needs transforming (Edelman, 1997), normalising or mentally rotating to establish alignment with the training view. The increase in recognition time arises simply from the view tuning of neurones whose selectivity has been established from a training experience with an object. This neuronal population will be the most appropriate for identifying the trained object. By listening to the activity of this cell population, evidence for the presence of the trained object in the image will accrue with a rate proportional to the similarity between test and training views.

Recognition depends only on how well the input image falls within the tolerance of neural representations of familiar objects. The speed of classification of an unfamiliar exemplar of a familiar class of objects (e.g. recognising a new car model as a car) should depend only on the novel item's similarity or resemblance to familiar exemplars (Moses et al., 1996; Gauthier and Tarr, 1997a). While this prediction is straightforward, the point is that recognition does not need to rely on a continuous imagined transformation of the visual appearance of the novel exemplar to match that of familiar exemplars. To recognise a new car model we do not need to imagine the new car gradually undergoing a change in shape until it conforms to the shape of a familiar car model or a generalised prototype of all cars.

2.1. Object symmetry

Generalisation functions are likely to be affected by the view chosen for training. Fig. 1 displays the response functions for cells whose optimal view was symmetric (i.e. face) and for rotations about the axis of symmetry. The situation is different for cells maximally responsive to a profile or 1/2 profile view of the head. Such cells are often maximally responsive to the profile pointing to one side of the viewer (e.g. left profile) but not all show a single peak of view sensitivity, a substantial number (25% of cells tuned to profile images) show a bimodal tuning function with two peaks of responsiveness, one for each of two mirror symmetric views (Perrett et al., 1991). In general terms this cellular sensitivity means that the behavioural performance after training on an asymmetric view (of a bilaterally symmetric object) will not be a monotonic function of the angle of perspective rotation between training and test. As the object is rotated away from the training view generalisation will first decline but then performance may show a subsidiary peak as the object is rotated to a test view that is the mirror image of the training view. Such effects have been seen at the behavioural level (Logothetis et al., 1994; Hill et al., 1997). Indeed humans and monkeys find it relatively hard to learn to discriminate between mirror symmetric patterns and damage to temporal cortex (removing neurones generalising across mirror reflection) can improve discrimination performance between mirror symmetric patterns (Holmes and Gross, 1984a).

3. Orientation

Studies of temporal cortex reveal that the majority of cells selectively responsive to faces are orientation-sensitive (Tanaka et al., 1991; Wachsmuth and Perrett, 1997; Wachsmuth et al., in preparation) as are the vast majority of cells sensitive to simpler features (Tanaka et al., 1991). Cell sensitivity to head orientation appears to show very similar tuning functions to the tuning functions for head view (Perrett et al., 1991; Wachsmuth et al., submitted). Changes in view or in orientation of approximately 60° from optimal conditions reduce cell responses by half. Particular cells in the superior temporal sulcus do generalise across all orientations and remain selectively responsive for face patterns throughout 360° of rotation in the picture plane

(Perrett et al., 1982, 1984, 1985, 1988b). Such orientation invariant cells, however, constitute a minority of those responsive to the head and body (16%, 4/25 of cells tested, Wachsmuth and Perrett, 1997; Wachsmuth et al., submitted).

The similar tuning function for orientation and view means that the above description of the neural responses to unusual views will apply to unusual orientations as well. For orientation, however, the physiological data provide an additional direct link between recognition and neural processing of unusual viewing conditions. More cells (15/21) are found tuned to the upright orientation than tuned to non-upright orientations (Wachsmuth and Perrett, 1997; Wachsmuth et al., submitted; Tanaka et al., 1991). This bias presumably arises because upright orientations are experienced more often than non-upright orientations.

The consequence of greater numbers of cells responsive to upright faces is evident in Fig. 3. This figure plots the activity of cells responsive to the sight of the head and body that were recorded in the superior temporal sulcus (STS) (Wachsmuth et al., 1994; Wachsmuth et al., submitted). Cells were included in the sample independent of their orientation sensitivity. Fig. 3 represents a limited estimate of the relative activity in the STS evoked by the sight of the head and body in different orientations. Fig. 3 displays how the cumulative response of this population varies with orientation. It is not surprising that the response to the upright stimuli is largest as this simply reflects the greater number of cells responsive to the normal orientation. The rate of accumulation of response declines as the stimuli are rotated from upright. This occurs despite the fact that the responses to different orientations commence at approximately the same latency. The lower part of Fig. 3 shows the time for the cumulative responses to exceed different threshold levels. Over a range of levels (>15 spikes), the time to exceed threshold increases as a function of angle of rotation from upright.

The curves plotted in Fig. 3 are an estimate of the population activity from a limited sample of cells. An analysis of a larger sample of cells tested with fewer orientations revealed equivalent results (the cumulative response to upright rising faster than horizontal and inverted orientations). Reduced numbers of cells responsive to inverted orientations have been revealed in recordings from 25 cells (Wachsmuth and Perrett, 1997) and in a previous study of 40 cells (Perrett et al., 1988a). Modelling based on the empirically defined orientation tuning function of the population (including its greater response to upright than inverted) and the distribution of cell response latencies, shows that the rank ordering of responses with rotation from upright to inverted is independent of the number of cells sampled and occurs within 5 ms of population response onset (Oram et al., submitted).

3.1. Behavioural effects of orientation

Most experience of faces or any mono-oriented object (Rock, 1973; Yin, 1969, 1970; Carey, 1992) occurs in the gravitationally upright orientation. As a result of this preferential experience it is suggested that more cells in the temporal cortex become selectively tuned for the upright orientation of these objects. This numerical bias in cell responsiveness to the upright orientation is sufficient to account for the

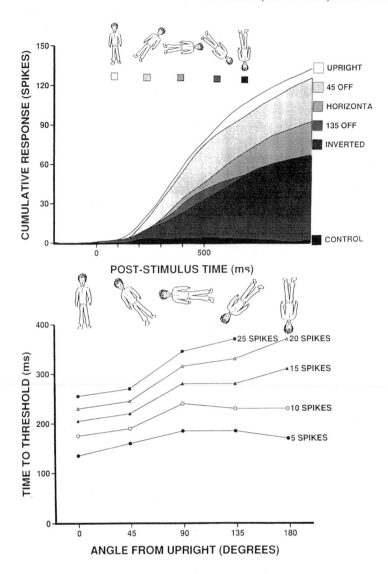

Fig. 3. Effect of orientation on the time course of cell responses. Upper: the cumulative difference in response from spontaneous activity of 11 cells selectively activated by the sight of the head and body (Wachsmuth et al., 1994; submitted). The 11 cells were selected on the basis that they had each been tested with eight face orientations and responded to one or more orientation at rates above control stimuli and spontaneous activity. The cells were chosen independent of their orientation tuning (most responded best to upright orientations but some responded best to non-upright orientations). Data are plotted for five stimulus orientations expressed as the angle from upright and control stimuli. Lower: the time for cumulative responses to exceed different threshold levels. For the horizontal, 45 and 135° orientations, responses to stimuli rotated clockwise and anticlockwise from upright have been pooled. Conventions as for Fig. 2.

greater ease of recognition of upright objects and the slower, less accurate recognition of more unusual orientations.

There are numerous studies of the effect of orientation change on recognition. The vast majority of studies report a reduced efficiency (increased reaction times and decreased accuracy) for recognising rotated images (Yin, 1969; Rock, 1973; Holmes and Gross, 1984b; Weiskrantz and Saunders, 1984; Jolicœur, 1985, 1990; Larsen, 1985; Corballis, 1988; Perrett et al., 1988b; Flin and Dziurawiec, 1989; Tarr and Pinker, 1989, 1990, 1991; Carey, 1992; Bülthoff and Edelman, 1992; Edelman and Bülthoff, 1992; McMullen and Jolicœur, 1992; Phelps and Roberts, 1994; for review see Wachsmuth and Perrett, 1997; Tarr, 1995).

Under special conditions it is possible that rotated images are processed with equal efficiency to upright images. One would not expect rotation to affect performance in tasks requiring only the detection of simple features that can differentiate target from non-targets at any orientation (e.g. colour or textural cues). Even without such obvious cues there are face recognition tasks which do not require coding of a face configuration per se but require only the detection of the presence of a feature (e.g. the presence of hair or the presence of a circular iris) which will be equally salient at any image orientation (Perrett et al., 1988b). The orientation dependence of recognition performance in object classification tasks also depends on similarity between stimuli (Edelman, 1995). Entry level or superordinate classification where subjects allocate the class name (car, face, chair, etc.) are situations where orientation (and view) effects are less likely to occur (Tarr, 1995) because they do not require discrimination of feature configuration. Superordinate tasks requiring face/non-face classification which include judgements of feature configuration do show sensitivity to stimulus orientation (e.g. Perrett et al., 1988b). The cells described here could participate in such tasks since they are sensitive to configuration, exhibiting reduced responses to displays of jumbled face or body parts (Perrett et al., 1982, 1988b).

Tasks which require differentiation of exemplars within the same class (subordinate classification) are ones in which the effects of orientation are more prevalent (for discussion see Tarr, 1995). The results described here are also appropriate for subordinate-class discriminations because the same view and orientation tuning is apparent for cells which show high degrees of selectivity amongst exemplars within a class, discriminating between different faces (Perrett et al., 1984, 1988b, 1991; Hasselmo et al., 1989; Young and Yamane, 1992) or different wire frame objects (Logothetis et al., 1995).

Even within these subordinate-level tasks the slope relating RT to stimulus orientation from behavioural studies can show various functions (linear, non-linear) depending on the paradigm and depending on the subjects' experience. For the cellular account described here, the nature of the RT-orientation function is determined only by the relative responsiveness of the cell population to different orientations. While this should parallel experience exceptions may arise due to the tuning of cells (e.g. cells tuned to horizontal eyes in an upright face may respond to eyes in an inverted face). Non-linear slopes are more of a problem for mental transformation models. A non-linear slope implies that the speed of transformation (mental rotation) depends on the object orientation. This does not appear to explain orientation-dependent processing but rather restates the phenomenon.

4. Size

Studies of cells responsive to the sight of the face and the body indicate that the majority are sensitive to image size (Wachsmuth and Perrett, 1997; Wachsmuth et al., submitted). While the cells generalise over a range of image sizes (Perrett et al., 1982, 1984), when unusually small images are presented the population response declines. Using a constant projection distance of 4 meters (the greatest distance our subjects see human faces), we have found that cells respond maximally to life-sized projected images of humans and have monotonically declining responses to 3/4, 1/2 and 1/4 sized images. Analysis, with the methods described above, reveals that the more unusual the image size, the smaller the population response and the longer the cumulative population response takes to exceed threshold levels. By similar arguments to those presented for view and orientation, it is, therefore, not necessary to postulate 'mental transformations of size' to account for the extra time taken to recognise objects seen at unusual image sizes (Shepard and Metzler, 1971; Bundesen and Larsen, 1975; Besner, 1983; Larsen, 1985).

5. Recognition from the whole or part of an object

Neuropsychological tests of object recognition from unusual views often include views of objects in which particular parts are occluded from sight or placed in less salient positions (Warrington and James, 1986; Humphreys and Riddoch, 1984; Warrington and Taylor, 1973). The analysis of the generalisation of temporal cortex neural responses across perspective view and orientation described so far extends easily to situations where object parts are occluded from sight.

Analysis of cells responsive to faces in the temporal cortex has revealed a spectrum of sensitivity to facial parts. Some cells respond only to one facial region (e.g. eyes). Most cells, however, exhibit independent tuning to several facial parts (e.g. eyes or mouth) and some cells respond only when multiple features are presented simultaneously (Perrett et al., 1982; Oram and Perrett, 1994). The face is just one component of a larger and more complex object (the body) and recent studies have analysed the contribution of body parts for cells in the STS that respond to the sight of the whole body (Wachsmuth et al., 1994; Oram et al., submitted).

Fig. 4 plots the responses of cells in the STS studied previously for sensitivity to two parts of the body (the head and the rest of the body; Wachsmuth et al., 1994). This study again revealed a spectrum of cell sensitivity to the two parts. Thirty-eight percent of cells responded to only one part. These included 28% which responded to the head presented in isolation but not to the rest of the body when the head was occluded from sight and 10% responded conversely to the body but not to the head. These cells continued to respond to images of the whole body that contained the effective and ineffective parts. A more common pattern of activity amongst the cell population studied (43%) was for cells to respond to the head or to the rest of the body. A final group of cells (19%) responded only when both the head and body were simultaneously visible. Fig. 4 displays the responses of all the cells in this study that were responsive to the whole body. The population therefore includes those

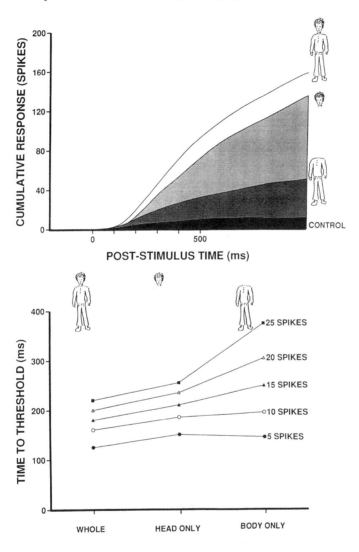

Fig. 4. Responses to an entire object and to object components. Data from a population of 35 cells responsive to the whole body (Wachsmuth et al., 1994). Cumulative response of the cell population activity is displayed for four types of stimulus: whole body (WHOLE), the head alone with the rest of the body occluded from sight (HEAD ONLY), the body alone with head occluded from sight (BODY ONLY) and objects other than faces and bodies (CONTROL). Lower: the time for cumulative responses to exceed different threshold levels. Conventions as for Fig. 2.

requiring the whole body before response, those responsive to the one component and those responsive independently to the head or the rest of the body.

From Fig. 4 it is evident that the population response to the head presented in isolation was greater than that to the rest of the body with the head covered. This reflects the greater number of cells responsive to the head alone (28%) than to the body alone (10%). It is also evident in the figure that the response to the whole body accumulates faster than the response to either part presented in isolation. The greater response occurs for two reasons. First, a sub-population of 19% of cells responds only when the whole body is presented and, second, the sight of the whole body will activate both sub-populations tuned to one part (i.e. both the 28% of cells responsive to the head alone and the 10% responsive to the body alone). (More generally, if one considers an object made up of two parts (A and B) and that 10% of the cells respond only to part A and 10% respond only to part B, then presenting the whole object will activate twice as many cells as presenting just one part). For these reasons it is apparent that the total brain activity will always be greater in response to the visual image of an entire object than to the image of one component of the object presented in isolation.

One can speculate from the data illustrated in Fig. 4 that the rate of accumulation of neural evidence for the parts and whole will have an impact at the behavioural level. Cumulative responses to the whole object will exceed a threshold level faster than responses to parts (Fig. 4, lower). Reaction times to detect an entire object (e.g. a human body) will be quicker for images containing the whole object than images displaying just one part of the object. The finding of Biederman (1987), that the more components visible in an object the quicker the time to name the object, follows this pattern. Similarly it is expected that recognition of famous individuals would be superior with whole face photographs than with photographs of isolated facial regions (eyes).

This relationship of speed of detection of parts and the whole may not be surprising but it suggests caution in inferring the order of stages of processing from differences in behavioural reaction times. Many theories of object recognition propose separate stages of processing for the definition of object parts and for access to the overall structure of the whole object (e.g. Biederman, 1987). Some theories of object recognition propose that the overall configuration of an object is processed first before the details of the object's parts (e.g. Baker Cave and Kosslyn, 1993). Quicker reaction times for naming whole objects as compared to object parts could be taken as evidence consistent with models in which the order of processing is 'whole' before 'parts'. Such inferences from the reaction time ordering as to the ordering of processing could be misleading. The data presented in Fig. 4 shows that the rate of accumulation of neuronal activity can be faster for the entire object even when cell responses to the entire object and to its separate parts begin at approximately the same latency.

It is interesting that a progressive ordering of reaction times for different types of judgements is often taken as evidence for a progressive ordering of processing stages in cognitive psychological models. For example, the finding that retrieving the name of a face takes longer than retrieving other forms of personal information (e.g.

profession) has been taken as supporting a serial processing model in which processes underlying naming are only initiated after accessing other person identity information (Bruce and Young, 1986). Similarly subordinate judgements between exemplars of the same object class (e.g. face identity) may take longer than superordinate judgements of object class (that a face is human). Smaller numbers of cells tuned to specific identities (Perrett et al., 1984, 1989; Young and Yamane, 1992) than tuned to the general structure of faces could produce this ordering of reaction times, even if cells responsive to general and specific facial characteristics were activated at the same time.

In this section, the neural responses to part and whole objects provide straightforward predictions for the speed of behavioural responses to part and whole objects. What is more interesting is the realisation that neural responses can accumulate at different rates when they have the same onset in time. Thus the relationship between behavioural reaction times and underlying neural stages of processing is not straightforward. One cannot assume that because two types of judgement take different lengths of time the judgements necessarily reflect two different stages of processing activated in serial order. Moreover, there is again no need to postulate an extra transformational process, such as 'mental completion' (extrapolating the presence of occluded parts), to explain slower recognition of parts than whole objects.

The terms word, object or face advantage (or superiority effect) have been used to describe the greater efficiency in recognition of normal configurations of words, objects or faces as compared to jumbled configurations (Purcell and Stewart, 1988). The difference between neural responses to whole objects and object parts can provide a basis for understanding the advantages conferred by normal configurations.

Cells responsive to one facial feature presented in isolation (and receiving no inputs from cells sensitive to other face parts) will respond equivalently to that feature in a jumbled face or a face with a correct configuration of features. Cells sensitive to multiple features in a face will respond preferentially to the normal configuration since jumbled configurations disrupt some local feature information (Perrett et al., 1982, 1988b; Perrett and Oram, submitted). For example moving the nose up in the face (a configuration change) will increase the gap between nose and mouth (a change in the local upper lip feature). Sensitivity to combined visual features imbues cells with selectivity for the configuration of face parts (Perrett et al., 1984; Yamane et al., 1988; Perrett and Oram, submitted). A normal face will excite more cells than a jumbled face; the normal configuration excites both cells responsive to whole faces and cells responsive to individual face parts but the jumbled face activates only the latter cell type. Therefore, the total response in the temporal cortex to a normal configuration of a face will be greater than the response to a jumbled face or an isolated part (Rolls et al., 1994). This is evident in local evoked potentials to faces in the temporal cortex of humans (Allison et al., 1994). From this one can predict that, provided subjects employ a search strategy utilising configuration, the latency to detect a normal face will be shorter than that required to detect a jumble (e.g. Perrett et al., 1988b). Likewise, if the visual patterns are degraded (e.g. by short exposure and backward masking), one can predict that the normal face pattern will become detectable before the jumbled configuration (Purcell and Stewart, 1988). The differences in recognition or perception times can be attributed to different numbers of cells activated at the same time by different stimuli.

6. Discussion

6.1. *Recognition of unusual views following brain damage*

One question which is left unanswered by the account here is why brain damage in the right parietal area should disrupt object recognition at all (Warrington and James, 1986; Warrington and Taylor, 1973). If viewer-centred representations in the ventral temporal cortex account for object recognition from typical and unusual views, then damage to ventral but not dorsal systems should produce impairment in tests of unusual views.

The impact of damage to the dorsal system on recognition may arise indirectly because any complex mental operation must have contributions from many brain systems. Outputs from temporal cortex may well provide evidence that a particular object is present in a particular orientation but if the amount of evidence is small (because the image is degraded, the view unfamiliar, or because early visual processing is defective), then the observer may need to check and form a considered opinion before reacting. If so, an entire strategy for gathering more visual information needs to be executed. For example, on the basis of the first fixation there may be evidence for a horizontal rabbit ear shape or a bird beak shape. Given the orientation and size of the object part and the current position of the eyes, a prediction can be made that moving the eyes to a new location should bring rabbit paws or a bird tail into central vision and window of attention. This prediction needs translating into action and the visual image resulting from the second fixation will need analysing. This cycle of operations might just be the first in a series of evaluations extending over several predictions and fixations. A single inspection saccade may fail to result in confirming evidence and a new test location would need to be chosen, alternatively the image interpretation and object hypothesis (Gregory, 1980) may need modifying after the first inspection saccade. As objects are presented at increasingly unusual orientations one expects the information processing requirements to increase. This could be reflected in number of inspections or their duration. Indeed, in the Shepard and Metzler matching paradigm, Carpenter and Just (1978) found that the time spent looking at each shape increased as the angle of rotation between the stimuli increased.

Visual search strategies of the type just described require planning (perhaps involving frontal cortex), awareness of position of eye fixation, decisions as to how to direct eye movements to selected locations (involving a whole variety of systems including parietal cortex, frontal eye fields and superior colliculus) in addition to information about the nature of visual features and object parts from ventral occipito-temporal cortex. One could add to the list of requirements the need for a short term memory to remember the object hypothesis from preceding fixations and the need for semantic associations (or object-centred representations) to predict the relationships between object parts and features and the capacity to translate these spatial relations into image co-ordinates. Damage in parietal or frontal regions could produce deficits in recognising unusual views for a variety of reasons, including difficulties in implementing an organised visual search.

Normal subjects may make decisions in speeded reaction tasks after a single pass through the ventral cortical system that engages the relevant detailed viewer-centred description of objects. Recognition under degraded viewing conditions or on the first trial with an object experienced in a completely novel view may involve many brain systems even for normal subjects with checks being made to assess the viability of the current interpretation. Damage, particularly in parietal systems, would impact on recognition not so much because this system contains detailed viewer-centred descriptions of objects but more because damage here disrupts search strategies, translation of spatial relations to action plans, or control of fixation and attention. All these processes are essential for gathering sufficient evidence for recognition in difficult circumstances.

This explanation might account for some aspects of the original mental rotation tasks of Shepard and Metzler (1971). The larger the difference between stimuli to be matched the more difficult and time consuming the checking processes. It should be noted, however, that the accumulation of cell responses described here does not depend on sequences of eye movements made after an image is presented. The effects on cell responses are seen before the onset of saccades and in situations in which the eyes remain on fixation points (e.g. Oram and Perrett, 1992; Logothetis et al., 1995).

6.2. The limits of generalisation

One question which arises concerns how generalisation is possible for totally novel objects or for a familiar object experienced in a totally novel view/orientation. If selective viewer-centred neural codes in temporal cortex are formed only after experience, then they cannot be used for generalisation on the initial trial with a totally novel object.

After becoming familiar with an object in just one specific circumstance (one view, orientation and retinal size), one can ask how does recognition occur after a dramatic rotation in depth or change in viewing circumstances? There are several mechanisms which might contribute to generalisation of recognition in this circumstance.

First, view sensitive cells, that we presume are formed through experience with an object from one view, may well aid recognition even after a dramatic change in viewing circumstance. The success of recognition depends on where the novel test view falls relative to the view, orientation and size tolerance functions of the relevant cells. If the test view falls within the tuning functions, then the speed of recognition will be a function of the difference between novel and familiar views.

When the novel view is dramatically different but still within the tuning function, the reaction time will be dramatically increased, and the recognition accuracy dramatically reduced (but still above chance). If the test view falls completely outside the tolerance, then the cells we describe will be irrelevant.

It should be realised that the pattern sensitive representations described here are tolerant to quite an extensive range of viewing conditions. Thus although the cells depicted in Fig. 1 are selective for view, their response remains above baseline even after 135° of rotation (baseline response to controls was approximately equal to the 180° rotated view). Generalisation on the initial trial after 135° of rotation should be possible for some familiar objects, although the rate of recognition would be very slow because of the slow rate of accumulation of evidence in the relevant cell populations. As noted the tuning functions of cells selective for a complex wire frame (trained in a specific view) are narrow. Recognition may fail when the test view is rotated 40° from a training view.

Second, some authors have argued that generalisations on initial and subsequent trials with a new view employ different mechanisms (Jolicœur, 1985, 1990); the account here may apply more to trials subsequent to the initial trial. It is relevant here to ask, 'what experience with an object from one view is necessary to derive selective neural populations in temporal cortex?' The answer will depend on how much experience the observer has already had with a particular class of stimuli. Evidence shows that cells in temporal cortex can show very quick adaptations to new patterns of input that are versions of familiar objects and faces (Dolan et al., 1997). Cells already responsive to faces can show modifications in selectivity to new faces within a relatively short time course of 1–2 trials (Rolls et al., 1989). Of course it may take far longer for temporal cortex cell populations to become selectively tuned to subtleties of new object classes (Logothetis et al., 1994, 1995; Gauthier and Tarr, 1997b). Even when the relevant cells are wired up and 'ready to go' in temporal cortex, one can assume that synaptic connections allowing such cells to have influence over neural control systems for arbitrary motor responses (such as those chosen by experimental psychologists as an index of recognition, e.g. 'press right button if the stimulus is familiar') take time and practice to optimise.

Third, the significance of an object (and semantic codes more generally) may be accessed through multiple routes, they may be reached not only from the high level view-centred pattern-selective cells described here but also from 'elaborate feature' sensitive cells in inferior temporal cortex or prestriate areas (Tanaka et al., 1991). These cells code simple characteristics that may be sufficient to differentiate objects on a coarse level. Some elaborate feature sensitive cells code features (e.g. brown and spiky, or spotted texture and round shaped) that are relatively unaffected by changes in orientation and view and size.

Recognition should be seen as a graded ability where performance depends on the similarity of the target to alternative distracters (non-targets). If the distracters are very dissimilar, then recognition is simple and can be made on the basis of simple view independent features (colour, texture, or idiosyncratic features visible from virtually any view).

6.3. *Measures of recognition: detection, discrimination, and categorisation*

To account for recognition of novel test views of an object, one needs to consider: (1) the angle between training and test views, (2) the tuning functions of cell populations that become adapted to the training view or views and (3) the task. After training on one view or orientation alone, then as the angle between training and test view increases so will the reaction time in detection tasks. This increase would continue up to the point where the training view falls outside the tuning function of cells selective for the training view. At this point reaction time would increase to infinity and recognition would fail.

For faces, view tuning at the cellular level is relatively broad: 60° of rotation is required to reduce cell responses to 1/2 maximal response (Perrett et al., 1991). After extensive training with paper clip and amoeboid figures the view tuning curves of cells in temporal cortex are narrower (Logothetis et al., 1995). Thus, one would expect generalisation across view to be more limited for paper clips than faces which is what is observed psychophysically (Edelman, 1995; Logothetis et al., 1994).

In the situation where two views of the same object have become equally familiar through training, we presume that two populations of cells would become tuned to the object, each population specialised for one view and each showing a tuning function. For recognition of the object class, activity in either population will provide evidence. One again predicts an increase in time for detection in proportion to the difference in angle between the test view and nearest training view. Unlike the mental rotation account, there is no need to define which training view is closest to the test view; recognition is successful when activity in either population exceeds a particular threshold.

If the two views have been associated with the same response or reward (i.e. the subject 'knows' that two views are known to belong to the same object), then cells higher up the processing stream will receive a convergent input from the two-view-specific populations. In this case, recognition of the object class will be successful when the summed activity of both view-specific populations exceeds a certain threshold. Such association would have the effect of smoothing out the reaction time dependence on view between the two trained views.

If a subject experiences two views of an object, the front view (0°) and the side or profile view rotated by 90°, experience would result in cells that become tuned to the features of the object. Amongst these cells there would be two populations of cells, tuned to the 0 and 90° views. If we assume that the view tuning is broad (equivalent to that observed for heads), seeing a novel 45° view (lying directly between the front view and side views) will activate both cell populations tuned to familiar front and side views. The novel view is not more detectable than training views because it will be sub-optimal for both front and side view-tuned cell populations. The combined activity in both populations to the new view will not exceed that evoked by one of the original training views.

It may help this description of generalisation to provide an analogy for colour vision. We have three cone mechanisms tuned to short (blue), middle (green) and long (red) wavelengths. The cones have wide spectral adsorption characteristics or tuning functions. If we take the red and green cones to stand for two populations of view tuned cells, then the novel intermediate 45° test view is equivalent to light of mid-long (yellow) wavelengths which will excite both red and green cones. Yellow light is sub-optimal for red and green cones since it does not match the peak spectral sensitivity of either cone. The total cone output to intermediate yellow light will not exceed that produced separately by red or green light. Hence detection will not be superior at stimulus values that fall between the peak sensitivities of two populations of neuronal detectors.

In some circumstances, object and face discrimination performance can be superior for the half profile view (with the front and side vies at 45° to the line of subject's sight, Palmer et al., 1981; Harries et al., 1991; Perrett et al., 1994). In these tasks the most efficiently recognised views may well be intermediate to the views represented most numerously by visual cells in the subjects' nervous system. This must, however, remain conjecture because the subjects' perceptual history of views of familiar objects and faces is usually unknown (though see Perrett et al., 1994).

In tasks where subjects are required to perform same-difference discriminations, performance can depend on how activity in neural populations is modified by small changes in the stimuli. Activity change in a neural population is greatest when a stimulus falls on the slope of a tuning function, rather than close to the peak sensitivity.

Supra-threshold wavelength discrimination is most efficient in the yellow region of the spectrum, intermediate to wavelengths matched to the peak spectral sensitivities of green and red cones. This is because a small change in wavelength in the yellow region of the spectrum will modulate the responses of red and green cones more than an equivalent change at wavelengths close to the peak sensitivities of the cones in the red or green regions of the spectrum. Thus, even for elementary sensory processing, 'intermediate stimuli' can produce superior or inferior psychophysical performance compared to stimuli matched to peak detector sensitivity depending on the nature of the task (detection or discrimination) and how the neural codes are being read (detecting any modulation above background activity or discriminating changes in the level of population activity when activity is already above background).

In higher level visual processing, detecting stimulus change is more efficient (just noticeable differences are smaller) at the boundary between two categories than detecting change for stimuli at the centre of categories. Indeed superior discrimination between categories is the hallmark of categorical judgements (Young et al., 1997). Superior discrimination at category boundaries has also been found for discriminating facial expression (Etcoff and Magee, 1992; Calder et al., 1996), facial identity (Beale and Keil, 1995) and discriminating object class (F. Newall, personal communication). Categorical judgements are assumed to reflect the existence of specialised neural populations with peak tuning matched to the centre of categories (i.e. the underlying neural 'detectors' are tuned to the prototypical or canonical examples of categories). Stimuli falling at the boundary between two categories will therefore fall on the slopes of the tuning functions of neurones tuned to the category prototypes. Superior same-difference judgements (in successive or simultaneous discriminations) at category boundaries can be interpreted as resulting from the fact that stimulus change at such boundaries will induce the greatest change in neuronal activity amongst the cells tuned to the category prototypes.

Classification of stimuli as examples of one or other of two categories will suffer further if the stimuli are moved away from the category prototypes. This will be because the stimuli will fall further from the peak sensitivity of cells tuned to the category prototypes, and evidence for the presence of either category prototype will accumulate progressively more slowly. Object categorisation like object detection will therefore show costs rather than benefits as one moves towards stimuli intermediate to familiar categories (Young et al., 1997). Both the costs and benefits for recognising intermediate stimuli in different types of recognition tasks can be seen to arise from consideration of the response functions of detectors tuned to category prototypes (Young et al., 1997).

For cells tuned to the front view of the head (the face or 0°), a 10° rotation of the head starting with the half profile view (45–55°) will produce a greater change in population activity than the same rotation starting with the face view (0–10°). Predicting performance for same-different discrimination for head views is complicated by unknown perceptual history with faces in general and by the fact that same-different judgements could be performed with other strategies (e.g. judging degree of symmetry). Predictions can be made from above considerations for the recognition of an asymmetric novel object (e.g. the paper clip stimuli of Poggio and Edelman, 1990; Logothetis et al., 1994; or symmetric 'greeble' stimuli of Gauthier and Tarr, 1997b) trained extensively at two views separated by a rotation equal to twice the band width of view sensitivity function for one view (1/2 width at 1/2 height). With such training, a task requiring same-difference discrimination between view pairs should peak in efficiency for views intermediate between the two training views. By contrast, a task requiring detection of the object from any view, or a task requiring categorical labels 'Training view 1' vs. 'Training view 2', should show the highest cost function (lowest accuracy and longest reaction time) for intermediate views.

6.4. Population vector hypothesis

Georgopoulos et al. (1982) and Georgopoulos (1995) have used 'population vector analysis' to read the activity of cell populations in motor cortex. Such analysis has also been used to analyse cell responses in the visual system (Young and Yamane, 1992; Földiák, 1993; Oram et al., 1998). Under this analysis each cell 'votes' for its preferred direction with strength proportional to the activity evoked in a test situation. Georgopoulos et al. (1989) observed that the population vector for cells in motor cortex rotated over time, during the interval between the presentation of a visual cue and an arm movement response made 90° to the direction of the cue. At the beginning of the trial the direction of the population vector pointed towards the sensory cue and later pointed in the direction of the monkey's reaching movement. The gradual rotation of the population vector direction through intermediate directions was likened to mental rotation (see also Lurito et al., 1991). Whatever neural mechanisms underlie this sensory-motor phenomenon in motor cortex, they need not necessarily relate to the recognition of familiar objects from unusual views and the processing in temporal cortex.

To study recognition of objects from unusual views, we have been recording activity in visual areas rather than in motor cortex since the subjects are not required to make movements. In our test situation objects were presented in a variety of views and orientation. When unusual views of familiar objects were presented, subjects in our test situation were not required to make any imagined rotations, though mental rotation accounts of recognition would suggest that such rotations take place whether they are consciously imagined or implemented without subjects awareness.

It is relevant to review the time course of activity in cells when an object is presented at some intermediate angle to the cells' preferred view. In this situation mental transformation models of recognition would predict that activity in such cells would commence at an intermediate time. Our findings show that cells tuned to views intermediate to the test stimulus are activated at intermediate rates, but not at intermediate times.

When an unusual orientation or view is presented our recordings show that cells tuned to a range of different views or orientations are activated. Each cell is activated in proportion to the angle between the test view and the cell's preferred view/orientation. For an inverted stimulus orientation, cells tuned to inverted orientations are activated most, those tuned to upright are activated least and those tuned to intermediate orientations at activated at intermediate amounts. The same is true for a back view with cells tuned to the back activated most, those tuned to the front are activated least and those tuned to intermediate side views activated to intermediate amounts. Our analysis shows that cells tuned to different orientations and views begin firing at the same latency but with different rates. We find that the cells tuned at intermediate views or orientations are activated at intermediate rates but not at intermediate latencies; they begin activity at the same time as those tuned to the test view or orientation. The relative degree of activation amongst cells (tuned to the test view, intermediate view or opposite view) does not change with time since stimulus appearance.

We hypothesis that the speed of recognition of the object is determined by the time for activity in the entire population of differently tuned cells to exceed a given criteria. This time to threshold reflects the frequency of cells with different orientation and view tuning. For unusual test views the small numbers of cells tuned to these unusual views will fire at high rates while larger numbers of cells tuned to more typical views will fire at medium to low rates. By contrast, for frequently experienced test views, large numbers of cells tuned to the typical views will fire at high rates, and the rare cells tuned to unusual views will fire at low rates.

Consideration of population vector coding with the present data from temporal cortex also suggests that there is no mental rotation in the recognition of faces. The rank order of stimulus effectiveness is apparent at response onset and is maintained throughout test periods of 1 s duration (Oram and Perrett, 1992). Moreover, the tuning of cells is independent of their preferred view/orientation (Oram and Perrett, 1992). Therefore the population vector analysis applied to the entire population of cells responsive to the face (from any view or orientation) points in the same direction from response onset to end of trial. If an inverted face image were presented, the population vector would indicate an inverted orientation throughout the trial period. While the direction of the population vector can be used to estimate stimulus identity (including head view) with limited accuracy (Sanger, 1996; Földiák, 1993; Oram et al., 1998), it does not predict changes in behavioural changes in recognition time from temporal cortical cell responses. The magnitude of the vector is related to the total population response and might be more appropriate for explanations of reaction times.

6.5. Evidence for mental transformations

The physiological explanation advanced here, accounts for the costs to object recognition (in time and accuracy) that are associated with change in view. It should be noted that the account does not address mechanisms underlying imagery. Imagery and imagined sensory-motor transformations may well have a role in a variety of tasks (e.g. subjects imagining moving their own hand to match an unusual view of a hand, Bonda et al., 1995; Parsons et al., 1995).

The cellular mechanisms within the ventral cortical stream that are described here are appropriate for the recognition of familiar objects encountered in unusual views. Other brain mechanisms may be involved in matching unfamiliar objects, in sensory-motor transformations or in the use of proprioceptive information to classify images of body parts (Bonda et al., 1995; Parsons et al., 1995). Indeed Cohen et al. (1996) note that classical mental rotation tasks do not engage the ventral visual stream but rather areas of the dorsal cortical pathway and frontal lobes.

The phenomena most often cited as evidence for a transformational process underling recognition of rotated stimuli include experiments in which prior information about stimulus orientation can null the extra time required to recognise rotated stimuli (e.g. Cooper and Shepard, 1973). These authors propose that 'the subject carries out a purely mental rotation of.... a mental image of the anticipated stimulus'. To account for these effects without invoking transformations, we propose that prior information about the upcoming stimulus (priming) acts on the same representation (i.e. cell populations) as the visual stimulus itself. We assume that the efficiency of priming is proportional to the degree to which the stimulus is therefore represented in the nervous system. The effectiveness of priming will parallel the effectiveness of visual activation during normal unprimed recognition. That is, priming will be less effective for more unusual views. Hence an increasing amount of time will be needed for prior information to prime increasingly rotated stimuli.

This explanation is post-hoc, as we do not have data on how cells are influenced by prior information during tasks equivalent to the Shepard and Metzler tasks. Some insight is available from 'delayed matching to sample' paradigms. With attention directed to stimuli within a cell's receptive field, then when the match stimulus is the same as the sample stimulus, cell responses are augmented during the match phase compared to when the sample and match differ. The augmentation is proportional to the cell's response to the stimulus when unprimed (McAdams and Maunsell, 1996).

In other words, the enhancement is greatest for cells optimally tuned to the stimulus in question. In this situation, priming due to prior information about the stimulus (seeing the sample) acts on the same cell population that represents the visual appearance of the stimulus itself. Furthermore, the magnitude of the priming is proportional to the strength of the stimulus representation in the nervous system.

A further effect interpreted as supporting internal transformation processes includes the impression that alternating presentations of differently oriented stimuli give a compelling demonstration of continuous rotation. Indeed, subjects can place a marker to indicate where the image passes at successive moments during the interpolated rotation. This phenomenon need not require the cellular explanation we have provided relating RTs to neural population responses. The perceptual impression of a smooth trajectory may be more related to the illusion of apparent motion. Early work by Wertheimer (1912) showed that apparent motion of objects can extend over large angles of rotation. Furthermore Kolers (1972) showed that the transition between start and end shapes during apparent motion is perceived to be a smooth transformation even when shape changes occur.

The perceptual history of apparent motion can influence the perceived trajectory. For example seeing a bar rotating back and forward around one end with rotations occurring over a gradually increasing angle, starting with an acute angle but slowly increasing to an obtuse angle, can induce apparent rotation through 180° rather than motion through the shorter path with than an angle less than 180°. In mental rotation tasks too when subjects are given enough biasing they appear to rotate stimuli 'the long way around'.

Mirror image stimuli are recognised according to reaction time (RT) functions that are predicted by the assumption that subjects mentally rotate stimuli along the most efficient axis. For some 2-D stimuli this would appear to include a flip in depth, since some 2-D stimuli rotated through 180° can produce faster RTs than stimuli rotated 90° (Tarr and Pinker, 1989; Tarr, 1995). Such phenomena appear to lie outside the physiological explanation advanced here. The unusually fast reaction times when matching mirror equivalent stimuli may arise in part from equivalence in orientation of some features across 180° rotation or mirror reflection. In general, the resolution of mechanism will depend on obtaining comparable physiological and psychological measures in the tasks requiring processing of the special stimulus classes and orientations that produce anomalous results.

The mental rotation explanation of the paths taken, including flips in depth is, however, not without problems. To rotate mentally the image (or its representation) along the optimal path, it is necessary to know the start and end points of the path. A difficulty with mental rotation accounts of object recognition concerns recognising which way to rotate the object when encountered in an unusual view. Information about an object might be pre-processed to establish which way to rotate it to bring it upright, prior to a matching process for identification. Admittedly, there are some cues from distinctive object features which might point to the relation of an object's axis to gravity and hence guide rotation (Ullman, 1989) but if one can recognise which way an image needs to be rotated, then to some extent the process of rotation is redundant since recognition has already been accomplished (Corballis, 1988).

In the account provided here, there is no need to pre-process an object to realise its likely orientation so that a mental rotation can take place subsequently. The system just accepts evidence in proportion to the activity of the relevant visually responsive cells in temporal cortex and elsewhere. Cells responsive to the face in temporal cortex will have outputs to brain systems capable of accessing semantic associations for faces (including verbal labels in the case of humans) and activating appropriate behavioural outputs. These associations will be more likely to be retrieved when face stimuli are presented in a frontal view, upright orientation and at a normal size, because under these conditions there will be more activity from cells in the temporal cortex already tuned to faces. Mental rotation has been invoked as an additional process to cope with unusual views. By contrast it is argued here that both typical and unusual views can be recognised using viewer-centred cells which operate in the same manner; unusual views take longer simply because there is less machinery dedicated to their processing.

Exposure to one particular view of an object increases the number of cells tuned to that view (Logothetis et al., 1995). This will decrease the time taken for the cumulative population response to exceed a threshold for that training view. This accounts for the selective improvement in recognition seen at the trained view or orientation (Logothetis et al., 1994; Perrett et al., 1988a; Tarr, 1995). Experience at all views during a task will increase the proportion of cells tuned to the previously unfamiliar views/orientations and may reduce the threshold of the population response required for behavioural output. This neural population account covers the wide variation in the RT-orientation slopes in different tasks without invoking different recognition strategies.

6.6. Explaining behavioural generalisation from physiological mechanisms

The proposed account suggests that people take longer to recognise an object in unusual orientations because the neural representation of that object is less strongly activated. This does not provide a full explanation of recognition of unusual views since it does not explain how and why the neurones fire as they do. This section briefly considers why the neural representation of familiar objects is sensitive to viewing conditions.

One can ask how individual cells exhibit response selectivity for complex stimuli and simultaneously show sensitivity to orientation, size and view. We suggest that the orientation and size sensitivity of cells at progressively higher levels of pattern processing is inherited from preceding stages, as cells in each level pool the activity of particular orientation and size specific feature detectors of lower levels (Perrett and Oram, 1993; Oram and Perrett, 1994; Fukushima, 1980). This process could establish the Elaborate feature detectors described by Tanaka et al. (1991) in the inferior temporal cortex from simpler features in prestriate cortex. Increased complexity of pattern selectivity and sensitivity to configuration can be achieved by combining several the outputs of several elaborate feature detectors which are themselves conjunctions of elements. Rearranged configurations (such as jumbled face parts) yield images lacking some of the 2-D visual features present in the normal configuration (Perrett and Oram, submitted). Sensitivity to the configuration of one view of a face can be generated in this way even when elaborate feature detection exhibits translation invariance over the parafovea.

While this scheme may explain the orientation sensitivity of individual cells to faces, it does not account for the overall tuning of the cell population. The population of cells responsive to faces exhibits tuning with respect to orientation and is biased to upright orientations. The bias can be explained by postulating that, through learning, the tuning of cells comes to reflect the statistics (e.g. frequency) of the images that we see. We see more upright than inverted faces. There is growing evidence that temporal cortex cell selectivity is indeed biased towards images experienced as an adult (Logothetis et al., 1995; Miyashita and Chang, 1988; Perrett et al., 1984). Competitive learning mechanisms (e.g. Földiák, 1991) coupled with visual experience may account both for cell selectivity for objects that are frequently seen and for the cell sensitivity to the viewing conditions in which the objects are seen.

What is important for the current paper is the inheritance of orientation and size specificity from early cortical processing. This specificity coupled with experience-dependent plasticity will produce bias in the population activity towards frequently seen views of faces. The dependence of RTs on orientation at the behavioural level is therefore explicable just from considering cellular mechanisms. There is no need to postulate additional mental operations to account for generalisation functions.

Examination of Fig. 1 shows that there is no systematic variation in onset latency of responses and viewing condition. Indeed, examination of cell responses to stimuli of different effectiveness shows that response latencies are coincident (within the 5 ms accuracy of measurement, Oram and Perrett, 1992, 1994). Previous reports of increased response latencies to rotated images of faces may reflect an artefact of measurement. Most, though not all, cell responses to non-upright faces are smaller and have slower rise times than responses to upright faces (Perrett et al., 1984, 1985, 1988b; Wachsmuth and Perrett, 1997). The smaller response magnitude means that with limited samples of trials it takes longer for a cell's response to a rotated face to exceed any statistical criterion (Perrett et al., 1984, 1985, 1988b).

If cell responses reflected mental transformations, then one would predict a systematic change in latency of response onset with change in view, orientation, size and part visibility. For example, a cell tuned to an upright face should not respond to an inverted face until the image has been mentally rotated by 180°. Thus inverted images should take longer to activate cells. We report here that cells do not show this predicted change in onset latency. Separation in the cumulative population response to different viewing circumstances occurs after response onset and amplifies over time. So the cells are not themselves implementing transformations nor are they reflecting the outputs of transformation processes occurring elsewhere. Since the behavioural RT-orientation functions can be predicted from the neural operations we describe, Occam's razor can be applied to conclude that there is no need to postulate additional transformation mechanisms for recognising familiar objects.

Acknowledgements

This work was supported by the MRC, BBSRC and the British Council British-German Academic Research Collaboration. W.S. received support from an SERC studentship. We thank Dr O. Turnbull, Dr. D. Carey, and Professor A. Georgopoulos for comments on earlier versions of manuscript. This model has been briefly presented elsewhere (Perrett, 1996). Since submission a similar computational model has been advanced (Bricolo et al., 1998).

References

Allison, T., McCarthy, G., Belger, A., Puce, A., Luby, M. Spencer, D.D., Bentin, S., 1994. What is a face: electrophysiological responsiveness of human extrastriate visual cortex to human faces. Society for Neuroscience Abstracts 20, 316.

Baker Cave, C., Kosslyn, M., 1993. The role of parts and spatial relations in object identification. Perception 22, 229–248.

Beale, J.M., Keil, F.C., 1995. Categorical effects in the perception of faces. Cognition 57, 217–239.

Besner, D., 1983. Visual pattern recognition: size pre-processing re-examined. Quarterly Journal of Experimental Psychology 35, 209–216.

Biederman, I., 1987. Recognition by components: a theory of human image understanding. Psychological Review 94, 115–145.

Bonda, E., Petrides, M., Frey, S., Evans, A., 1995. Neural correlates of mental transformations of the body-in-space. Proceedings of the National Academy of Science USA 92, 11180–11184.

Bricolo, E., Poggio, T., Logothetis, N.K., 1998. 3D object recognition: a model of view tuned neurons. In: Advances in Neural Information Processing Systems, Vol. 9. Morgan Kaufman, Los Altos, CA, in press.

Bruce, V., Young, A., 1986. Understanding face recognition. British Journal of Psychology 77, 103–327.

Bundesen, C., Larsen, A., 1975. Visual transformation of size. Journal of Experimental Psychology: Human Perception and Performance 1, 214–220.

Bülthoff, H.H., Edelman, S., 1992. Psychophysical support for a two-dimensional view interpolation theory of object recognition. Proceedings of the National Academy of Science USA 89, 60–64.

Calder, A.J., Young, A.W., Perrett, D.I., Etcoff, N.L., Rowland, D., 1996. Categorical perception of morphed facial expressions. Visual Cognition 3, 81–117.

Carey, S., 1992. Becoming a face expert. Philosophical Transactions of the Royal Society of London B 335, 95–103.

Carpenter, P.A., Just, M.A., 1978. Eye fixations during mental rotation. In: J.W. Senders, D.F. Fisher, R.A. Monty (Eds.), Eye Movements and Higher Psychological Functions. Erlbaum, Hillsdale, NJ.

Cohen, M.S., Kosslyn, S.M., Breiter, H.C., Digirolamo, G.J., Thompson, W.L., Anderson, A.K., Bookheimer, S.Y., Rosen, B.R., Belliveau, J.W., 1996. Changes in cortical activity during mental rotation – a mapping study using functional MRI. Brain 119, 89–100.

Cooper, L.A., Shepard, R.N., 1973. In: W.G. Chase (Ed.), Chronometric Studies of the Rotation of Mental Images. Academic Press, New York, pp. 75–176.

Corballis, M., 1988. Recognition of disoriented shapes. Psychological Review 95, 115–123.

Dolan, R.J., Fink, G.R., Rolls, E.T., Booth, M., Holmes, A., Frackowiak, R.S.J., Friston, K.L., 1997. How the brain learns to see objects and faces in an impoverished context. Nature 389, 596–599.

Edelman, S., Bülthoff, H.H., 1992. Orientation dependence in the recognition of familiar and novel views of three-dimensional objects. Vision Research 32, 2385–2400.

Edelman, S., Weinshall, D., 1991. A self-organising multiple-view representation of 3D objects. Biological Cybernetics 63, 209–219.

Edelman, S., 1995. Class similarity and viewpoint invariance in the recognition of 3D objects. Biological Cybernetics 72, 207–220.

Edelman, S., 1997. Representation is representation of similarities. Behavioural and Brain Sciences, in press.

Ellis, R., Allport, D.A., Humphreys, G.W., Collis, J., 1989. Varieties of object constancy. Quarterly Journal of Experimental Psychology 41, 775–796.

Etcoff, N.L., Magee, J.J., 1992. Categorical perception of emotion. Cognition 44, 227–240.

Farah, M.J., Hammond, K.M., 1988. Mental rotation and orientation-invariant object recognition: dissociable processes. Cognition 29, 29–46.

Flin, R., Dziurawiec, S., 1989. Development factors in face processing. In: A.W. Young, H.D. Ellis. Handbook of Research on Face Processing. North Holland, Amsterdam.

Földiák, P., 1991. Learning invariance from transformation sequences. Neural Computation 3, 194–200.

Földiák, P., 1993. The 'ideal homunculus': statistical inference from neural population responses. In F.H. Eeckman, J.M. Bower (Eds.), Computation and Neural System. Kluwer Academic Publishers, Norwell, MA, pp. 55–60.

Fukushima, K., 1980. Neocognition: a self-organizing neural network model for a mechanism of pattern recognition unaffected by shift in position. Biological Cybernetics 36, 193–202.

Gauthier, I., Tarr, M.J., 1997. Orientation priming of novel shapes in the context of viewpoint dependent processing. Perception 26, 51–73.

Gauthier, I., Tarr, M.J., 1997b. Becoming a 'Greeble' expert: exploring the mechanisms for face recognition. Vision Research, in press.

Georgopoulos, A.P., Kalaska, J.F., Caminiti, R., Massey, J.T., 1982. On the relations between the direction of two-dimensional arm movements and cell discharge in primate motor cortex. Journal of Neuroscience 2, 1527–1537.

Georgopoulos, A.P., Luroto, J.T., Petrides, M., Schwartz, A.B., Masey, J.T., 1989. Mental rotation of the neuronal population vector. Science 243, 234–243.

Georgopoulos, A.P., 1995. Current issues in directional motor control. Trends in Neuroscience 18, 506–510.

Goodale, M.A., Milner, A.D., 1992. Separate visual pathways for perception and action. Trends in Neurosciences 15, 20–25.

Gregory, R.L., 1980. Perceptions as hypotheses. Philosophical Transactions of the Royal Society of London B 290, 181–197.

Hasselmo, M.E., Rolls, E.T., Baylis, G.C., Nalwa, V., 1989. Object centred encoding by face-selective neurons in the cortex of the superior temporal sulcus of the monkey. Experimental Brain Research 75, 417–429.

Harries, M.H., Perrett, D.I., Lavender, A., 1991. Preferential inspection of views of 3-D model heads. Perception 20, 669–680.

Hill, H., Schyns, P.G., Akamatsu, S., 1997. Information and viewpoint dependence in face recognition. Cognition 62, 201–222.

Holmes, E.J., Gross, C.G., 1984. Stimulus equivalence after inferior temporal lesions in monkeys. Behavioural Neuroscience 98, 898–901.

Holmes, E.J., Gross, C.G., 1984. Effects of inferior temporal lesions on discrimination of stimuli differing in orientation. Journal of Neuroscience 4, 3063–3068.

Humphreys, G.W., Kahn, S.C., 1992. Recognizing novel views of three-dimensional objects. Canadian Journal of Psychology 46, 170–190.

Humphreys, G.W., Riddoch, M.J., 1984. Routes to object constancy: implications from neurological impairments of object constancy. Quarterly Journal of Experimental Psychology 36, 385–415.

Humphreys, G.W., Quinlan, P.T., 1987. Normal and pathological processes in visual constancy. In: G.W. Humphreys, M.J. Riddoch (Eds.), Visual Object Processing: a Cognitive Neuropsychological Approach. Lawrence Erlbaum Associates, Hillsdale, NJ, pp. 281–301.

Jolicœur, P., 1985. The time to name disorientated natural objects. Memory and Cognition 13, 289–303.

Jolicœur, P., 1987. A size-congruency effect in memory for visual shape. Memory and Cognition 15, 531–543.

Jolicœur, P., 1990. Identification of disoriented objects: a dual-system theory. Mind and Language 5, 387–410.

Jolicœur, P., Besner, D., 1987. Additivity and interaction between size ratio and response category in the comparison of size-discrepant shapes. Journal of Experimental Psychology 38, 80–93.

Koenderink, J.J., van Doorn, A.J., 1979. The internal representation of solid shape with respect to vision. Biological Cybernetics 32, 211–216.

Kolers, P., 1972. Aspects of Motion Perception. Pergamon Press, Elmsford, NY.

Larsen, A., 1985. Pattern matching: effects of size ratio, angular difference in orientation, and familiarity. Perception and Psychophysics 38, 63–68.

Lennie, P., 1981. The physiological basis of variations in visual latency. Vision Research 21, 815–824.

Logothetis, N.K., Pauls, J., Bülthoff, H.H., Poggio, T., 1994. View-dependent object recognition by monkeys. Current Biology 4, 401–414.

Logothetis, N.K., Pauls, J., Poggio, T., 1995. Shape representation in the inferior temporal cortex of monkeys. Current Biology 5, 552–563.

Lurito, J.T., Georgopoulos, T., Georgopoulos, A.P., 1991. Cognitive spatial-motor processes. 7. The making of movements at an angle from stimulus direction: studies of motor cortical activity at the single cell and population level. Experimental Brain Research 87, 562–580.

McAdams, C.J., Maunsell, J.H.R., 1996. Attention enhances neuronal responses without altering orientation selectivity in macaque area V4. Society for Neuroscience Abstracts 22, 1197.

McMullen, P.A., Jolicœur, P., 1992. The reference frame and effects of orientation on finding the top of rotated objects. Journal of Experimental Psychology: Human Perception and Performance 18, 807–820.

Miyashita, Y., Chang, H.-S., 1988. Neuronal correlate of pictorial short-term memory in the primate temporal cortex. Nature 331, 68–70.

Moses, Y., Ullman, S., Edelman, S., 1996. Generalization to novel images in upright and inverted faces. Perception 25, 443–462.

Oram, M.W., Perrett, D.I., 1992. Time course of neural responses discriminating different views of the face and head. Journal of Neurophysiology 68, 70–84.

Oram, M.W., Perrett, D.I., 1994. Modelling visual recognition from neurobiological constraints. Neural Networks 7, 945–972.

Oram, M.W., Wachsmuth, E., Perrett, D.I., Emery, N.J., submitted. Visual coding of body-part and whole body motion in the temporal cortex of the macaque monkey. Cerebral Cortex.

Oram, M.W., Foldiak, P., Perrett, D.I., Sengpiel, F., 1998. The ideal Homunculus: decoding neural population signals. Trends in Neuroscience, in press.

Palmer, S.E., Rosch, E., Chase, P., Baddely, D., 1981. Canonical perspective and the perception of objects. In: J. Long, A. Baddeley (Eds.), Attention and Performance IX. Lawrence Erlbaum Associates, Hillsdale, NJ, pp. 135–151.

Parsons, L.M., Fox, P.T., Downs, J.H., Glass, T., Hirsch, T.B., Martin, C.C., Jerabek, P.A., Lancaster, J.L., 1995. Use of implicit motor imagery for visual shape discrimination as revealed by PET. Nature 375, 54–58.

Perrett, D.I., 1996. View-dependent coding in the ventral stream and its consequences for recognition. In: R. Caminiti, K.-P. Hoffmann, F. Lacquaniti, J. Altman (Eds.), Vision and Movement Mechanisms in the Cerebral Cortex. HFSP, Strasbourg, pp. 142–151.

Perrett, D.I., Oram, M.W. Visual recognition based on temporal cortex cells: viewer-centered processing of pattern configuration. Zeilschrift für Naturforschung, in press.

Perrett, D.I., Oram, M.W., Hietanen, J.K., Benson, P.J., 1994. Issues of representation in object vision. In: M. Farah, G. Ratcliff (Eds.), The Neuropsychology of Higher Vision: Collated Tutorial Essays. Lawrence Erlbaum Associates, Hillsdale, NJ, pp. 33–61.

Perrett, D.I., Oram, M.W., 1993. The neurophysiology of shape processing. Image and Visual Computing 11, 317–333.

Perrett, D.I., Oram, M.W., Harries, M.H., Bevan, R., Hietanen, J.K., Benson, P.J., Thomas, S., 1991. Viewer-centred and object-centred coding of heads in the macaque temporal cortex. Experimental Brain Research 86, 159–173.

Perrett, D.I., Mistlin, A.J., Chitty, A.J., Smith, P.A.J., Potter, D.D., Brönnimann, R., Harries, M.H., 1988. Specialised face processing and hemispheric asymmetry in man and monkey: evidence from single unit and reaction time studies. Behavioural Brain Research 29, 245–258.

Perrett, D.I., Mistlin, A.J., Chitty, A.J., Harries, M., Newcombe, F., De Haan, E., 1988a. Neuronal mechanisms of face perception and their pathology. In: C. Kennard, F. Clifford Rose (Eds.), Physiological Aspects of Clinical Neuro-opthalmology. Chapman and Hall, London, pp. 137–154.

Perrett, D.I., Harries, M.H., Bevan, R., Thomas, S., Benson, P.J., Mistlin, A.J., Chitty, A.J., Hietanen, J.K., Ortega, J.E., 1989. Frameworks of analysis for the neural representation of animate objects and actions. Journal of Experimental Biology 146, 87–114.

Perrett, D.I., Smith, P.A.J., Potter, D.D., Mistlin, A.J., Head, A.S., Milner, A.D., Jeeves, M.A., 1985. Visual cells in the temporal cortex sensitive to face view and gaze direction. Proceedings Royal Society London B 223, 293–317.

Perrett, D.I., Smith, P.A.J., Potter, D.D., Mistlin, A.J., Head, A.S., Milner, A.D., Jeeves, M.A., 1984. Neurons responsive to faces in the temporal cortex: Studies of functional organization, sensitivity to identity and relation to perception. Human Neurobiology 3, 197–208.

Perrett, D.I., Rolls, E.T., Caan, W., 1982. Visual neurons responsive to faces in the monkey temporal cortex. Experimental Brain Research 47, 329–342.

Phelps, M.T., Roberts, W.A., 1994. Memory for pictures of upright and inverted primate faces in humans (*homo sapiens*), squirrel monkeys (*saimiri sciureus*), and pigeons (*columba livia*). Journal of Comparative Psychology 108, 114–125.

Poggio, T., Edelman, S., 1990. A network that learns to recognise three-dimensional objects. Nature 343, 263–266.

Purcell, D.G., Stewart, A.L., 1988. The face-detection effect: configuration enhances detection. Perception and Psychophysics 43, 355–366.

Rock, I., 1973. Orientation and Forms. Academic Press, New York.

Rock, I., DiVita, J., 1987. A case of viewer-centred object perception. Cognitive Psychology 19, 280–293.

Rolls, E.T., Baylis, G.C., Hasselmo, M.E., Nalwa, V., 1989. The effect of learning on the face selective properties of neurons in the cortex in the superior temporal sulcus of the monkey. Experimental Brain Research 76, 153–164.

Rolls, E.T., Tovee, M.J., Purcell, D.G., Stewart, A.L., Azzopardi, P., 1994. The response of neurons in the temporal cortex of primates and face identification and detection. Experimental Brain Research 101, 473–484.

Sanger, T.D., 1996. Probability density estimation for the interpretation of neural population codes. Journal of Neurophysiology 76, 2790–2793.

Shepard, R.N., Metzler, J., 1971. Mental rotation of three-dimensional objects. Science 171, 701–703.

Stratford, K., Mason, A., Larkman, A., Major, G., Jack, J., 1989. The modeling of pyramidal neurones in the visual cortex. In: R. Durbin, C. Miall, G. Mitchison (Eds.), The Computing Neurone. Addison–Wesley, New York, pp. 296–321.

Tanaka, K., Saito, H., Fukada, Y., Moriya, M., 1991. Coding visual images of objects in the inferotemporal cortex of the macaque monkey. Journal of Neurophysiology 66, 170–189.

Tarr, M.J., Pinker, S., 1989. Mental rotation and orientation dependence in shape recognition. Cognitive Psychology 5, 233–282.

Tarr, M.J., Pinker, S., 1990. When does human object vision use a viewer-centred reference. Psychological Science 2, 207–209.

Tarr, M.J., Pinker, S., 1991. Orientation-dependent mechanisms in shape-recognition – further issues. Psychological Science 2, 207–209.

Tarr, M.J., 1995. Rotating objects to recognise them: a case study on the role of viewpoint dependency in the recognition of three-dimensional objects. Psychonomic Bulletin and Review 2, 55–82.

Turnbull, O.H., Laws, K.R., McCarthy, R.A., 1995. Object recognition without knowledge of object orientation. Cortex 31, 387–395.

Ullman, S., 1989. Aligning pictorial descriptions: an approach to object recognition. Cognition 32, 193–254.

Vaughan, H.G. Jr., Costa, L.D., Gilden, L., 1966. Functional relation of visual evoked response and reaction time to stimulus intensity. Vision Research 6, 645–656.

Vetter, T., Poggio, T., Bülthoff, H.H., 1994. The importance of symmetry and virtual views in three-dimensional object recognition. Current Biology 4, 18–23.

Wachsmuth, E., Oram, M.W., Perrett, D.I., 1994. Recognition of objects and their component parts: responses of single units in the temporal cortex of the macaque. Cerebral Cortex 4, 509–522.

Wachsmuth, E., Perrett, D.I., Oram, M.W., submitted. Effect of image orientation and size on cells responsive to faces in the cortex of the superior temporal sulcus of macaque. Cognitive Neuropsychology.

Wachsmuth, E., Perrett, D.I., 1997. Generalising across object orientation and size. In: V. Walsh, S. Butler (Eds.), Perceptual Constancies. Oxford University Press, Oxford, in press.

Weiskrantz, L., Saunders, R.C., 1984. Impairments of visual object transforms in monkeys. Brain 107, 1033–1072.

Warrington, E.K., James, M., 1986. Visual object recognition in patients with right hemisphere lesions: axes or features? Perception 15, 355–366.

Warrington, E.K., Taylor, A.M., 1973. The contribution of the right parietal lobe to object recognition. Cortex 9, 152–164.

Wertheimer, M., 1912. Experimentelle Stuidien uber das Sehen von Beuegung. Zeitschrift fuer Psychologie 61, 161–265.

Yamane, S., Kaji, S., Kawano, K., 1988. What facial features activate face neurons in the inferotemporal cortex of the monkey. Experimental Brain Research 73, 209–214.

Yin, R.K., 1969. Looking at upside-down faces. Journal of Experimental Psychology 81, 141–145.

Yin, R.K., 1970. Face recognition by brain-injured patients, a dissociable ability? Neuropsychologia 8, 395–402.

Young, A.W., Rowland, D., Calder, A.J., Etcoff, N. L, Seth, A., Perrett, D.I., 1997. Facial expression megamix: tests of dimensional and category accounts of emotional recognition. Cognition 63, 271–313.

Young, M.P., Yamane, S., 1992. Sparse population coding of faces in the inferotemporal cortex. Science 256, 1327–1331.

6

Diagnostic recognition: task constraints, object information, and their interactions

Philippe G. Schyns*

Department of Psychology 56, Hillhead St., University of Glasgow, Glasgow G12 8QB, UK

Abstract

Object recognition and categorization research are both concerned with understanding how input information matches object information in memory. It is therefore surprising that these two fields have evolved independently, without much cross-fertilization. It is the main objective of this paper to lay out the basis of a dialogue between object recognition and categorization research, with the hope of raising issues that could cross-fertilize both domains. To this end, the paper develops *diagnostic recognition*, a framework which formulates recognition performance as an interaction of task constraints and object information. I argue and present examples suggesting that diagnostic recognition could be fruitfully applied to the understanding of everyday object recognition. Issues are raised regarding the psychological status of the interactions specified in the framework. © 1998 Elsevier Science B.V. All rights reserved

Keywords: Object recognition; Categorization research; Diagnostic recognition

1. Introduction

Object recognition and categorization research are both concerned with the question 'what is this object?' To recognize an object as a car is not very different from placing the object in the *car* category. In both cases, the problem is to understand how input information matches with information in memory. Thus, both categorization and object recognition research are concerned with the same fundamental issues of 'which input information should be used?' 'what is the organization of information in memory?' and 'how do input and memory information interact to explain performance?'

* E-mail: philippe@psy.gla.ac.uk

Given such profound similarity, it is surprising that object recognition and categorization research have evolved separately, without much cross-fertilization between the two. The reason for this could be a difference of focus: typical categorization studies have sought to understand the rules governing the formation of categories (the idea that the visual attributes *feathers*, *wings*, *legs*, *beak*, *black*, but also functional attributes such as *fly*, *lay eggs*, *live in the trees* represent a crow which is also a bird, an animal and a living thing), while recognition researchers have mostly looked into the perceptual characteristics of the recognition process (e.g. the representation of the visual attributes of a crow that authorize its initial recognition as a member of the *bird* category). However, recent debates on the possible interactions between categorization and perception have suggested that the principles governing the formation of categories should be more tightly coupled with the perceptual aspects of recognition (Schyns et al., 1998). It is proposed that such interactions will promote the emergence of new, more powerful theories of visual cognition.

It is the main objective of this paper to lay out the basis of a dialogue between object recognition and categorization studies, to raise issues that could cross-fertilize both fields. To this end, the first section develops *diagnostic recognition*, a framework which integrates two main factors: the task constraints of categorization studies, and the perceptual information of recognition theories. I wish to stress from the outset that diagnostic recognition is *not* a new theory of object recognition. Instead, it is a generic framework which proposes one possible answer to the question: 'how could we frame issues common to object recognition and categorization theories?'

The paper is organized as follows: the first section develops the diagnostic recognition framework and its main motivations. Two examples are then presented to illustrate how both object recognition and categorization could benefit from the framework. Subsequent sections apply diagnostic recognition to the explanation of 'everyday recognition', discuss its task constraints, its perceptual information, and the psychological status of their interactions.

2. The diagnostic recognition framework: interactions of task constraints and object information

Everyday observation reveals that a single object fits into many possible categories. For example, the same object may be recognized as a *Porsche*, a *car*, or a *vehicle*. On other occasions, it may be called a *toy*, an *expensive gift*, a *public nuisance*, or a *public danger* which sometimes leads to *scrap metal*. Categorization is a flexible process and people tend to place a single object into one category or another depending on a number of factors including their goals and actions, environmental contingencies, and so forth (e.g. Barsalou, 1983).

It is always worth stressing that different categorizations of an identical object tend to change the information requirements of the task at hand. For example, when assigning a visual event to the *Porsche*, *collie*, *sparrow*, *Mary* or *New York* category comparatively more specific information might be necessary than when categorizing it as a *car*, *dog*, *bird*, *human face* or *city*. I will not consider here all possible object classifications, but instead focus on the information requirements associated with the hierarchical organization of categories; the idea that an object belongs to a sequence of progressively more inclusive categories such as *Porsche, car, vehicle*. Within this hierarchy, I will concentrate on the initial, or so-called 'perceptual' classifications (e.g. *Porsche* or *car*), instead of the abstract functional classifications (e.g. *vehicle*) which are arguably more detached from the perceptual input. Henceforth, *task constraints* relate to the visual information required to place the input into the hierarchy of perceptual categories. Section 3.1 will detail what these task constraints might be. For now, it suffices to treat them as the demands for perceptual information that emanate from different categorizations. Although task constraints have traditionally been the province of categorization research, they are an irreducible factor of *any* recognition task, and the first factor considered in diagnostic recognition.

The second factor is the structure of the perceptual information available to form hierarchically organized categories. Objects form categories because they 'look alike' – i.e. they share cues such as a similar silhouette or global shape, distinctive sets of parts similarly organized (e.g. nose, mouth, eyes, ears, hair and their structural relationships), or characteristic surface properties (e.g. smooth vs. discontinuous, symmetric vs. asymmetric, and textural, color and illumination cues). Generally speaking, there are perceptual limitations to the extraction of image cues. For instance, the neural wiring of early vision could promote an earlier recovery of shape from luminance variations and shading, at the expense of color and textural cues (e.g. Livingstone and Hubel, 1987; Weisstein et al., 1992). Alternatively, real-world objects could be so structured that their shapes vary much more than their colors and textures, resulting in comparatively more information for visual processing along the shape dimension. Issues of perceptual availability of object information have traditionally been the province of perceptually-oriented object recognition researchers. However, perceptual cues are an irreducible factor of any object categorization, and the second factor of diagnostic recognition. Section 3.3 will review how the main theories of human object recognition assume that we use different kinds of perceptual information.

Diagnostic recognition attempts to frame a recognition problem as an interaction between task constraints and perceptual object information, the two factors just discussed (see Fig. 1). Here is how it would work: when the information required to assign an object to a category matches with input information, a subset of object cues become particularly useful (i.e. diagnostic) for the task at hand. Diagnosticity is the first component of recognition performance. However, perceptual limitations on the extraction of diagnostic cues should also affect performance. Thus, diagnostic recognition frames explanations of performance as interactions between cue diagnosticity and cue availability. The nature and the implications of these interactions have been neglected both in object recognition and in object categorization research.

For example, even though the diagnosticity of cues for different classifications has been thoroughly modeled in categorization theories (e.g. Elio and Anderson, 1981; Nosofsky, 1984, 1986; Estes, 1986; Gluck and Bower, 1988; Anderson, 1991;

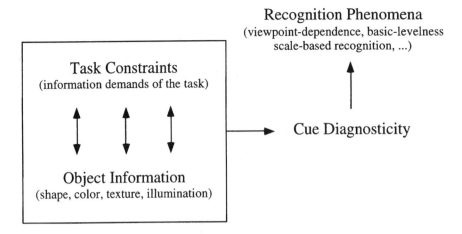

Fig. 1. This figure illustrates the main components of diagnostic recognition: task constraints and object information, whose interactions give rise to cue diagnosticity. According to diagnostic recognition, cue diagnosticity could explain the usage of image information subtending many recognition phenomena.

Kruschke, 1992; and many others), these often adopt a stance of: 'you tell me what the object cues are, and I will tell you how they are integrated to perform the object categorization' (Schyns et al., 1998). Consequently, they place few perceptual constraints on what may count as an object cue and they tend not to incorporate perceptual limitations on cue availability in their explanations of performance. However, recent studies have suggested that the simple fact of placing an object in one category or another could change the perception of its cues (Goldstone, 1994), or even its analysis into perceptual cues (Schyns and Murphy, 1991; Schyns and Rodet, 1997). If categorization does not start where perception ends, constraints on the perceptual availability of visual cues should supplement explanations of even very simple categorizations.

In contrast, whereas recognition researchers are well aware of the role of cue availability in their explanations of performance, they still tend to overlook the influence of task constraints. For example, researchers often assume that shape cues always supersede color and textural cues in everyday recognition (e.g. Biederman, 1987; Biederman and Ju, 1988; Tarr and Kriegman, 1998). Cutzu and Edelman (1997) even argued that the visual system could support 'veridical' representations of the objective similarities existing between the shapes of distal three-dimensional (3D) objects. These findings open the possibility of veridical, exhaustive representations of the object shapes themselves. However, would these always be exhaustive, irrespective of the diagnosticity of other cues? If this was the case, people who would distinguish different fruits in a basket on the basis of their colors and textures would also construct complete representations of their shapes. Alternatively, the diagnosticity of color and textural cues in this task could affect the *accuracy* of shape representations. People who categorize a chair as *chair* or *Art Deco chair* might also construct slightly different representations of its shape. Cutzu and Edelman's findings suggest that the shape of 3D objects can sometimes be represented in detail. The circumstances of exhaustive or task-dependent representations remain to be explored. These issues arise from considering the potential impact of cue diagnosticity on object perceptions and representations in recognition research.

Together, these considerations should justify the importance of bridging the gap between object categorization and object recognition research. A complete object recognition and categorization theory will need to integrate the factors affecting the diagnosticity of object cues and the perceptual constraints on their availability. It is the first aim of this paper to illustrate that the interactions between cue diagnosticity and cue availability could account for a wide range of phenomena (including feature learning, viewpoint-dependence vs. independence, basic and subordinate level recognition, the basic-to-subordinate shift, and scale-dependent recognition).

The second aim of the paper is to address the psychological status of the interactions between the task and the object cues. If several object cues are highly diagnostic of a categorization, their perception is essential to accomplish the task. What happens, then, to the other, less informative cues? Are they all perceived, or are some of them left out of the perception? When perceived, are non-diagnostic cues processed as extensively as when they are diagnostic? In the example discussed earlier, would one encode all the complex arabesques of a 3D Art Deco chair when one simply categorizes it as a chair? Simply put, is object perception driven to a certain extent (yet to be determined) by the diagnosticity of cues in a task, or does it reflect all the information of the distal object? There are psychological (O'Regan, 1992; Rensink et al., 1997; Schyns and Oliva, 1997) philosophical (Dennett, 1991) and computational (Cutzu and Edelman, 1997) indications that an exhaustive view is misguided. Later in the paper, I will present an instance of partial, flexible and diagnosticity-driven perceptions of complex visual stimuli. I will also argue that flexible perceptions could arise as psychological byproducts of the interactions between cue diagnosticity and cue availability. For the time being, let us turn to an important object recognition phenomenon (viewpoint-dependence) and examine how it might be fruitfully expressed within the diagnostic recognition framework.

2.1. Example 1: diagnostic recognition and viewpoint-dependence

One of the most challenging problems of object recognition is to explain the relative invariance of recognition to changes in object orientation. This is not to say that object recognition is fully viewpoint-invariant; there are now many independent sources of evidence suggesting that a large number of object classes are better recognized when shown from particular viewpoints (e.g. Palmer et al., 1981; Rock and Di Vita, 1987; Tarr and Pinker, 1989; Perrett et al., 1991; Bülthoff and Edelman, 1992; Edelman and Bülthoff, 1992; Vetter et al., 1994). Subjects label such object views as 'better' and are faster to categorize the objects shown in these views. Typically, 'viewpoint-dependent recognition' refers to a monotonic increase in recognition performance (reaction times and/or error rates) with increasing misorientation from the preferred views. Evidence of such viewpoint-dependent recognition has been reported for familiar (e.g. Palmer et al., 1981), unfamiliar (e.g. Rock and Di Vita, 1987), realistic and artificial objects (e.g. Tarr and Pinker,

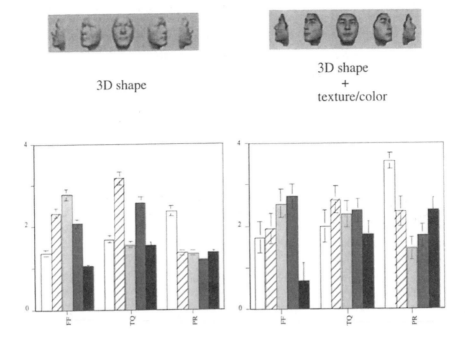

3D shape

3D shape
+
texture/color

Fig. 2. This figure (adapted from Hill et al., 1997) illustrates the main results of an experiment on viewpoint-dependence in face identification. The top left picture shows the face views of the shape-from-shading condition. The bottom left histogram presents patterns of viewpoint-dependent performance for the identification of shaded stimuli. The top right picture shows the face views of the shape plus texture conditions, and the bottom right histogram presents the viewpoint-dependent performance for the identification of these stimuli. A version of d' measured performance. Each of the three learning conditions (full-face, FF; three-quarter, TQ; profile, PR) is associated with a different histogram. In each histogram, the height of each bar corresponds to generalization performance to one of the test views (from left to right, left PR, left TQ, FF, right TQ, right PR).

1989; Bülthoff and Edelman, 1992), and the detailed conditions of viewpoint-dependence have become a central issue in object recognition research.

However, the debate is still open as to the interpretation of the phenomenon. Evidence of viewpoint-dependence or viewpoint-independence is often used to tease apart formats of object representation (see Biederman and Gerhardstein, 1995; Tarr and Bülthoff, 1995). For example, the 'view-based approach' claims that objects are stored in memory as collections of discrete views and that dependence on a view reveals that it is effectively stored in memory. In contrast, Biederman's recognition-by-components theory argues that the recognition of an object is viewpoint-independent over the range of viewpoints in which the geons that represent this object in memory are visible (Biederman, 1987; Biederman and Gerhardstein, 1993).[1]

Diagnostic recognition suggests that viewpoint-dependence might arise from the

[1]The precise conditions for viewpoint invariance specified in Biederman and Gerhardstein (1993) are listed in Section 3.3.

interaction between the diagnosticity of cues in a task and the availability of those cues in the input image. The presence of diagnostic information in these views, rather that the specific format (part or view) used to represent this information in memory, could then determine dependence of recognition on one (or a subset of) view(s). For example, two different categorizations of an identical face might change the information requirement of the task, the face cues that are diagnostic, and the subset of views that are preferred for recognition. To illustrate, many views would convey sufficient information to categorize Mary's face as *face*. However, fewer views would allow one to classify the same face as *Mary* (because Mary's features are visible from only a restricted subset of views). Within the range of views in which diagnostic cues are visible, there could be geometrical and perceptual limitations on their extraction from the image. For example, although the nose of a face is visible in all views between the two profiles, its length (if it was important to identify Mary) might be easier to measure from a 3/4, or profile view than from the frontal view. These limitations, interacting with task constraints, would predict that *length-of-nose* (in fact, its perceptual implementation) would only affect viewpoint-dependence when this cue was diagnostic for the task – i.e. in the *Mary*, not the *face* categorization.

Hill et al. (1997) tested the possibility of such relative patterns of viewpoint-dependent face recognition. Their subjects learned only one view of a face (either the full-face, FF, one three-quarter, TQ, or one profile view, PR, see Fig. 2) and were subsequently tested on their generalization capabilities to other views of the same face (FF, the two TQ and the two PR views). The top pictures of Fig. 2 illustrate what these views looked like. Different subject groups were assigned a different learning view, and all groups participated in the same generalization task which tested all views. This allowed a comparison of patterns of viewpoint-dependence when people extracted object information from a single, different view, but had to recognize all views. One set of experiments used shaded models of 3D laser-scanned faces, to isolate the influence of shape-from-shading cues (see Fig. 2, the top left picture). A second set of experiments added color and texture to the shaded models, to examine the role of these supplementary cues (see Fig. 2, the top right picture). Together, these designs framed viewpoint-dependence as an interaction between fixed task demands and variable stimulus information.

As an object class, faces share geometrical information to which perception could be attuned. One such property is their approximate bilateral symmetry (Vetter et al., 1994) which allows occluded cues to be inferred from a single learned view. Consequently, the learned view and its symmetrical view might be identified with equal accuracy, and possibly better than any other unseen views. Such effects of symmetric object information should be particularly salient with shaded face models, for which no other cue than shape is available from the image (compare the top pictures of Fig. 2).

The results of Hill et al. (1997) are summarized in the histograms of Fig. 2. The bottom left histogram illustrates that subjects who learned a TQ view recognized almost as efficiently the symmetric three-quarter, while performance decreased monotonically with rotation in depth for subjects who learned the profile, or the full-face view, confirming the role of symmetric face information in explanations of viewpoint-dependent identification, or that the TQ view conveys more face information for identity decisions (see also Schyns and Bülthoff, 1994; Troje and Bülthoff, 1996).

The addition of color and textural cues in an otherwise identical task affected performance (see Fig. 2, bottom right histogram). It was found that learning a TQ view now elicited good generalization to all views (of those tested). Also, a symmetric peak appeared to the other profile when learning a colored profile. Color and textural cues offered supplementary object information which reduced the overall viewpoint-dependence for identity. Together, these two experiments illustrate how a different availability of object cues can change patterns of viewpoint-dependence.

Diagnostic recognition also predicts that the task and its associated cue diagnosticity could affect viewpoint-dependence. Pilot studies were run in a paradigm identical to Hill et al. (1997), with only one variation: the task. Rather than judging whether or not the learned and tested view were of the same person, subjects were now asked to judge whether they had the same gender. With shaded faces, performance was close to chance, but it was near ceiling with textured faces, with no marked dependence on viewpoint in either case. This contrasted with the viewpoint-dependent performance observed for identity judgments.

In sum, this example suggests that viewpoint-dependence can be framed as an interaction between the multiple categorizations of an object and its perceptual information. If a categorization requires selective input information, and if its extraction depends on viewpoint, recognition performance might reflect the requirement of 'getting a good view' of the diagnostic cues. Evidence of such preferred views could prompt an object recognition researcher to hypothesize that these views (or their information content) actually represent faces in memory. However, there would be a difficulty with this strategy if each change in task elicited a change in preferred views. We come back to this point in the General Discussion, in Section 5.2. The next example examines the impact of cue availability on explanations of even very simple categorizations.

2.2. Example 2: object information and categorization

As explained earlier, categorization research as a whole has underplayed the role of perceptual factors in its theories. In a typical categorization experiment, subjects are instructed to learn the rules to categorize simple colored geometric shapes (see e.g. Bruner et al., 1956; Shepard et al., 1961; Bourne, 1982). For example subjects could learn that 'green and square' defined the objects of a category. Importantly, there is no ambiguity as to which features characterize which objects. Although categorization research has considerably evolved since these pioneering experiments, tight control of stimulus dimensions is still required (e.g. Murphy and Smith, 1982; Gluck and Bower, 1988; Wattenmaker, 1991; among many others). Modern category learning models still adhere to a similar approach: They specify a number of dimensions along which the stimuli can vary, and these form the basis of the similarity comparisons which underlie category learning (see, among many others, Elio and Anderson, 1981; Estes, 1986; Gluck and Bower, 1988; Anderson, 1991; Kruschke, 1992; Nosofsky et al., 1994).

The idea that categorization processes operate on a 'pre-perceived' input has led researchers to concentrate comparatively more on the ways in which object cues combine to represent categories than on the origin of the cues themselves. However, it is legitimate to question whether object cues are fixed and independent of the categorization being performed, or whether they can flexibly tune to the perceptual characteristics of the object categories they must differentiate.

This issue comes into sharper focus once the perceptual availability of object cues is taken seriously. The medical expertise literature abounds with illustrations of category learning that do not seem to fit well with the idea that relevant cues are a given. For example, when complete novices categorize dermatosis (Norman et al., 1992), sex chicks (Biederman and Shiffrar, 1987) and read chest X-rays (Christensen et al., 1981; Lesgold, 1984) they are not always able to see the relevant cues of the stimuli. Expertise with these categories involves as much learning which cue goes with which categories as learning the object cues themselves.

Object cues are the first inputs to categorization; they provide a perceptual organization of the stimulus on which categorization processes operate. One function of object cues is therefore to represent important perceptual differences between categories. Reasoning backwards from this property, Schyns and Murphy (1994) suggested that the need to distinguish categories that initially 'look alike' could prompt the creation of new object cues that change the perception of the stimuli. The *Functionality Principle* summarizes this view (Schyns and Murphy, 1994): 'if a fragment of a stimulus categorizes objects (distinguishes members from non-members), the fragment is instantiated as a unit in the representational code of object concepts' (p. 310).

Schyns and Rodet (1997) tested one implication of the Functionality Principle, that orthogonal categorizations of the same stimulus could arise from its perceptual organization with different object cues. They reasoned that a different history of categorization of unfamiliar objects could change the cues people learn to perceptually organize the visual input. Their experiments involved categories of unfamiliar objects called 'Martian cells' (examples of cells are presented in Fig. 3). Not only were these objects unfamiliar to subjects, but their cues were also unfamiliar. Learning to categorize the cells involved as much learning which cues goes with which category as the cues themselves.

Categories were defined by specific blobs common to all members to which irrelevant blobs were added (to simulate various cell bodies). X cells shared the x cue, Y exemplars shared y, and the components x and y were always adjacent to one another in XY cells. (Fig. 3 shows, from left to right, an XY, an X, and a Y exemplar. It also shows their defining xy, x and y cues.). A difference in categorization history simply resulted from one group learning X before Y before XY ($X \rightarrow Y \rightarrow XY$) while the other group learned the same three categories, but in a different order ($XY \rightarrow X \rightarrow Y$). The idea was that this simple difference would elicit orthogonal perceptions and representations of the identical XY Martian cells.

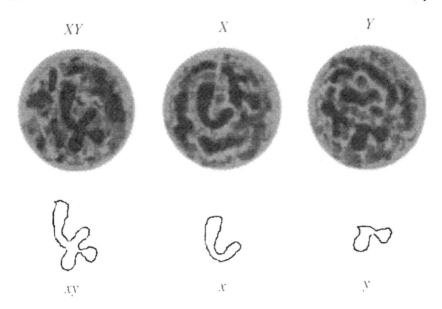

Fig. 3. This figure illustrates the design of Schyns and Rodet's feature creation experiment (Schyns and Rodet, 1997). From left to right, the top pictures are Martian cell exemplars from the *XY*, *X*, and *Y* categories, respectively. From left to right, the bottom pictures are the features *xy*, *x*, and *y*, defining the categories. Note that the feature xy is a conjunction of feature x and feature y. Subjects in the $XY \to X \to Y$ (vs. $X \to Y \to XY$) group learned the category in this order.

Results revealed that $X \to Y \to XY$ subjects initially created the cues x and y when they learned their X and Y categories, respectively. The incoming XY category was then perceived and represented as a conjunction of the acquired x and y cues. Cue creation was different in the group initially exposed to the XY category. Unlike the other group, when $XY \to X \to Y$ subjects initially learned XY, they did not possess the x and y components that allowed a conjunctive analysis. Instead, subjects learned to perceive and represent XY with a configural cue (that we call xy, but whose perceptual status is really more like an independent z unit) without even noticing the $x\&y$ conjunction that the other group perceived.

This example illustrates that one cannot simply assume the cues on which classification processes operate. A simple change in the history of categorization of unfamiliar materials changed the cues that were learned, the perceptual analyses, perceptions and representations of identical objects. Because object cues form the basis of the similarity judgments that determine category learning, complete explanations of categorization behavior will need to integrate cue availability.

In summary of the examples reviewed so far, it appears that both object recognition and object categorization could benefit from framing their problems in a bidirectional framework that integrates cue diagnosticity and cue availability. The recognition example insisted on the impact task constraints and cue diagnosticity could exert on explanations of viewpoint-dependence in face recognition. The categorization example stressed the importance of the availability of perceptual cues in explanations of simple categorization rules. We now turn to the nature of cue diagnosticity and cue availability in everyday object recognition.

3. Everyday object recognition

What is everyday object recognition? Specifically, what are the information requirements and the input information used when people categorize common objects such as a car, a chair, a dog, and so forth? These issues are essentially intertwined, but we will first explore the task demands of everyday object recognition before discussing input information.

3.1. The task demands of 'everyday object recognition'

Classic categorization research has shown that the interactions between the human perceiver and the objects of his or her world specify several hierarchical levels of categorization. Following Rosch et al.'s seminal research, three of these levels are often isolated: the superordinate *(animal, vehicle, furniture)*, the basic *(dog, car, chair)*, and the subordinate *(collie, Porsche, Chippendale chair)* (Rosch et al., 1976). Although these categorizations are all important, Rosch et al. showed that one of them had a privileged status. When subjects were asked to spontaneously name pictures of common objects, Rosch demonstrated that they preferentially used basic-level names (see also Jolicoeur et al., 1984). Similarly, when asked to verify that a picture belonged to a particular category, subjects' decisions were faster for the basic-level (Rosch et al., 1976). Together, these findings suggested that the initial contact between the object percept and its semantic information occurs at the *basic level*, also known in object recognition research as *primal access* (Biederman, 1987), or *entry point* (Jolicoeur et al., 1984)[2].

It is usually thought that supplementary visual processing is required for subordinate categorizations. For example, Jolicoeur et al. (1984) asked subjects to categorize common object pictures at their superordinate *(animal)*, basic *(dog)* and subordinate *(collie)* levels. In one condition (long exposure), pictures were presented for 250 ms, in the other condition (short exposure) pictures were presented for 75 ms. Their finding was that while basic level categorizations were equally fast at long and short exposures, short exposures disrupted the perceptually more taxing subordinate level categorizations.

The superordinate level is markedly different from the basic and subordinate levels. For example, Rosch et al. (1976) determined that the shapes of objects within basic and subordinate categories were generally more similar than those of objects within superordinate categories (e.g. *animal, vehicle, healthy food*). Functional, not so much perceptual, attributes tend to define superordinate categories. This explains why Rosch and her colleagues found that basic and subordinate names facilitated identification, at least more so than superordinate names. The functional attributes

---

[2]There are important differences between these concepts that will be discussed in Section 5.1.

associated with superordinate names would not allow the construction of a visual image that could facilitate the subsequent identification of a category exemplar.

For the reasons discussed so far, a significant portion of object recognition research has focused on faster basic level categorizations, and when it has not done so this has been considered a shortcoming. If common recognition tasks mirror basic level categorizations, then it is crucial to understand the organization of object categories at this level, to grasp the information requirements of the recognition task, and to explain why these elicit faster recognition. The basic level is often pictured as the most inclusive level at which objects 'look alike' in terms of their shape. One determinant of shape is part structure: objects with common parts tend to have a common shape. Tanaka and Gauthier (1998) define parts as 'divisible, local components of an object that are segmented at points of discontinuity, are perceptually salient, and are usually identified by a linguistic label' (p. 5). For example, the attributes 'legs', and 'seat' are the parts of the basic-level category *chair*.

Tversky and Hemenway (1984) found a dramatic increase in the number of parts listed from the superordinate to the basic level; non-part cues increased from the basic to the subordinate level, but little increase was found for parts. Thus, Tversky and Hemenway (1984) suggested that 'the natural breaks among basic-level categories are between clusters of parts' (p. 186). This claim is the basis of Biederman's influential recognition-by-components (RBC) theory, which represents basic-level categories with the parts of their objects – specifically, with different geon structural descriptions (Biederman, 1987; Biederman and Gerhardstein, 1993). Hence, the widely-held assumption in the recognition literature that shape, as is represented by parts, is the most important information used in everyday, basic-level categorizations. Categories subordinate to the basic level are distinguishable on the basis of transformed parts and surface properties (Tversky and Hemenway, 1984). For example, the attribute *legs* and *seat* distinguishes *chair* from its contrast categories while *long legs* is a transformed part which distinguishes the subordinate category *stool* from its contrast categories. Thus, goes the argument, a qualitative identification of parts at the basic level must precede metrical computations between transformed parts at the subordinate level; the basic level is the entry point to the recognition hierarchy.

3.1.1. Difficulties with part information for all basic-level tasks

Two issues should be distinguished in explanations of the basic-level phenomenon. (1) The information requirements of basic level tasks: are parts really necessary and sufficient to distinguish between all memorized basic-level categories? (2) The available object information: is perception so organized that parts are the most salient object cues? On the one hand, if parts define the information requirements of everyday recognition, perceivers could have evolved to become primarily attuned to these object cues. On the other hand, if parts were not strictly necessary to distinguish between basic-level categories, a perceptual primacy for this information would be harder to justify in visual development.

Note that the issue here is not whether shape differences are relevant for basic level categorizations, but whether one representation of these shape differences –

part structure – is necessarily tied to the basic level. There is evidence that a 'part-centric' account of the basic level could be misguided. For example, Murphy (1991) demonstrated that cues other than parts could determine basic-level performance. Furthermore, findings in expert categorizations (Tanaka and Taylor, 1991) have revealed that the basic level was neither absolute nor unimodally specified, but could instead fluctuate with category expertise. Finally, available evidence that parts are the point of contact for basic-level categories is either based on feature listings, or reaction times. Without a conclusive argument for a necessary association between parts and the basic-level, evidence for parts is compatible with alternative shape representations that comprise part structures – e.g. silhouette, 2D edge configurations, or representations of the image at a coarser descriptive level. The following sections review each of these arguments in turn.

3.1.2. A basic level without parts

Since Rosch's seminal research, an important issue has always been the extent to which the basic-level originates in the abstract organization of categories, or in the concrete constraints of perception. Murphy (1991), see also Murphy and Brownell (1985) suggested that the basic level was a consequence of the *informativeness* and the *distinctiveness* of a category representation in memory. Informative representations have many concrete object features; a representation is distinctive when it differs from contrast representations. In general, more specific representations tend to be more informative, but they are also less distinctive from other representations (Murphy, 1991). Thus, subordinate categories tend to score high on informativeness (e.g. two brands of cars convey detailed information), but low on distinctiveness (e.g. two brands of car are similar in overall appearance, at least more so than a brand of car and a type of shoe). In contrast, superordinate categories score low on informativeness, but high on distinctiveness (e.g. *vehicle* and *furniture* have different functions, shapes, parts, colors, textures, and so forth). On this account, the basic level would be a compromise between the accuracy of categorization at a maximally general level and the predictive power of a maximally specific level (Murphy and Lassaline, 1998).

Informativeness and distinctiveness are two constraints that apply to the abstract organization of categories in memory. Any type of object cue (including function, shape, color and textural cues) could functionally serve to optimize the informativeness and distinctiveness of categories, independently of its perceptual availability. Thus, the prediction is that parts should only specify the entry point when they optimize the informativeness and distinctiveness of the organization of the categories in memory.

In a series of experiments with artificial stimuli, Murphy (1991) questioned the necessity of parts for the basic level. His reasoning was that the addition of non-part information (here, mainly color and textural cues) to a basic level already structured with parts should not speed up its recognition advantage, if parts were the sole determinant of performance. Alternatively, if the informativeness and the distinctiveness of categories determined basic-level performance, then the addition of other cues to this level should enhance its informativeness and distinctiveness, and consequently speed up its identification time. Results revealed that the additional colors and textures enhanced the basic-level advantage. Furthermore, categorization times increased with the addition of new cues at the subordinate level (because these categories were now less distinctive, sharing similar color and texture across exemplars) while superordinate categorizations were now faster (because they were more distinctive). A separate experiment showed that massing non-part information (color, size and texture) at the superordinate level eliminated the advantage of a basic level defined by parts: The diagnosticity of non-part cues at one level suppressed the diagnosticity of part information at the basic level. These results led Murphy (1991) to conclude that '... parts are neither necessary, nor sufficient to establish a basic-level structure... categorization into basic categories uses all kinds of information, not just part-based information' (p. 436).

Although these conclusions could have profound implications for object recognition, there is an important rider. The experiments Murphy (1991) reviewed only demonstrate that a basic-level *effect* can be obtained with other cues than parts. Although the effect contrasts with the standard assumption that parts are necessary, it was obtained with artificial 2D stimuli whose part structures are different from those of typical 3D objects and might not tap into the same perceptual processes. This exemplifies the shortcoming that was leveled at categorization explanations that do not account for perceptual constraints. A differential availability of object cues might very well offer a speed advantage for real-world parts, or more generally shape cues, irrespective of the memory organization of categories, and so categorization theories must integrate this factor in their explanation of performance; distinctiveness should also concern perception, not just memory organization.

Bearing in mind that part descriptions are only one form of shape representation, a basic level effect could in principle also be obtained with alternative shape descriptions that comprise part representations (e.g. silhouettes and coarse-scale edge descriptions, fine-scale contours, depth maps and so forth). It should be an important goal of object recognition studies to tease out the relative contributions of different aspects of shape to basic level performance. Thus, it still is an empirical challenge to determine the information demands that structure basic level categories and the entry point to everyday recognition. The following discussion will suggest that these demands might not be the same for all object categories, but could instead change with category expertise.

3.1.3. A relative basic-level

If perceptual organization was such that parts from a fixed set (e.g. Biederman's geons) were the primary 'search keys' into object memory, the level at which parts differentiate categories would fix the entry point to recognition. Research in conceptual expertise has questioned this idea of uniform information demands at the basic level. Tanaka and Taylor (1991) showed that extensive expertise with a category enhanced the speed of access of its subordinate categories, which became at least as accessible as basic-level categories. In a category-verification task, their subjects (*dog* and *bird* experts) first heard a category label (superordinate, basic or subordinate) and were then asked to indicate whether a subsequently presented picture was an exemplar of the labeled category. For expert categories (*bird* or *dog*), the subordinate and basic categorizations were equally fast. Interestingly, the authors also discovered that the subordinate categories of experts were associated with more cues than their novice categories. Note that these cues were not supplementary parts (beagles do not have an extra nose, ear or leg that German shepherds lack), but cues that increased the informativity and distinctiveness (and the accessibility) of the expert category at its subordinate level. As Tanaka and Taylor (1991) put it succinctly, the basic-level could be in the eye of the beholder.

Although the 'basic-to-subordinate shift' was only ascertained in limited domains, expertise with a category is a continuum and the acquired salience of a subordinate level might unveil a pervasive principle of knowledge reorganization. There is suggestive evidence that perceptual expertise changes the defining cues and the categorization speed of other important object classes. For example, face identification is often thought to be a clear-cut 'subordinate' categorization because the similar global shape of faces makes them perceptually more taxing to discern.[3] However, we are all 'natural' face experts, even if the 'other race effect', in which people discriminate faces of their own race with greater facility than those of another race (Brigham, 1986) suggests that this expertise is probably limited to faces of our own race. To the human observer, different views of an individual tend to be more alike than the same views of different persons. For faces of our own race, the entry point could therefore be the level of the individual (the level at which face views are more alike) instead of their assumed, 'face' basic level categorization (the level at which faces views differ more). Note that this could be reversed with faces of another race. Less familiar faces could appear comparatively more similar when seen from the same viewpoint. This illustrates another domain where a basic-to-subordinate shift might account for categorization differences between novices and experts.

One question that arises is the nature of the perceptual learning that would accompany such basic-to-subordinate shift. It has often been suggested that face expertise involves holistic recognition strategies (e.g. Carey, 1992). Tanaka and Farah (1993), see also Tanaka and Sengco (1997) showed that the identification of face parts was optimal when they were presented in their original configuration. Performance was impaired when parts were included in transformed configurations, and worse when they were presented in isolation. This suggests 'holistic', rather than independent representations of face parts. Recently, Gauthier and Tarr (1997) demonstrated that expertise with 'Greebles' (3D, computer synthesized 'Martian beings' designed to have the same kind of geometric homogeneity as faces) increased experts' sensitivity to their configural cues. The principles underlying such expertise acquisition are reminiscent of those presented in Example 2 (see

---

[3]It is worth noting that the usage of 'subordinate' and 'basic-level' in object recognition and object categorization research do not always correspond. Object recognition researchers tend to use subordinate when the shapes of categories are alike, and basic-level when the shapes differ. Similarly, they tend to use subordinate for the identification of an individual face or object. In categorization, a subordinate level is the level immediately underneath the basic level (e.g. *Ford Mustang* is subordinate to *car*), which is first identified.

also Schyns and Murphy, 1994) in which new configural cues were created to distinguish between objects that initially look alike. The basic-to-subordinate shift could originate in the contribution of acquired configural cues to the informativeness and distinctiveness of expert subordinate categories. If the informativeness and distinctiveness of categories in memory determine the basic level, then the information requirements at this level might not be uniform for all categories, but instead depend on the individual's level of expertise with them.

3.2. Towards a formal model of task constraints

In an attempt to formalize the notion of task constraints, Gosselin and Schyns (1997) developed a model that accounts for the basic-to-subordinate shift and other basic level phenomena. Their model, termed SLIP (strategy length information proxility), builds on Murphy and Brownell's (Murphy and Brownell, 1985) idea that the 'basic-levelness' of a category originates in its informativeness and distinctiveness in a hierarchy of categories. The model assumes that categorization is a succession of tests on object cues such as 'is X blue?' and so forth. Some of these tests are highly informative and almost sufficient to isolate a category (e.g. 'does X possess feathers?' individuates birds) whereas others overlap between categories (e.g. 'does X possess two wings?' would be positive for birds and planes). SLIP derives its two main computational factors from this observation. To illustrate the first factor, consider the category hierarchy of Murphy and Smith (1982); Experiment 1, see also Murphy, 1991; Tanaka and Taylor, 1991) shown on the top structure of Fig. 4. Underneath the category names (e.g. *hob*, *bot*, *com*), the letters (e.g. *a*, *b*, *c*, d) designate the object cues that define three distinct category levels (the point preceding the cues corresponds to the cues inherited from the level(s) above the considered level – e.g. at the lowest level, a *com is* the feature conjunction *acdeo*). A careful observation of the structure should reveal that a single feature test is sufficient to identify each category, irrespective of its level. For example, the presence of *o* isolates *com*. Of course, several features often define categories, and in fact, three of them define mid-level categories in the top structure of Fig. 4. However, testing more than one feature does not add any information to the diagnosis; object cues are redundant for this categorization. The *number of redundant cues* at any category level in a hierarchy is the first computational factor of SLIP (it is three for the mid-level, and one for the other two levels).

In the real-world, however, features tend to overlap between categories. For example, to identify a helicopter, one needs to perform at least two tests: 'does X fly?' and 'does X possess a rotor?'. Two tests are also necessary to identify a plane: 'does X fly?' and 'does X possess two wings?'. *Feature overlap* in a category structure is the second computational factor of SLIP. It determines the minimal number of tests to arrive at a decision. To illustrate, consider the bottom structure of Fig. 4. To arrive at a *com* categorization, three tests (not just one, as in the top structure) must be executed: 'does X possess *a*?' 'does X possess c?' and 'does X possess *e*?'. Two tests are necessary for *bot*, and only one for *hob*.

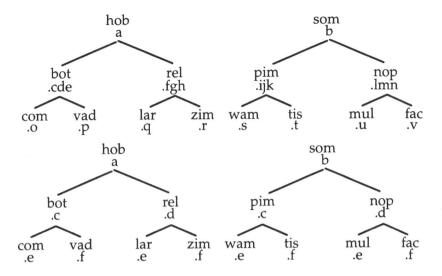

Fig. 4. This figure, adapted from Gosselin and Schyns (1997), illustrates the two main factor of SLIP. Underneath the category names (e.g. *hob, bot, com*), the letters (e.g. *a, b, c, d*) designate the object cues that define three distinct category levels (the point preceding the cues corresponds to the cues inherited from the level(s) above the considered level – e.g. at the lowest level, a *com is* the feature conjunction *acdeo*). The top structure (adapted from Murphy and Smith (1982) Experiment 1) illustrates the first computational factor of the model. In the structure, a single feature test is sufficient to identify each category. The middle level is defined by three features, but they are redundant. The redundancy of features at different categorization levels is the first factor of SLIP. The second factor, illustrated on the bottom structure, is the overlap of features across categories. To identify a *com*, for example, one has to ensure that it has three features *(a, c* and *e)*. Only two tests are necessary for *bot (a* and *c)* and one test for *hob (a)*.

Category attentional slip integrates these two factors in a probabilistic model which performs the minimal number of tests to arrive at a category decision. High feature overlap between categories tend to increase their identification times. The model's attention, however, sometimes slips from the ideal series of feature tests to a randomly chosen object cue. All things being equal, categories with high feature redundancy are more likely to benefit from attentional slip to a randomly chosen feature.

In a series of numerical simulations (see Gosselin and Schyns, 1997), the model predicted 20 out of 24 results from eight classic basic level experiments (including Murphy and Smith, 1982; (experiments 1 and 3) Murphy, 1991; (experiments 3 and 4 simple and enhanced, 5) Tanaka and Taylor, 1991; (Experiment 3, the basic-to-subordinate shift)). One established model of basic-level performance (Corter and Gluck, 1992; *Category Utility*) only predicted 12 of these results but that of Jones (1983), *Category Feature Possession* also predicted 20 results. It must be stressed that classic basic-level experiments only used categories organized with non-overlapping features. In other words, strategies of length 1 could be deployed and feature redundancy was the only factor affecting performance. However, the length of strategies which results from feature redundancy should also affect basic-levelness, but this has so far been neglected in experiments on the basic level.

SLIP offers a powerful platform to explore the issues of basic level categorization and task constraints discussed so far. Starting from an objectively defined category structure (with its associated cue redundancy and cue overlap at different levels), an ideal categorizer can be constructed that predicts the relative accessibility (and speed of access) of each level in the hierarchy. Performance of the ideal is then compared to human subjects who categorize perceptually plausible experimental materials (e.g. computer-synthesized 3D objects composed of different parts, colors and textures). The comparative strategy enables us to explore how basic-levelness results from the interactions between objectively defined information demands and their relative perceptual availabilities. For example, if the presence of parts is the main determinant of faster recognition, then a basic level effect could occur at any level of the two hierarchies of Fig. 4. However, systematic variations of the objective information demands at each level (in the form of different shape, color or textural cues) could elicit performance discrepancies between the ideal and human subjects, revealing a contrast between objectively defined information demands and the perceptual limitations on their availability. This strategy could be applied to the understanding of the perceptual conditions of a basic-to-subordinate shift. Features created to solve expert categorizations must necessarily be diagnostic of these categories, have little overlap with other categories and have sufficient perceptual salience. Thus, newly-created features tend to augment feature redundancy at the subordinate level (the first component of category attentional slip) and minimize feature overlap and the length of categorization strategies at this level (the second component of the model). Such comparisons between an ideal categorizer (with its clearly-specified task constraints) and human performance might be one way forward in understanding basic level phenomena.

3.2.1. Lessons from task constraints

Everyday object recognition probably occurs at the basic-level and it is therefore important to understand the information demands it imposes on recognition tasks. The reviewed literature suggests that the basic level might not be designated by a unique, necessary and sufficient criterion (demands for parts) that determines the entry point to recognition. In contrast, there is suggestive evidence (1) that the basic level is the optimal level of informativity and distinctiveness of a category, (2) that parts are neither necessary, nor sufficient to determine basic level performance, but that other cues (e.g. color, texture, size, other shape cues such as shape configurations, an object silhouette and so forth) can also determine entry level, and (3) that perceptual experience with a category could change its defining cues and its basic-levelness. In sum, the information demands of a basic task could be relative and partially dependent on the individual's experience (i.e. history of categorization) with an object category. Category attentional slip was proposed as a platform with which to oppose objectively defined information demands and their perceptual availability. Section 5 discusses implications of flexible basic level demands for recognition and categorization theories.

3.3. *Perceptual information in object everyday recognition*

Although task constraints depend on the functional organization of categories in memory and its associated information requirements, it is also important to understand how perception facilitates, or taxes, the extraction of relevant information. We know that object information is ultimately bounded by the retinal output (a million-dimensional space), but neuroanatomical and computational data suggest that this space is gradually projected (recoded) onto a much smaller-dimensional space of object cues. Unfortunately, too little is known about this dimensionality reduction process and the perceptual constraints it imposes on classification processes. Instead of attempting the impossible task of listing all likely information sources, this section examines the reduced set of object cues that determine performance in leading object recognition theories. We then relate these cues to the information demands of the categorization tasks they subtend, and discuss how task constraints and object information interact to determine performance.

Current thinking in recognition assumes that perception delivers shape cues to match against spatio-visual object representations in memory. To illustrate, in the RBC theory of Biederman (1987) the assumption that parts underlie the demands of basic-level recognition justifies the gradual projection of the 2D retinal input onto a space of geon structural descriptions (GSD, Biederman and Gerhardstein, 1993). The reduced object description is obtained in two stages. The first stage computes the edges of the input image. The second stage seeks 2D, non-accidental, viewpoint-invariant properties of edge descriptions (e.g. colinearity, curvilinearity, symmetry, parallelism, cotermination, see Lowe, 1987; Kanade, 1981). Collections of viewpoint-invariant labeled edges individuate the geons that compose the input object.

Together, these mechanisms should implement viewpoint-invariant recognition at the basic-level. More precisely, RBC predicts viewpoint-invariant performance whenever (1) the input object is decomposable into geons, (2) different GSDs represent different objects in memory, and (3) the same GSD is recoverable from different viewpoints (Biederman and Gerhardstein, 1993). Note that explanations of recognition performance that involve geons will, by construction of RBC, necessarily overlap with explanations that involve the viewpoint-invariant properties that individuate geons. Strictly speaking, it is these viewpoint-invariant properties of edges that determine the viewpoint-invariance of recognition.

In opposition to RBC, the view-based approach predicts viewpoint-dependent performance to stored object views. In attempting to define more precisely what constitutes a 'view', Tarr and Kriegman (1998) began to explore how viewpoint-dependent shape cues could determine performance. As an observer changes its vantage point, drastic changes often occur in the qualitative appearance of an object. For a given geometrical object class (e.g. smooth objects), a vocabulary of viewpoint-dependent labeled edges (local and multi-local edge configurations, see Tarr and Kriegman, 1998) can describe these qualitative changes. These cues partition the viewpoint space of an object into stable regions (in fact, into the views of an *aspect graph* of this object, Koenderink and Van Doorn, 1982). Viewpoint-dependent recognition performance could partially result from enhanced perceptual sensitivity to viewpoint-dependent shape cues. Tarr and Kriegman's psychophysical experiments demonstrated that this was the case, at least for some of the visual cues of their theory (Tarr and Kriegman, 1998).

From the above discussion, it appears that although RBC and the view-based approach both use shape information for recognition, the theories differ radically on the specific shape cues that they use. RBC suggests that perception detects 2D, viewpoint-independent cues that serve to reconstruct 3D geons, but Tarr and Kriegman showed that humans were sensitive to 2D, viewpoint-dependent edge configurations. Consequently, RBC and the view-based approach should in principle predict different recognition performance[4]. In what follows, I will interpret performance as the interaction between the availability of cues and the information demands of the task at hand.

The image formation process entirely determines the availability of viewpoint-dependent and viewpoint-independent cues. The image formation process concerns the 2D retinal projection of the 3D geometry of an input object. It is likely that the 2D projection of a given 3D object comprises viewpoint-dependent and viewpoint-independent cues. Both types of cues should then be available to object recognition mechanisms, independently of whether or not a recognition theory advocates viewpoint-dependent (e.g. view-based) or viewpoint-independent (e.g. geon-based) representations of objects in memory. With this in mind, the explanation of performance shifts from the format of object representations in memory to a task analysis. Diagnostic recognition suggests that specific image cues are used when they become diagnostic for a particular task. What could be the object categorizations that would systematically require viewpoint-dependent versus viewpoint-independent object cues? Object recognition theories suggest a generic answer: basic-level categorizations would generally require viewpoint-independent image cues, and subordinate categorizations would demand viewpoint-dependent cues (e.g. Biederman, 1987; Jolicoeur, 1990; Tarr and Pinker, 1991; Farah, 1992). There are several difficulties with this claim.

A first difficulty arises from the recent results of Tarr and his colleagues (see Tarr et al., 1997) which revealed that even diagnostic combinations of shaded parts elicit viewpoint-dependent performance. Their experiments involved either a sequential matching or a naming of artificial, geon-based objects which varied in viewpoint between learning and testing. The objects comprised five parts, one, three or five of which were diagnostic geons, the remaining parts being non-diagnostic tubes. All objects were computer-synthesized and shaded. Results revealed a viewpoint-dependent performance in conditions in which Biederman and Gerhardstein's criteria would predict viewpoint invariance (Biederman and Gerhardstein, 1993). This

---

[4]RBC predicts viewpoint-dependent performance in many practical situations of recognition. Rotation in depth of many real-world objects is such that different views will often convey different information (parts included, think, e.g. of a human body rotating in depth). Consequently, Biederman and Gerhardstein's condition number three for viewpoint-independent performance (that the same part structural description is recovered from different viewpoints, Biederman and Gerhardstein, 1993) will not always be met, and both RBC and view-based theories will predict viewpoint-dependence.

questioned the overall viewpoint invariance of realistically-rendered geons, and the viewpoint-invariance of RBC (see also Edelman, 1995; Liu, 1996).

A second problem arises from evidence of basic-to-subordinate shifts with category experience. If these shifts occur together with the acquisition of new cues that change the informativeness and distinctiveness of categories, then it becomes difficult to systematically associate viewpoint-dependent or viewpoint-independent performance with a generic categorization level (either basic or subordinate). Instead, the issue really becomes whether the acquired cues that support faster categorizations at this level are viewpoint-dependent or not. As explained earlier, this depends on their projection on the 2D retina. The conclusion, then, is that the relationship between categorization levels and viewpoint-dependence should be treated with greater caution than is often the case in object recognition.

In sum, this section reviewed the object information assumed in major object recognition theories, and how it determines recognition performance. The analysis suggests (1) that the image formation process, not the format of object representations in memory, determines the availability of viewpoint-dependent and viewpoint-independent cues in the retinal input, (2) that dependence on viewpoint might therefore be better explained as an interaction between the cues requested for a given categorization and their dependence or independence on viewpoint in the input (see also Edelman, 1995; Liu, 1996; Tarr and Kriegman, 1998; for a similar view), and (3) that a systematic association between basic level information demands with viewpoint invariance and subordinate information demands with viewpoint-dependence might be misguided.

4. Interactions of spatial scales and diagnostic cues in scene recognition

The second aim of the paper concerns the psychological implications of the interactions between cue diagnosticity and cue availability. This section illustrates that the perception of a scene can change with the diagnosticity of its cues. Although a scene is not an object, but many objects, the example will raise issues that can directly be applied to studies of object recognition and categorization.

Computational vision and psychophysics have often emphasized the importance of simultaneously processing stimuli at multiple spatial resolutions, called 'spatial scales' (Campbell and Robson, 1968; Blackmore and Campbell, 1969; Breitmeyer and Ganz, 1976; Marr, 1982; Burt and Adelson, 1983; Canny, 1986; Ginsburg, 1986; Mallet, 1989; de Valois and de Valois, 1990; among many others). Starting with the observation that recognition algorithms could hardly operate on the raw pixel values of digitized images, vision researchers investigated multi-scale representations to organize and to simplify the description of events. *Coarse-to-fine processing* suggests that it may be computationally more efficient to derive a coarse and global (but imprecise) skeleton of the image before fleshing it out with fine grain (but considerably noisier) object cues (Marr, 1982; Watt, 1987). Evidence of coarse-to-fine processing in human psychophysics has been reported for face (e.g. Sergent,

1982, 1986; Fiorentini et al., 1983), object (e.g. Ginsburg, 1986) and scene recognition (e.g. Parker et al., 1992; Schyns and Oliva, 1994).

Fig. 5 illustrates the perceptual scales that are available to recognition mechanisms (adapted from Schyns and Oliva, 1994). Reconstruction of the image from fine scale edges (technically, the high spatial frequencies, HSF) should unveil a city scene in the top picture and a highway in the bottom picture. However, if this information is made unavailable (either by squinting or blinking while looking at the pictures) your perception of the top picture should turn into a highway and a city in the bottom picture (step back from Fig. 5 if this demonstration does not work). You would then perceive the coarse scale of the pictures (technically, the low spatial frequencies, LSF).

Even though there is now little doubt that the visual system operates at multiple scales, their selection for recognition is still a matter of current debate. According to psychophysical evidence, the earlier availability of coarse scales should force a coarse-to-fine recognition scheme. However, this claim disregards the influence the task could exert on scale selection. In the diagnosticity framework, the information requirements of a task change the diagnosticity of the cues which are actively sought in the input. If diagnostic cues were preferentially associated with a different spatial scale, then the task at hand could determine scale selection. For example, whereas coarse scale information might be sufficient for a *city* categorization of a city picture, its *New York* categorization might necessitate comparatively finer scale cues (see Fig. 5). Such top-down influence of task constraints on scale perception is particularly interesting given the precedence the latter has on many processes of early vision such as stereopsis (Schor et al., 1984; Legge and Gu, 1989), motion (Morgan, 1992), depth perception (Marshall et al., 1996) and saccade programming (Findlay et al., 1993).

In their Experiment 2, Oliva and Schyns (1997) tested the prediction that the diagnosticity of scale cues could change the perception of identical hybrid scenes. Hybrids have the main advantage that they multiplex (i.e. combine) information across spatial scales. They can control which scale supports which categorization. To illustrate, a *city* categorization of the top picture of Fig. 5 would unambiguously attest the usage of coarse scale cues (LSF), whereas its *highway* categorization would indicate the usage of its fine scale cues (HSF). The issue was whether such distinct categorizations could simply originate from one scale of the picture (either coarse of fine) being more diagnostic than the other for the task at hand.

In a sensitization phase, two subject groups (the LSF and the HSF groups) were asked to categorize hybrids which presented a scene at only one spatial scale-the other scale represented meaningless patterns, see Fig. 6. Each hybrid was presented for 135 ms on a computer screen, and subjects were instructed to name aloud the scene they saw. It was expected that these stimuli would implicitly sensitize perceptual processes to tune to the informative scale (either LSF or HSF, depending on the group). In a testing phase immediately following sensitization, subjects were shown hybrids whose LSF and HSF represented two different scenes (as in Fig. 5). The sensitization and testing phases were appended so that subjects did not notice a transition, or a change of stimuli; from their viewpoint, they were categorizing a single series of pictures.

Fig. 5. This figure (adapted from Schyns and Oliva, 1994) shows examples of the hybrid stimuli. Hybrids were constructed by combining the low spatial frequency (LSF) components of one scene (e.g. a highway) with the high spatial frequency (HSF) components of another scene. The top picture mixes the LSF of a highway and the HSF of a city. The bottom picture mixes the LSF of a city with the HSF of a highway.

Categorization data revealed that subjects maintained their categorizations of ambiguous hybrids at the scale congruent with their sensitization. For example,

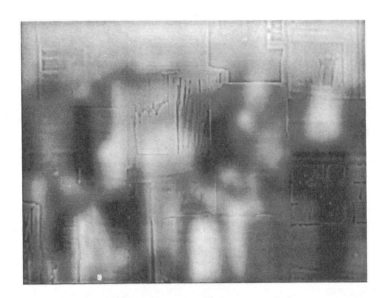

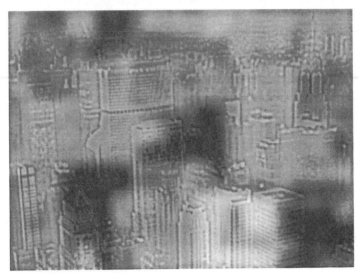

Fig. 6. This figure (adapted from Oliva and Schyns, 1997) illustrates the stimuli used in the sensitization phase of the reported experiment. The top picture is an LSF/noise hybrid composed of the LSF of a city added to structured noise in HSF. The bottom picture is a HSF/noise resulting from the addition of the HSF of the same city and LSF structured noise.

LSF subjects categorized the top hybrid of Fig. 5 as *highway* while HSF participants categorized the same picture as *city*. Orthogonal categorizations of identical pictures indicate that different cues were used, but they do not necessarily imply, however, that the stimuli were orthogonally perceived. Subjects might have perceived the two scenes composing the ambiguous hybrids but strategically decided to report only one of them. Alternatively, the requirement of locating diagnostic cues for the task might have changed scale usage to the point of changing the perception of identical pictures. In a debriefing following the experiment, participants were told what hybrid stimuli were and were asked whether they saw any such stimulus during the experiment. Out of 24 subjects, only one reported seeing two scenes; all others were surprised to learn that they were exposed to ambiguous stimuli. Follow-up studies (see Oliva and Schyns, 1997) confirmed that neglected information at the non-diagnostic scale did not enter the scene percept, but was nonetheless registered at a lower level of processing.

In sum, the example illustrates that another recognition phenomenon, scale-based recognition, might be better explained in a bi-directional framework, as an interaction between the perceptual availability of multiple spatial scales and the requirement of locating diagnostic scale cues, rather than as a unidirectional, perceptually determined process. The example also shows that the information demands of a categorization can flexibly change the immediate appearance of an identical stimulus. Flexible perceptions could be the psychological byproduct of the interactions between task and cues. It is unclear whether task-driven perception generalizes from the experimental room to everyday situations of face, object and scene recognition. However, entertaining its possibility opens a number of issues that we address in Section 5.

5. General discussion

It was the main goal of this paper to establish a dialogue between object recognition and object categorization theories, with the intention of raising issues that could cross-fertilize their research. To this end, I presented diagnostic recognition, a framework which expresses object recognition and categorization phenomena as interactions between the information requirements of specific categorization tasks and the perceptual information available from visual inputs. Diagnostic recognition insists on the diagnosticity of perceptual object cues in a task to understand object recognition and categorization phenomena. Two examples illustrated the opposite benefits that object recognition and categorization theories could gain from explicitly considering the two factors of diagnostic recognition in their explanations of performance. The face example showed how object recognition could benefit from more extensive studies of task constraints, and the Martian cells categorizations suggested that the availability of perceptual cues might need further consideration in explanations of even very simple categorization problems.

The second part of the paper extrapolated the approach of diagnostic recognition to the account of 'everyday recognition' performance. Everyday recognition was equated with the basic level of a categorization hierarchy. Examination of information demands at the basic level from a categorization perspective suggested that it was the optimal level of informativity and distinctiveness of a category, that parts were neither necessary nor sufficient to structure this level, but that many other cues could elicit a basic level effect. It was also suggested that the individual's perceptual experience with an object category could change its defining perceptual cues, as well as its entry point. Category attentional slip was proposed as a platform to formalize task constraints and to explore how they fit, or contrast with the perceptual availability of object cues.

Turning to the object information of leading recognition theories, it was first observed that perception is often assumed to initially deliver shape cues to match into object memory. These are either viewpoint-dependent or viewpoint-invariant depending on the 3D geometry of the object and its projection on the 2D retina. The usage of one type of cue or another (and the viewpoint-dependent or viewpoint-independent nature of recognition performance) was then related to the information demands of the task at hand. The faster recognition of subordinate categories by experts suggests that information demands at the basic level will vary with the acquisition of category expertise. Hence, it is unlikely that the basic level (or the subordinate level) will be uniformly viewpoint-independent (or viewpoint-dependent).

The scene recognition example addressed the problem of multiple categorizations in the perceptually plausible materials of spatial scales. The behavioral data suggested that a bi-directional account including top-down task constraints provided a better explanation of the opposite categorizations of identical scene pictures than a unilateral, bottom-up flow of constraints. The example also illustrated a situation in which different information demands induced the flexible perceptions of complex visual stimuli, which suggests that the diagnosticity of cues not only changes their use in the input, but also the immediate appearance of the stimulus.

5.1. Implications of diagnostic recognition for studies of object recognition, categorization and perception

The idea of a flexible basic level raises a number of new issues for object recognition and categorization theories. Consider the example of an Asian person who has had sufficient experience with Caucasian faces that she can individuate them. Presumably, this person has learned the cues that enable precise discriminations within the homogeneous category of Caucasians (the example is of course reversible). We could expect face identity to stand out in informativeness and distinctiveness, and she should classify Caucasians the way Caucasians do, equally fast at their subordinate and basic levels (Tanaka and Gauthier, 1998).

Equal accessibility of categorization levels, however, does not necessarily imply replacement of one level by the other. One could legitimately ask whether, following even extensive expertise, the categorization sequence is still basic before subordinate (e.g. *face* before *Sara*, or *car* before *Mustang*), or whether the entry point has genuinely changed to the subordinate level (e.g. *Sara* and *Mustang*). This issue is difficult because too little is known about the nature of the perceptual changes that can accompany category expertise. If new diagnostic features are simply added at the subordinate level, then it is difficult to assume that object information at the inclusive basic level would simply be dismissed. For example, even if Dalmatians have a diagnostic texture, they still have a typical dog shape, and the dog expert would probably not confuse a Dalmatian dog with a Dalmatian texture wrapped around a car.

There are alternatives to an additive version of category expertise which might support independent access to the subordinate level. For instance, extensive experience with a category could involve non-linear feature-learning mechanisms. Subordinate features could then represent an altogether different encoding of the entire object – much in the way in which the xy configural encoding was not reducible to the additive perception of feature x and feature y in Example 2. In fact, the argument has been made (e.g. Diamond and Carey, 1986) and evidence exists (Schyns and Rodet, 1997; Gauthier and Tarr, 1997) that expertise with geometrically homogeneous objects enhances sensitivity to their configural cues – cues that are not perceived as a simple addition of their components. If expertise with a category involves such non-linear recodings of its objects, then independent access at the subordinate level would not necessarily lead to the information loss implied by an additive model. The relationships between independent entry levels and feature learning mechanisms clearly deserve further research.

These speculations about the nature of the entry point to recognition are important because they directly question the nature of 'the right' representation of an object. For example, the idea of a basic level that can progressively shift as people acquire new features that increase the informativeness and distinctiveness of subordinate categories implies that the most stringent task (e.g. face identity) in which an object is used determines its representation. Do we maintain in memory different representations of the same object for different categorization tasks, or do we acquire and progressively transform a unique perceptual representation that encodes the information demands of the most stringent subordinate tasks while preserving those of less taxing tasks (such as the former basic level)? If visual cognition constructs multiple representations, then independent entry points for recognition would mean that different tasks access different representation systems. By contrast, independent entry points to a unique representation would mean that certain information of this representation elicits faster recognition times. This dichotomy reflects the ambiguity existing between basic-levelness (which is a functional measure of recognition performance computed over a category organization) and entry point (which is a structural statement about the access to internal systems of object representations). The relationship between multiple categorizations of an object and its representation(s) should be carefully considered.

Intertwined with these issues are the relationships existing between the information demands of a categorization task (the diagnosticity of object cues) and the perceptual appearance of the visual input. The logic of diagnostic recognition implies that diagnostic cues must be clearly perceived in the visual input for the task to succeed. What happens, then, to the other, non-diagnostic cues? Is perception flexible and correlated with the information demands of a categorization task, or is it instead 'veridical' and independent of the task at hand? The scene example presented earlier illustrated one intriguing instance of a flexible, task-dependent influence on the perceptual appearance of stimuli. Do flexible percepts also arise when people categorize the same chair as a *chair*, or as an *Art Deco chair*, or a scene picture as *city* or *New York*, or a face as *face* or *Mary*? In short, do perceptions follow, even in part, task constraints? It is difficult to derive predictions from existing recognition and categorization theories because most simply do not address the question. However, these issues are fundamental because they tap into the 'cognitive penetrability' (Fodor, 1983) of early visual processes and suggest that cue diagnosticity could partially determine object perception. I believe there is much to be gained from studying how categorization influences perception.

5.2. *Limitations of diagnostic recognition for studies of object representations*

Diagnostic recognition is a framework in which the information goals of object categorization tasks are considered before their perceptual representations.

Although this is a good, generally recommended approach to theory construction (e.g. Marr, 1982), it nevertheless presents serious limitations for the study of object representations.

The reason is simply that thinking from task constraints to their perceptual representations could over-represent the considered information demands in the proposed representation. For example, if it were discovered that the information requirements of an object categorization were X, then it would be an easy step to assume that the representation of this object was effectively that X. But then, how would we know whether X represents the object, or the task itself?

It is interesting to note that major recognition theories sit on the opposite sides of the spectrum of independence of representations from task demands. Biederman's geons directly mirror the assumed information demands (parts) of the basic level (Biederman, 1987). The view-based approach stands on the other side of the spectrum. Unless more clearly specified, an object view could potentially represent all the information that can ever be requested from an object seen from this view, including parts. In other words, a view is too powerful a representation, and it is an important research goal to attempt to reduce the high dimensionality of a view to a low-dimensional subset of object cues (e.g. Edelman and Intrator, 1998; Tarr and Kriegman, 1998).

However, it still is the case that diagnostic recognition might be better suited to explain recognition performance and to study object perceptions than to infer representation formats in memory. Performance involves both object *and* input representations: The input image must first be encoded with object cues for matching against memorized representations. Because there is no general theory specifying the information content of the 2D projections of 3D objects, behavioral performance might not be sufficiently powerful to isolate issues of object formats in memory from issues of input information and perception (Liu, 1996). Performance that might be attributed to a particular object format might also be attributed to the interaction between task demands and the usage of specific image cues. For these reasons, diagnostic recognition suggests that object and input representations should be unified and constitute the set of image cues that are available and perceived for different object categorization tasks. Hence, it insists on flexible perceptions rather than various systems of object representations.

There is a similarity between the framework presented here and the ideal observer approach to recognition (Bennett et al., 1993; Liu et al., 1995). Both diagnostic recognition and the ideal observer stress that the available object information and the perceptual constraints on its extraction influence performance (see also Liu, 1996). However, actual developments of the ideal observer do not include task constraints which 'act' on different object cues to assign them different diagnosticities. For example, Liu (1996) suggests that a viewpoint-independent framework for representation should predict that the performance only depends on the information content of the input image. However, there is suggestive evidence that recognition performance is also dependent on the task itself. Extensions of ideal observers might need to include the notion of flexible task constraints.

6. Concluding remarks

This paper started with a question: 'how could we frame issues common to object recognition and categorization?' A bi-directional framework was presented which expresses recognition and categorization phenomena as interactions between the information demands of categorization tasks and the perceptual availability of object information. This integrative framework raises new issues that could shed some light on the nature of face, object and scene perception.

Acknowledgements

The author wishes to thank Michael Burton, Simon Garrod, Frédéric Gosselin, Gregory Murphy, Martin Pickering and two anonymous reviewers for helpful comments on an earlier version of this manuscript.

References

Anderson, J.R., 1991. The adaptive nature of human categorization. Psychological Review 98, 409–429.

Barsalou, L.W., 1983. Ad hoc categories. Memory and Cognition 11, 211–227.

Bennett, B.M., Hoffman, D.D., Prakash, C., 1993. Recognition polynomials. Journal of Optical Society of America A 10, 759–764.

Biederman, I., 1987. Recognition-by-components: a theory of human image understanding. Psychological Review 94, 115–147.

Biederman, I., Gerhardstein, P.C., 1993. Recognizing depth rotated objects: evidence and conditions for three-dimensional viewpoint invariance. Journal of Experimental Psychology: Human Perception and Performance 18, 121–133.

Biederman, I., Gerhardstein, P.C., 1995. Viewpoint-dependent mechanisms in visual object recognition: a critical analysis. Journal of Experimental Psychology: Human Perception and Performance 21, 1506–1514.

Biederman, I., Ju, G., 1988. Surface versus edge-based determinants of visual recognition. Cognitive Psychology 94, 115–147.

Biederman, I., Shiffrar, M.M., 1987. Sexing day-old chicks: a case study and expert systems analysis of a difficult perceptual-learning task. Journal of Experimental Psychology: Learning, Memory and Cognition 13, 640–645.

Blackmore, C., Campbell, F.W., 1969. On the existence of neurons in the human visual system selectively sensitive to the orientation and size of retinal images. Journal of Physiology (London) 203, 237–260.

Bourne, L.E. Jr., 1982. Typicality effects in logically defined categories. Memory and Cognition 10, 3–9.

Breitmeyer, B.G., Ganz, L., 1976. Implications of sustained and transient channels for theories of visual pattern masking, saccadic suppression and information processing. Psychological Review 83, 1–35.

Brigham, J.C., 1986. The influence of race on face recognition. In: Ellis, H.D., Jeeves, M.A., Newcombe, F., Young, A.W. (Eds.), Aspects of Face Processing. Martinus Nijhoff, Dordrecht.

Bruner, J.S., Goodnow, J., Austin, G.A., 1956. A Study of Thinking. Wiley, New York.

Bülthoff, H.H., Edelman, S., 1992. Psychophysical support for a two-dimensional view theory of object recognition. Proceedings of the National Academy of Science USA 89, 60–64.

Burt, P., Adelson, E.H., 1983. The Laplacian pyramid as a compact image code. IEEE Transactions on Communications 31, 532–540.

Campbell, F.W., Robson, J.G., 1968. Application of the Fourier analysis to the visibility of gratings. Journal of Physiology (London) 88, 551–556.

Canny, J.F., 1986. A computational approach to edge detection. IEEE Pattern Analysis and Machine Intelligence 8, 100–105.

Carey, S., 1992. Becoming a face expert. Philoshophical Transactions of the Royal Society of London B355, 95–103.

Christensen, E.E., Murry, R.C., Holland, K., Reynolds, J., Landay, M.J., Moore, J.G., 1981. The effect of search time on perception. Radiology 138, 361–365.

Corter, J.E., Gluck, M.A., 1992. Explaining basic categories: features predictability and information. Psychological Bulletin 111 (2), 291–303.

Cutzu, F., Edelman, S., 1997. Faithful representation of similarities among 3-dimensional shapes in human vision. Proceedings of the National Academy of Sciences USA 93, 12046–12050.

Diamond, R., Carey, S., 1986. Why faces are not special: an effect of expertise. Journal of Experimental Psychology: General 115, 107–117.

de Valois, R.L., de Valois, K.K., 1990. Spatial Vision. Oxford University Press, New York.

Dennett, D.C., 1991. Consciousness Explained. Little and Brown, Boston, MA.

Edelman, S., 1995. Class similarity and viewpoint invariance in the recognition of 3D objects. Biological Cybernetics 72, 207–220.

Edelman, S., Bülthoff, H.H., 1992. Orientation dependence in the recognition of familiar and novel views of three-dimensional objects. Vision Research 32, 2385–2400.

Edelman, S., Intrator, N., 1998. Learning as extraction of low-dimensional representations. In: Goldstone, R., Schyns, P.G., Medin, D.E. (Eds.). Mechanisms of Perceptual Learning. Academic Press, San Diego, CA, pp. 353–376.

Elio, R., Anderson, J.R., 1981. The effect of category generalizations and instance similarity on schema abstraction. Journal of Experimental Psychology: Human Learning and Memory 7, 397–417.

Estes, W.K., 1986. Array models of category learning. Cognitive Psychology 18, 500–549.

Fodor, J., 1983. The Modularity of Mind. MIT Press, Cambridge, MA.

Farah, M.J., 1992. Is an object an object an object? Cognitive and neuropsychological investigations of domain-specificity in visual object recognition. Current Directions in Psychological Science 1, 164–169.

Findlay, J.M., Brogan, D., Wenban-Smith, M., 1993. The visual signal for saccadic eye movements emphasizes visual boundaries. Perception and Psychophysics 53, 633–641.

Fiorentini, A., Maffei, L., Sandini, G., 1983. The role of high spatial frequencies in face perception. Perception 12, 195–201.

Gauthier, I., Tarr, M.J., 1997. Becoming a 'Greeble' expert: exploring mechanisms for face recognition. Vision Research 37, 1673–1689.

Ginsburg, A.P., 1986. Spatial filtering and visual form perception. In: Boff, K.R., Kaufman, L., Thomas, J.P. (Eds.), Handbook of Perception and Human Performance, II: Cognitive Processes and Performance. Wiley, New York.

Gluck, M.A., Bower, G.H., 1988. Evaluating an adaptive network model of human learning. Journal of Memory and Language 27, 166–195.

Goldstone, R.L., 1994. Influences of categorization on perceptual discrimination. Journal of Experimental Psychology: General 123, 178–200.

Gosselin, F., Schyns, P.G., 1997. Debunking the basic level. In: Proceedings of the XIX Meeting of the Cognitive Science Society. Lawrence Erlbaum, Hilldsale, NJ, pp. 277–282.

Hill, H., Schyns, P.G., Akamatsu, S., 1997. Information and viewpoint dependence in face recognition. Cognition 62, 201–222.

Jolicoeur, P., 1990. Identification of disoriented objects: a dual-systems theory. Mind and Language 5, 387–410.

Jolicoeur, P., Gluck, M., Kosslyn, S.M., 1984. Pictures and names: making the connexion. Cognitive Psychology 19, 31–53.

Jones, G.V., 1983. Identifying basic categories. Psychological Bulletin 94, 423–428.

Kanade, T., 1981. Recovery of the three-dimensional shape of an object from a single view. Artificial Intelligence 17, 409–460.

Koenderink, K., Van Doorn, A., 1982. The shape of smooth objects and the way contours end. Perception 11, 129–137.

Kruschke, J.K., 1992. ALCOVE: an exemplar-based connectionist model of category learning. Psychological Review 99, 22–44.

Legge, G.E., Gu, Y., 1989. Stereopsis and contrast. Vision Research 29, 989–1004.

Lesgold, A.M., 1984. Acquiring expertise. In: Anderson, J.R., Kosslyn, S.M. (Eds.), Tutorials in Learning and Memory: Essays in Honor of Gordon Bower. W.H. Freeman, San Francisco, pp. 31–60.

Liu, Z., 1996. Viewpoint-dependency in object representation and recognition. Spatial Vision 9, 491–521.

Liu, Z., Knill, D.C., Kersten, D., 1995. Object classification for human and ideal observers. Vision Research 35, 549–568.

Livingstone, M.S., Hubel, D.H., 1987. Psychophysical evidence for separate channels for the perception of form, color, movement and depth. Journal of Neuroscience 7, 3416–3468.

Lowe, D.G., 1987. The viewpoint consistency constraint. International Journal of Computer Vision 1, 57–72.

Mallet, S.G., 1989. A theory for multiresolution signal decomposition: the wavelet representation. IEEE Pattern Analysis and Machine Intelligence 11, 674–693.

Marr, D., 1982. Vision. W.H. Freeman, San Francisco.

Marshall, J.A., Burbeck, C.A., Ariely, J.P., Rolland, J.P., Martin, K.E.., 1996. Journal of the Optical Society of America A 13, 681–688.

Morgan, M.J., 1992. Spatial filtering precedes motion detection. Nature 355, 344–346.

Murphy, G.L., 1991. Parts in object concepts: experiments with artificial categories. Memory and Cognition 18, 407–418.

Murphy, G.L., Brownell, H.H., 1985. Category differentiation in object recognition: typicality constraints on the basic category advantage. Journal of Experimental Psychology: Learning, Memory and Cognition 11, 70–84.

Murphy, G.L., Lassaline, M.E. (1998). Hierarchical structure in concepts and the basic level of categorization. In: Lamberts, K. Shanks, D. (Eds.), Knowledge, Concepts and Categories. Psychology Press, London, pp. 93–131.

Murphy, G.L., Smith, E.E., 1982. Basic-level superiority in picture categorization. Journal of Verbal Learning and Verbal Behavior 21, 1–20.

Norman, G.R., Brooks, L.R., Coblentz, C.L., Babcock, C.J., 1992. The correlation of feature identification and category judgments in diagnostic radiology. Memory and Cognition 20, 344–355.

Nosofsky, R.M., 1984. Choice, similarity, and the context of categorization. Journal of Experimental Psychology: Learning, Memory, and Cognition 10, 104–114.

Nosofsky, R.M., 1986. Attention, similarity, and the identification-categorization relationship. Journal of Experimental Psychology: General 115, 39–57.

Nosofsky, R.M., Gluck, M.A., Palmeri, T.J., McKinley, S.C., Glauthier, P., 1994. Comparing models of rule-based classification learning: a replication and an extension of Shepard, Hovland, and Jenkins (1961). Memory and Cognition 22, 352–369.

Oliva, A., Schyns, P.G., 1997. Coarse blobs or fine edges? Evidence that information diagnosticity changes the perception of complex visual stimuli. Cognitive Psychology 34, 72–107.

O'Regan, J.K., 1992. Solving the real mysteries of visual perception: the world as an outside memory. Canadian Journal of Psychology. 46, 461–488.

Palmer, S., Rosch, E., Chase, P., 1981. Canonical perspective and the perception of objects. In: Long, J., Baddeley, A. (Eds.), Attention and Performances IX. Lawrence Erlbaum, Hillsdale, NJ.

Parker, D.M., Lishman, J.R., Hughes, J., 1992. Temporal integration of spatially filtered visual images. Perception 21, 147–160.

Perrett, D.I., Oram, M.W., Harries, M.H., Bevan, R., Benson, P.J., Thomas, S., 1991. Viewer-centred and object-centred coding of heads in the macaque temporal cortex. Experimental Brain Research 86, 159–173.

Rensink, R.A., O'Regan, J.K., Clark, J.J., 1997. To see or not to see: the need for attention to perceive changes in scenes. Psychological Science 8, 368–373.

Rock, I., Di Vita, J., 1987. A case of viewer-centered object representation. Cognitive Psychology 19, 280–293.

Rosch, E., Mervis, C.B., Gray, W., Johnson, D., Boyes-Braem, P., 1976. Basic objects in natural categories. Cognitive Psychology 8, 382–439.

Schor, C.M., Wood, I.C., Ogawa, J., 1984. Spatial tuning of static and dynamic local stereopsis. Vision Research 24, 573–578.

Schyns, P.G., Bülthoff, H.H., 1994. Viewpoint dependence and face recognition. Proceedings of the XVI Meeting of the Cognitive Science Society. Lawrence Erlbaum, Hilldsale, NJ, pp. 789–793.

Schyns, P.G., Murphy, G.L., 1991. The ontogeny of units in object categories. Proceeding of the XIII Meeting of the Cognitive Science Society. Lawrence Erlbaum, Hilldsale, NJ, pp. 197–202.

Schyns, P.G., Murphy, G.L., 1994. The ontogeny of part representation in object concepts. In: Medin, D.L. (Ed.), The Psychology of Learning and Motivation, Vol. 31, pp. 301–349.

Schyns, P.G., Oliva, A., 1994. From blobs to boundary edges: evidence for time and spatial scale dependent scene recognition. Psychological Science 5, 195–200.

Schyns, P.G., and Oliva, A., 1997. Flexible, diagnosticity-driven, rather than fixed, perceptually determined scale selection in scene and face recognition. Perception 26, 1027–1038.

Schyns, P.G., Rodet, L., 1997. Categorization creates functional features. Journal of Experimental Psychology: Learning, Memory and Cognition 23, 681–696.

Schyns, P.G., Goldstone, R.L., Thibaut, J.P., 1998. The development of features in object concepts. Brain and Behavioral Sciences 21, 17–54.

Sergent, J., 1982. Theoretical and methodological consequences of variations in exposure duration in visual laterality studies. Perception and Psychophysics 31, 451–461.

Sergent, J., 1986. Microgenesis of face perception. In: Ellis, H.D., Jeeves, M.A., Newcombe, F., Young, A.M. (Eds.), Aspects of Face Processing. Martinus Nijhoff, Dordrecht.

Shepard, R.N., Hovland, C.I., Jenkins, H.M., 1961. Learning and memorization of classifications. Psychological Monographs 75.

Tanaka, J., Gauthier, I., 1998. Expertise in object and face recognition. In: Goldstone, R., Schyns, P.G., Medin, D.E. (Eds.). Mechanisms of Perceptual Learning. Academic Press, San Diego, CA, pp. 85–121.

Tanaka, J., Farah, M.J., 1993. Parts and wholes in face recognition. Quarterly Journal of Experimental Psychology 46A, 225–245.

Tanaka, J., Sengco, J.A., 1997. Features and their configuration in face recognition. Memory and Cognition 25, 583–592.

Tanaka, J., Taylor, M.E., 1991. Object categories and expertise: is the basic level in the eye of the beholder? Cognitive Psychology 15, 121–149.

Tarr, M.J., Bülthoff, H.H., 1995. Is human object recognition better described by geon structural descriptions or by multiple views? Journal of Experimental Psychology: Human Perception and Performance 21, 1494–1505.

Tarr, M.J., Kriegman, D.J., 1998. Toward understanding human object recognition: aspect graphs and view-based representations. Submitted.

Tarr, M.J., Pinker, S., 1989. Mental rotation and orientation – dependence in shape recognition. Cognitive Psychology 21, 233–282.

Tarr, M.J., Pinker, S., 1991. Orientation-dependent mechanisms in shape recognition: further issues. Psychological Science 2, 207–209.

Tarr, M.J., Bülthoff, H.H., Zabinski, M., Blanz, V., 1997. To what extent do unique parts influence recognition across changes in viewpoints? Psychological Science 8, 282–289.

Troje, N., Bülthoff, H.H., 1996. Face recognition under varying pose: the role of texture and shape. Vision Research 36, 1761–1771.

Tversky, B., Hemenway, K., 1984. Objects, parts and categories. Journal of Experimental Psychology: General 113, 169–193.

Vetter, T., Poggio, T., Bülthoff, H.H., 1994. The importance of symmetry and virtual views in three-dimensional object recognition. Current Biology 4, 18–23.

Watt, R., 1987. Scanning from coarse to fine spatial scales in the human visual system after the onset of a stimulus. Journal of Optical Society of America A 4, 2006–2021.

Wattenmaker, W.D., 1991. Learning modes, feature correlations, and memory-based categorization. Journal of Experimental Psychology: Learning, Memory, and Cognition 17, 908–923.

Weisstein, N., Maguire, W., Brannan, J., 1992. M and P pathways and the perception of figure and ground. In: Brannan, J. (Ed.), Applications of Parallel Processing in Vision. North Holland, Amsterdam.

7

The objects of action and perception

Melvyn A. Goodale*, G. Keith Humphrey

Department of Psychology, University of Western Ontario, London, ON N6A 5C2, Canada

Abstract

Two major functions of the visual system are discussed and contrasted. One function of vision is the creation of an internal model or percept of the external world. Most research in object perception has concentrated on this aspect of vision. Vision also guides the control of object-directed action. In the latter case, vision directs our actions with respect to the world by transforming visual inputs into appropriate motor outputs. We argue that separate, but interactive, visual systems have evolved for the perception of objects on the one hand and the control of actions directed at those objects on the other. This 'duplex' approach to high-level vision suggests that Marrian or 'reconstructive' approaches and Gibsonian or 'purposive-animate-behaviorist' approaches need not be seen as mutually exclusive, but rather as complementary in their emphases on different aspects of visual function. © 1998 Elsevier Science B.V. All rights reserved

Keywords: Vision; Action; Perception

1. Introduction

It is a common assertion that the fundamental task of vision is to construct a representation of the three-dimensional layout of the world and the objects and events within it. But such an assertion begs at least two fundamental and interrelated questions. First, what is vision? Second, what is the nature of the representation that vision delivers? These questions, which are central to the entire research enterprise in understanding human vision, form the framework for the present paper. In attempting to answer these questions, we will contrast what we believe are two major functions of the visual system. One function of vision is the creation of an internal model or percept of the external world – a model that can be used in the

* Corresponding author. Tel.: +1 519 6612070; fax: +1 519 6613961; e-mail: mgoodale@julian.uwo.ca

recognition of objects and understanding their interrelations. Most research in object vision has concentrated on this function (witness the current volume). There is another function of vision, however, which is concerned not with object recognition, but with object-directed action. In this case, vision guides our actions with respect to the world by transforming visual inputs into appropriate motor outputs. We will suggest that separate, but interacting, visual systems have evolved for the perception of objects on the one hand and the control of actions directed at those objects on the other. This 'duplex' approach to high-level vision suggests that Marrian or 'reconstructive' approaches and Gibsonian or 'purposive-animate-behaviorist' approaches need not be mutually exclusive and may be actually complementary.

2. What is vision?

Vision gives us sight. In other words, vision gives us an experience of the world beyond our immediate body surface, a world full of objects and events that are imbued with meaning and significance. Research in human psychophysics and perception has concentrated almost entirely on the way in which the visual system delivers this visual experience (for related discussions of this issue see Georgeson, 1997; Watt, 1991, 1992). Although a good deal of this research has concentrated on 'low-level' visual computations, even here it has been generally assumed that the mechanisms supporting such computations are all part of the same general-purpose system dedicated to the construction of the visual percept. This fascination with what and how we 'see' has meant that many other functions of vision have either been ignored or been assumed to depend on the same mechanisms supporting sight. This preoccupation with vision as sight was nicely described 20 years ago by Weimer (1977):

> Since the time of Aristotle the mind has been regarded as intrinsically sensory in nature, as a passive black box or window that is (somehow) sensibly impressed with input from the environment. A root metaphor of mind has evolved from the common-sense, everyday experience of looking at the world. Vision, conceived as the passive reception of information that both exists and possesses an intrinsic psychological character independently of the organism, became the paradigm exemplar of mental processing (p. 268).

For most people then vision is synonymous with sight; there is nothing more to vision than visual experience. Even Marr, who was perhaps the most influential visual theorist in recent years, appears to endorse this 'plain man's' conception of vision (see p. 3 of Marr, 1982). Yet there is plenty of evidence that much of the work done by the visual system has nothing to do with sight or experiential perception. The pupillary light reflex, the synchronization of circadian rhythms with the local light-dark cycle, and the visual control of posture are but three examples of a range of visually modulated outputs where we have no direct experience of the controlling stimuli and where the underlying control mechanisms have little to do with our perception of the world. Yet most contemporary accounts of vision, while acknowledging the existence of these 'extraperceptual' visual phenomena, still assume that the main function of the visual system is the construction of some sort of internal model or percept of the external world (for a detailed discussion of this issue, see Goodale, 1983a, 1988, 1997). In such accounts, phenomena such as the pupillary light reflex are seen as simple servomechanisms which, while useful, are not part of the essential machinery for the construction of the visual percept. But, as we shall see later, the visual control of much more complex behaviours, such as reaching out and grasping an object, also appear to depend on mechanisms that are functionally and neurally separate from those mediating our perception of that object. Indeed, the origins of vision may be related more to its contribution to the control of action than to its role in conscious perception, a function which appears to be a relative newcomer on the evolutionary scene (Goodale, 1983a, 1988; Goodale et al., 1996).

2.1. Vision for acting on the world

Vision in many animals can be studied without appealing to the idea of vision as sight. The reason for this, of course, is that vision evolved in animals, not to enable them to 'see' the world, but to guide their movements through it. Indeed, the visual system of most animals, rather than being a general-purpose network dedicated to reconstructing the rather limited world in which they live, consists instead of a set of relatively independent input-output lines, or visuomotor 'modules', each of which is responsible for the visual control of a particular class of motor outputs.

While evidence for separate visuomotor modules can be found in a broad range of anatomical, electrophysiological, and behavioral studies, some of the most compelling demonstrations have been provided by experiments with so-called 'rewired' frogs. Because the amphibian brain is capable of far more regeneration following damage than the mammalian brain, it is possible to 're-wire' some retinal projections, such as those going to the optic tectum in the midbrain, while leaving all the other retinal projections intact. Thus, the retinotectal projections can be induced to project to the optic tectum on the same side of the frog's brain instead of to the optic tectum on the opposite side, as is the case in the normal animal. In one such experiment, these unfortunate creatures were shown to demonstrate 'mirror-image' feeding – directing their snapping movements to positions in space that were mirror-symmetrical to the location of prey objects (Ingle, 1973). They also showed mirror-image predator avoidance and jumped towards rather than away from the looming visual stimuli. These results suggest that the optic tectum plays a critical role in the visual control of these patterns of behavior in the frog. Remarkably, however, the same 'rewired' frogs showed quite normal visually-guided barrier avoidance as they locomoted from one place to another, even when the edge of the barrier was placed in the visual field where mirror-image feeding and predator avoidance could be elicited. As it turns out, the reason they showed normal visual control of barrier avoidance is quite straightforward; the retinal projections to the pretectum, a structure in the thalamus just in front of the optic tectum, were still intact and had not been redirected to the opposite side of the brain. A number of lesion studies have shown that this structure plays a critical role in the visual control of barrier avoidance (Ingle, 1980, 1982). Thus, it would appear that there are at least two independent visuomotor systems in the frog: a tectal system, which mediates visually elicited prey-catching and predator-avoidance, and a pretectal system which mediates visually guided locomotion around barriers. In fact, more recent work suggests that there may be upwards of five or more distinct visuomotor networks in the amphibian brain, each with its own set of retinal inputs and each controlling different arrays of motor outputs (Ewert, 1987; Ingle, 1991).

The results of such studies, which point to a good deal of modularity in the organization of the visuomotor circuitry in the frog, do not fit well with the common view of a visual system dedicated to the construction of a general-purpose representation of the external world. Although the outputs from the different visuomotor systems described above need to be coordinated, it makes no sense to argue that the different actions controlled by these networks are guided by a single visual representation of the world residing somewhere in the animal's brain. Of course, the idea of separate visuomotor channels is consistent with the views of some visual theorists who have argued that vision does more than mediate perception and subserves the visual control of many the different actions that organisms carry out in their daily lives. 'Purposive vision', as this approach is sometimes described, has emphasized the role of vision in the direct control of actions rather than its contribution to constructing percepts of the world in which those actions might unfold (e.g. Aloimonos, 1990).

While there is certainly plenty of evidence to suggest that visuomotor modularity of the kind found in the frog also exists in the mammalian brain (e.g. Ellard and Goodale, 1986, 1988; Goodale, 1983b, 1996; Goodale and Carey, 1990; Goodale and Milner, 1982), the very complexity of day-to-day living in many mammals, particularly in higher primates, demands much more flexible organization of the circuitry. In monkeys (and thus presumably in humans as well), there is evidence that many of the phylogenetically ancient visuomotor circuits that were present in more primitive vertebrates are now modulated by more recently evolved control systems in the cerebral cortex (for review, see Milner and Goodale, 1995). Thus, the highly adaptive visuomotor behavior of humans and other higher primates is made possible by the evolution of another layer of control in a series of hierarchically organized networks. This idea is reminiscent of the views of John Hughlings Jackson (e.g. Jackson, 1875), an eminent nineteenth-century British neurologist who was heavily influenced by concepts of evolution. Jackson tried to explain the effects of damage to human cerebral cortex by suggesting that such damage removed the more highly evolved aspects of brain function, so that what one saw in the performance of many patients was the expression of evolutionarily older mechanisms residing elsewhere in the brain. The emergence of more flexible visuomotor control has not been accomplished entirely by cortical modulation of older circuitry however. The basic subcortical circuitry has itself changed to some extent and new visuomotor control systems have also emerged in which visual control of an almost limitless range of motor outputs is possible. Nevertheless, as we shall see later, for the most part, these networks have remained functionally and neurally separate from those mediating our visual perception of the world.

2.2. *Vision for perceiving the world*

Although the need for more flexible visuomotor control was one of the demands on the evolving primate brain, another was related to the need to identify the objects, to understand their significance and causal relations, to plan a course of action, and to communicate with other members of the species. In short, the emergence of cognitive systems and complex social behavior created a whole new set of demands on vision and the organization of the visual system. Direct sensory control of action was not enough. As interactions with the world become more complicated and subtle, motor outputs became quite arbitrary with respect to sensory input. In fact, many animals particularly humans and other primates, behave as though their actions are driven by some sort of internal model of the world in which they live. The representational systems that use vision to generate such models or percepts of the world must carry out very different transformations on visual input than the transformations carried out by the visuomotor modules described earlier (the nature of these differences will be explored later). Moreover, these systems, which generate our perception of the world, are not linked directly to specific motor outputs but are linked instead to cognitive systems involving memory, semantics, spatial reasoning, planning, and communication. But even though such higher-order representational systems permit the formation of goals and the decision to engage in a specific act without reference to particular motor outputs, the actual execution of an action may nevertheless be mediated by dedicated visuomotor modules that are not dissimilar in principle from those found in frogs and toads. In summary, vision in humans and other primates (and perhaps in other animals as well) has two distinct but interactive functions: (1) the perception of objects and their relations, which provides a foundation for the organism's cognitive life; and (2) the control of actions directed at (or with respect to) those objects, in which specific sets of motor outputs are programmed and guided 'on-line'.

3. Action and perception systems in the primate brain: dorsal and ventral streams

The evolution of separate systems for visual perception and for the visual control of action is reflected in the organization of the visual pathways in the primate cerebral cortex. Over fifteen years ago, Ungerleider and Mishkin (1982) identified two distinct 'streams of processing' in the macaque monkey brain: a so-called ventral stream projecting from primary visual cortex to inferotemporal cortex and a so-called dorsal stream projecting from primary visual cortex to posterior parietal cortex (Fig. 1). Although one must always be cautious when drawing homologies between monkey and human neuroanatomy (Crick and Jones, 1993), it seems likely that the visual projections from the primary visual cortex to the temporal and parietal

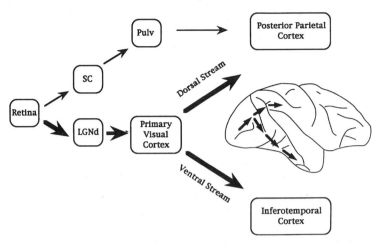

Fig. 1. Major routes whereby retinal input reaches the dorsal and ventral streams. The diagram of the macaque brain (right hemisphere) on the right of the figure shows the approximate routes of the cortico-cortical projections from the primary visual cortex to the posterior parietal and the inferotemporal cortex respectively. LGNd, lateral geniculate nucleus, pars dorsalis; Pulv, pulvinar; SC, superior colliculus.

lobes in the human brain may involve a separation into ventral and dorsal streams similar to that seen in the macaque brain. Ungerleider and Mishkin (1982) suggested, on the basis of a number of electrophysiological studies in the monkey, that the ventral stream plays a critical role in object vision, enabling the monkey to identify an object, while the dorsal stream is involved in spatial vision, enabling the monkey to localize the object in space. This interpretation, in which a distinction is made between identification and localization, is similar to an earlier functional dichotomy proposed by Schneider (1969), who argued that primary visual cortex plays an essential role in identifying visual stimuli while the more ancient midbrain structure, the superior colliculus (another name for the optic tectum in mammals), is responsible for localizing the stimulus. Ungerleider and Mishkin (1982) have taken this same distinction and moved it into the cerebral cortex. More recently, however, Goodale and Milner (1992) (and Milner and Goodale, 1995) have offered a re-interpretation of the apparent differences in the visual processing carried out by the two streams of processing emanating from primary visual cortex. Rather than emphasizing differences in the visual information handled by the two streams (object vision versus spatial vision or 'what' versus 'where'), their account has instead focused on the difference in the requirements of the output systems that each stream of processing serves.

According to Goodale and Milner, the ventral stream plays the major role in constructing the perceptual representation of the world and the objects within it, while the dorsal stream mediates the visual control of actions directed at those objects (for a more detailed discussion, see Goodale and Milner, 1992; Milner and Goodale, 1995). In other words, processing within the ventral stream allows the monkey to recognize an object, such as a ripe piece of fruit dangling from a tree, while processing within the dorsal stream provides critical information about the location, size, and shape of that fruit so that the animal can accurately reach out and grasp it with its hand or mouth. Notice that in this account, information about object attributes, such as size, shape, orientation, and spatial location, are processed by both streams but the nature of that processing is very different. The functional distinction is not between 'what' and 'where', but between the way in which the visual information about a broad range of object parameters are transformed either for perceptual purposes or for the control of goal-directed actions. This is not to say that the distribution of retinogeniculate inputs does not differ between the two streams, but rather that the main difference lies in the nature of the transformations that each stream performs on those two sets of inputs.

3.1. Neuropsychological studies of the dorsal stream

In the intact brain, the two streams of processing work together in a seamless and unified fashion. Nevertheless, by studying individuals who have sustained brain damage that spares one of these systems but not the other, it is possible to get a glimpse of how the two streams differ in the way they each deal with incoming visual information. For example, patients who have sustained damage to the superior portion of the posterior parietal cortex, the major terminus of the dorsal stream, are unable to use visual information to reach out and grasp objects in the hemifield contralateral to the lesion. Clinically, this deficit is called optic ataxia (Bálint, 1909). Such patients have no difficulty using other sensory information, such as proprioception, to control their reaching; nor do they usually have difficulty recognizing or describing objects that are presented in that part of the visual field. Thus, their deficit is neither 'purely' visual nor 'purely' motor; it is a visuomotor deficit.

Observations in several laboratories have shown that patients with optic ataxia not only have difficulty reaching in the correct direction, but they also show deficits in their ability to adjust the orientation of their hand when reaching toward an object, even though they have no difficulty in verbally describing the orientation of the object (e.g. Perenin and Vighetto, 1988). Such patients can also have trouble adjusting their grasp to reflect the size of an object they are asked to pick up – although again their perceptual estimates of object size remain quite accurate (Jakobson et al., 1991; Goodale et al., 1993). To pick up an object successfully, however, it is not enough to orient the hand and scale the grip appropriately; the fingers and thumb must be placed at appropriate opposition points on the object's surface. To do this, the visuomotor system has to compute the outline shape or boundaries of the object. In a recent experiment (Goodale et al., 1994b), a patient (RV) with bilateral lesions of the occipitoparietal region, was asked to pick up a series of small, flat, non-symmetrical smoothly contoured objects using a precision grip, which required her to place her index finger and thumb in appropriate positions on either side of each object. If the fingers were incorrectly positioned, the computation of the correct opposition points ('grasp points') can be achieved only if the overall shape or form of the object is taken into account. Despite the fact that the patient could readily distinguish these objects from one another, she often failed to place her fingers on the appropriate grasp points when she attempted to pick up the objects (Fig. 2).

Such studies suggest that it is not only the spatial location of the object that is apparently inaccessible for controlling movement in patients with dorsal-stream lesions, but the intrinsic characteristics of the object as well. It would be incorrect to characterize the deficits in these patients simply in terms of a disturbance of spatial vision. In fact, in one clear sense their 'spatial vision' is quite intact, since they can often describe the relative location of objects in the visual field contralateral to their lesion, even though they cannot pick them up (Jeannerod, 1988). This pattern of deficits is quite consistent with Goodale and Milner's proposal that the dorsal stream plays a critical role in the visuomotor transformations required for skilled actions, such as visually guided prehension – in which the control of an accurate grasp requires information about an object's location as well as its orientation, size, and shape. It should be emphasized, however, that not all patients with damage to the posterior parietal region have difficulty shaping their hand to correspond to the structural features and orientation of the target object. Some have difficulty with hand postures, some with controlling the direction of their grasp, and some with foveating the target. Indeed, depending upon the size and locus of the lesion, a patient can demonstrate any combination of these visuomotor deficits (for review, see Milner and Goodale, 1995). Different sub-regions of the posterior parietal cor-

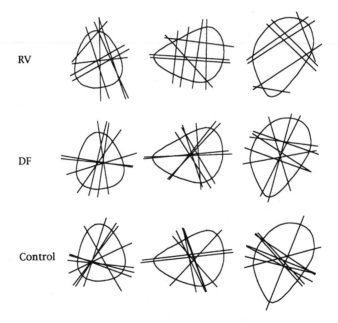

Fig. 2. The 'grasp lines' (joining points where the index finger and the thumb first made contact with the shape) selected by the optic ataxic patient (RV), the visual form agnosic patient (DF), and the control subject when picking up three of the twelve shapes. The four different orientations in which each shape was presented have been rotated so that they are aligned. No distinction is made between the points of contact for the thumb and finger in these plots.

tex, it appears, support transformations related to different motor outputs. Such modularity within the dorsal stream means that a particular skilled action would invoke certain combinations of these visuomotor networks and other actions would invoke quite different combinations.

3.2. Neuropsychological studies of the ventral stream

As we have just seen, patients with optic ataxia often have difficulty reaching towards and/or picking up objects that they have no difficulty identifying. Are there patients who show the opposite pattern of visual deficits and spared visual abilities? In other words, are there patients who can grasp objects quite accurately despite their failure to recognize what it is they are attempting to pick up? One such patient is DF, a young woman who developed a profound visual form agnosia following near-asphyxiation by carbon monoxide. Not only is she unable to recognize the faces of her relatives and friends or the visual shape of common objects, but she is also unable to discriminate between such simple geometric forms as a triangle and a circle. DF has no difficulty identifying people from their voices and she has no problem identifying objects placed in her hands. Her perceptual problems are exclusively visual. Moreover, her deficit, seems largely restricted to the form of objects. She can use color and other surface features to identify objects and she can even use shape from shading to some extent (Humphrey et al., 1994, 1996; Servos et al., 1993). What she seems unable to perceive are the contours of objects – no matter how the contours are defined (Milner et al., 1991). Thus, she cannot identify, shapes whose contours are defined by differences in luminance or color, or by differences in the direction of motion or the plane of depth. Not surprisingly, DF is also unable to recognize shapes that are defined by the similarity or proximity of individual elements of the visual array. A selective deficit in form perception with spared color and other surface information is characteristic of the severe visual agnosia that sometimes follows an anoxic episode. Although MRI shows a pattern of diffuse brain damage in DF that is consistent with anoxia, most of the damage was evident in the ventrolateral region of the occipital lobe sparing primary visual cortex.

The profound deficit in DF's form perception cannot be explained by disturbances in 'low-level' sensory processing. In perimetry testing, she was able to detect luminance-defined targets at least as far out as 30 degrees (Milner et al., 1991). Her spatial contrast sensitivity also appeared to be normal above about 10 cycles/degree and was only moderately impaired at lower spatial frequencies (of course, even though she could detect the presence of the gratings used to measure her contrast sensitivity, she could not report their orientation; see also Humphrey et al., 1991). But the most compelling reason to doubt that her perceptual deficit is due to some sort of low level disturbance in processing is the fact that in another domain, visuomotor control, she remains exquisitely sensitive to the form of objects! Thus, despite her inability to recognize the shape, size, and orientation of objects, she shows strikingly accurate guidance of hand and finger movements directed at those very same objects. Thus, when she was presented with a pair of rectangular blocks of the same or different dimensions, she was unable to distinguish between them. Even when she was asked to indicate the width of a single block by means of her index finger and thumb, her matches bore no relationship to the dimensions of the object and showed considerable trial to trial variability. In contrast, when she was asked simply to reach out and pick up the block, the aperture between her index finger and thumb changed systematically with the width of the object as the movement unfolded, just as in normal subjects (Goodale et al., 1991). In other words, DF scaled her grip to the dimensions of the object she was about to pick up, even though she appeared to be unable to perceive those object dimensions.

A similar dissociation was seen in DF's responses to the orientation of stimuli. Thus, when presented with a large slot which could placed in one of a number of different orientations, she showed great difficulty in indicating the orientation of the slot either verbally or even manually by rotating a hand-held card (see Fig. 3, left). Nevertheless, when she was asked simply to reach out and insert the card, she performed as well as normal subjects, rotating her hand in the appropriate direction as soon as she began the movement (see Fig. 3, right). Finally, even though DF could not discriminate between target objects that differed in outline shape, she could nevertheless pick up such objects successfully, placing her index finger and thumb on stable grasp points (see Fig. 2).

Findings such as these are difficult to reconcile with the idea of Ungerleider and Mishkin (1982) that object vision is the preserve of the ventral stream – for here we have a patient in whom a profound loss of object perception exists alongside a preserved ability to use object features such as size, outline shape, and orientation to guide skilled actions. Such a dissociation, of course, is consistent with the idea

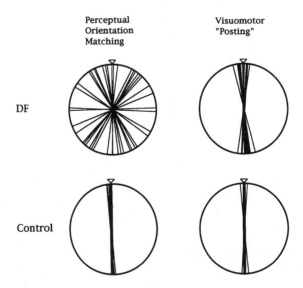

Fig. 3. Polar plots of the orientation of the hand-held card when DF and a control subject were each asked to rotate the card to match the orientation of the slot (left column) or to 'post' the card into the slot (right column). The orientation of the card on the visuomotor task was measured at the instant before the card was placed in the slot. In both plots, the actual orientations of the slot have been normalized to vertical.

proposed by Goodale and Milner (1992) that there are separate neural pathways for transforming incoming visual information for action and perception. Presumably it is the latter and not the former that is compromised in DF. In other words, the brain damage that she suffered as a consequence of anoxia appears to have interrupted the normal flow of shape and contour information into her perceptual system without affecting the processing of shape and contour information by the visuomotor modules comprising her action system. If, as Goodale and Milner have suggested, the perception of objects and events is mediated by the ventral stream of visual projections to inferotemporal cortex, then DF should show evidence for damage relatively early in this pathway. Certainly, the pattern of damage revealed by MRI is consistent with this interpretation; the major focus of cortical damage is in the ventrolateral region of the occipital cortex, an area that is thought to be part of the human homologue of the ventral stream. Primary visual cortex, which provides input for both the dorsal and ventral streams, appears to be largely intact. Thus, although input from primary visual cortex to the ventral stream may have been compromised in DF, input from this structure to the dorsal stream appears to be essentially intact. In addition, the dorsal stream, unlike the ventral stream, also receives input from the superior colliculus via the pulvinar, a nucleus in the thalamus (see Fig. 1). Input to the dorsal stream from both the superior colliculus (via the pulvinar) and the lateral geniculate nucleus (via primary visual cortex) could continue to mediate well-formed visuomotor responses in DF.

Nevertheless, it must not be forgotten that DF's problems arose, not from a discrete lesion, but from anoxia. Therefore, the brain damage in DF, while localized to some extent, is much more diffuse than it would be in a patient with a stroke or tumour. For this reason, any attempt to map the striking dissociation between perceptual and visuomotor abilities in DF onto the ventral and dorsal streams of visual processing must be regarded as tentative. The proposal is strengthened, however, by observations in the patients described earlier whose pattern of deficits is complementary to DF's and whose brain damage can be confidently localized to the dorsal stream.

4. Electrophysiological and behavioural studies in the monkey

The functional division of labour between the two streams proposed by Goodale and Milner is also supported by a large number of studies in the macaque monkey. Thus, monkeys which show profound deficits in object recognition following inferotemporal lesions are nevertheless as capable as normal animals at picking up small food objects (Klüver and Bucy, 1939), at catching flying insects (Pribram, 1967), and at orienting their fingers in a precision grip to grasp morsels of food embedded in small slots placed at different orientations (Buchbinder et al., 1980). In short, these animals behave much the same way as DF: they are unable to discriminate between objects on the basis of visual features that they can clearly use to direct their grasping movements. In addition, there is a long history of electrophysiological work showing that cells in this area are tuned to specific objects or object features.

Moreover, the responses of these cells are not affected by the animal's motor behavior, but are instead sensitive to the reinforcement history and significance of the visual stimuli that drive them (for review, see Goodale, 1993; Milner and Goodale, 1995). Indeed, sensitivity to particular objects can be created in ensembles of cells in inferotemporal cortex simply by training the animals to discriminate between different objects (Logothetis et al., 1995). Finally, there is evidence for a specialization within separate regions of the ventral stream for the coding of certain categories of objects, such as faces and hands, which are of particular social significance to the monkey (for review, see Logothetis and Sheinberg, 1996; Perrett et al., 1995).

In contrast to cells in the ventral stream, most visually-sensitive cells in the dorsal stream are modulated by the concurrent motor behavior of the animal (e.g. Hyvärinen and Poranen, 1974; Mountcastle et al., 1975). In reviewing the electrophysiological studies that have been carried out on the posterior parietal cortex, Andersen (1987) concluded that most neurons in these areas 'exhibit both sensory-related and movement-related activity'. The activity of some visually-driven cells in this region have been shown to be linked to saccadic eye movements; the activity of others to whether or not the animal is fixating a stimulus; and the activity of still other cells to whether or not the animal is engaged in visual pursuit or is making goal-directed reaching movements (e.g. Snyder et al., 1997). Some cells in the posterior parietal area that fire when monkeys reach out to pick up objects are selective not for the spatially directed movement of the arm, but for the movements of the wrist, hand, and fingers that are made prior to and during the act of grasping the target (Hyvärinen and Poranen, 1974; Mountcastle et al., 1975). In a particularly interesting recent development, Sakata and his colleagues have shown that many of these so-called 'manipulation' cells are visually selective and are tuned for objects of a particular shape (Sakata et al., 1992; Taira et al., 1990; for review see Sakata and Taira, 1994; Sakata et al., 1997). These manipulation neurons thus appear to be tied to the properties of the goal object as well as to the distal movements that are required for grasping that object. Finally, it should be noted that lesions in the posterior parietal area in the monkey produce deficits in the visual control of reaching and grasping similar in many respects to those seen in humans following damage to the homologous region (e.g. Haaxma and Kuypers, 1975; Ettlinger, 1977). This review of the monkey literature is clearly far from complete. Interested readers are directed to Milner and Goodale (1993; 1995).

5. Neuro-imaging studies in humans

Ten years ago little was known about the organization of the cerebral visual pathways beyond V1 in humans. With the advent of functional neuroimaging, however, a wealth of data has suddenly become available. The careful work of Tootell et al. (1996) has revealed an organization of visual areas in the human brain that is remarkably similar to that seen in the macaque. Although clear differences in the topography of these areas emerges as one moves from monkey to human, the functional separation into a ventral occipitotemporal and a dorsal occipitoparietal pathway appears to be preserved. Thus, areas in the occipitotemporal region appear to be specialized for the processing of colour, texture, and form differences of objects (e.g. Puce et al., 1996; Price et al., 1996; Malach et al., 1995; Kanwisher et al., 1996). In contrast, regions in the posterior parietal cortex have been found that are activated when subjects engage in visually guided movements such as saccades, reaching movements, and grasping (Matsumura et al., 1996).

As in the monkey, there is evidence for specialization within the occipitotemporal and occipitoparietal visual pathways. Thus, activation studies have identified regions in the occipitotemporal pathway for the processing of faces that are distinct from those involved in the processing of other objects (Kanwisher et al., 1997; Gauthier et al., 1997). Similarly, there is evidence that different areas in and around the intraparietal sulcus are activated when subjects make saccadic eye movements as opposed to manual pointing movements towards visual targets (e g. Kawashima et al., 1996).

Thus, the neuroimaging data are consistent with the idea of two visual streams. In addition, the results of several studies indicate that areas in the posterior parietal cortex are involved in the visual control of action while areas in the occipitotemporal region appear to play a role in object recognition.

6. Differences in the visual transformations mediating action and perception

The division of labour within the organization of the cerebral visual pathways in primates reflects the two important trends in the evolution of vision in higher vertebrates that were identified earlier. First, the emergence of a dorsal 'action' stream reflects the need for more flexible programming and on-line control of visually guided motor outputs. It is interesting to note that this stream is intimately connected not only with the primate forebrain but also with those brainstem structures such as the superior colliculus and various pontine nuclei that play a critical role in the programming and control of movement in all vertebrates (Milner and Goodale, 1995). Thus, one way that the dorsal stream may mediate the visual control of skilled actions is by modulating the activity of these more phylogenetically ancient visuomotor networks.

Second, the emergence of a ventral 'perception' stream which can parse the visual array into discrete objects and events means that animals like ourselves can use perceptual representations of those objects and their relations for long-range planning, communication and other cognitive activities. Although a separate system for this kind of reconstructive visual activity is evident in the cerebral cortex of many mammals (Goodale and Carey, 1990), it is particularly well-developed in humans and other higher primates. Indeed, the ventral stream projections to the inferotemporal cortex, which is intimately connected with structures in the medial temporal lobe and prefrontal cortex involved in long-term memory and other cognitive activities, is exquisitely poised to serve as interface between vision and cognition. In short, while the dorsal stream allows us visual control of our movements through the world, it is the ventral stream that gives us sight.

The distinction between vision for perception and vision for action is similar in many respects to a distinction that Neisser (1989, 1994) has drawn between what he calls 'recognition systems' on the one hand and 'direct perception systems' on the other. According to Neisser, recognition systems mediate the identification and classification of objects through the accumulation of evidence in relation to stored representations. Recognition is always defined as a relation of present input to the past, i.e. in relation to stored information about objects. Direct perception for Neisser is something quite different. Following Gibson (1979), he proposes that the direct perception system provides information about where we are, where objects are, and what physical actions those objects can afford – information that is provided as the animal moves through the world and interacts with it. He proposes that Gibson's concept of affordance be limited to the notion of a 'physical affordance' since such affordances are entirely specified by the physics of light and do not depend on stored semantic knowledge about the objects – which is the business of the recognition systems. The possibility of picking up an object such as a rock and throwing it does not depend on identifying the object but rather the 'fit', or physical relationship, between our effector organs and the object. In short, the task of direct perception is the programming and on-line control of action.

The type of information stored and used in recognition is quite different from that used in the control of action. One example that Neisser (1989) uses to illustrate the difference between recognition and direct perception is the way each system deals with the orientation of objects. As several papers in this volume attest to, a large amount of recent research on object orientation has been concerned with the effects of object orientation on recognition. Our recognition of an object often suffers greatly if its orientation does not match the orientation that we have experienced in the past (e.g. Edelman and Bülthoff, 1992; Humphrey and Khan, 1992; Rock and DiVita, 1987; Tarr, 1995; see also Biederman and Gerhardstein, 1995; Tarr and Bülthoff, 1995; for review see Jolicoeur and Humphrey, 1998). In sharp contrast, our ability to direct a well-formed grasp at an object is not dependent on prior familiarity with a particular orientation; in fact, we do not need to recognize the object to grasp it efficiently.

While Neisser's distinction between recognition and direct perception converges on our own ideas to some extent, there are some critical differences. For us, the action system (similar to Neisser's direct perception system) is entirely concerned with providing visual information for the programming and control of motor outputs. This system contains an array of dedicated visuomotor modules which, when activated in various combinations, transform visual inputs into directed motor acts. Neisser, however, suggests that our perception of the spatial location of objects and their relations is dependent on the direct perception system; the recognition system for Neisser seems to be concerned only with identifying and classifying objects. In our scheme, the visuomotor modules that make up the action system do not participate in the construction of perceptual representations of the layout or disposition of objects for cognitive purposes. Instead, it is the perception system which does this.

Like Neisser, we see the perception system (similar to his recognition system) as being intimately linked with cognitive processes such as long-term memory; but unlike Neisser, we see the perception system as providing information, not only about the identity of objects, but also about their spatial and temporal relations. In our scheme, the perception system delivers our experience of the world and the objects within it.

Clearly what distinguishes the perception system from the visuomotor modules making up the action system is the way in which the visual world is represented in the brain. Of course, the notion of representation is one of the central ideas in perception and cognition, although the type(s) of representations used in visual perception and the very notion of representation itself have been the source of much debate. Nevertheless, the goal of visual perception is often taken to be the creation of a representation that is in some sense an internal model of the three-dimensional world. In this sense, a representation is a reconstruction of the world (for further critical discussion of this approach see Ballard and Brown, 1992; Churchland et al., 1994; Tarr and Black, 1994 and accompanying commentaries). This approach to vision is exemplified by Marr (1982) who concentrated on the representation of information about objects for the purposes of recognition. According to this approach, the major task of recognition is to reconstruct a detailed and accurate model or replica of the three-dimensional world on the basis of the two-dimensional data present at the retinas.

Presumably, the proposed representation is not only important for recognition, but plays a crucial role in other cognitive activities related to spatial reasoning and the semantics of objects and scenes. It is the construction of this kind of representation that we see as the major function of the perception system – a kind of 'general purpose' representation that can serve as the substrate upon which a large range of cognitive operations can be mounted (in fact, the cognitive operations are themselves intimately involved in the construction of the representation upon which they operate). Of course, the nature of representations used for recognition and other cognitive acts is far from settled. A large proportion of recent research in object vision has been directed at uncovering the nature of this presentation as other papers in this volume attest. It is also clear that although Marr's approach to object recognition has been very influential, recognition need not entail reconstruction in the way he envisaged.

Our perception of the world certainly appears remarkably rich and detailed. Nevertheless much of this perceptual representation is 'virtual' and is derived from memory rather than visual input, (e.g. McConkie and Currie, 1996; O'Regan, 1992; Rensink et al., 1997). Much of the metric information about objects and their relations is inaccurate and even unavailable (for review, see Intraub, 1997). And in any case, the metrical information is not computed with reference to the observer as much as it is to other objects in a visual array (Goodale and Haffenden, 1998). Indeed, if perceptual representations were to attempt to deliver the real metrics of all objects in the visual array, the computational load would be astronomical. The solution that perception appears to have adopted is to use world-based coordinates – in which the real metric of that world need not be computed. Only the relative position, orientation, size and motion of objects is of concern to perception. For example, we can watch the same scene unfold on television or on a movie screen without be confused by the enormous change in the coordinate frame.

As soon as we direct a motor act towards an object, an entirely different set of constraints applies. We can no longer rely on the perception system's 'general purpose' representation. We could not, for example, direct actions towards what we see on television, however compelling and 'real' the depicted scene might be. To be accurate, the actions must be finely tuned to the metrics of the real world. Moreover, different actions will engage different effectors. As a consequence, the computations for the visual control of actions must not only take into account the real metrics of the world, they must be specific to the particular motor output required. Directing a saccadic eye movement, for example, will demand different transformations of visual input to motor output from those required to direct a manual grasping movement. The former will involve coordinate systems centred on the retina and/or head, while the latter will involve shoulder and/or wrist centered coordinates. While it is theoretically possible that a highly sophisticated 'general-purpose' representation could accommodate such transformations, such a possibility seems unlikely and unnecessary. Indeed, as we saw earlier, the empirical evidence from a broad range of studies indicates that visuomotor control in humans and other primates is organized in much the same way as it is in simpler vertebrates, such as the frog (for review see Milner and Goodale, 1995). Moreover, these different visuomotor modules work in real time with only limited 'memory'. In other words, once a movement is made the visuomotor coordinates used to program and guide that movement are lost. Even if the movement is not performed, the coordinates cannot be stored much beyond a second or two (e.g. Gnadt et al., 1991; Goodale et al., 1994a). Perception of course has a much longer time course and stores information perhaps in some cases for a lifetime. In summary, the visuomotor modules within the action system transform sensory information directly into motor output rather than using reconstructions of visual scenes. Moreover, as will be described below, such transformations are not available to consciousness in the way that outputs of perceptual processes usually are.

7. Dissociations between action and perception in normal subjects

Although the visual fields of the two eyes together span about 200°, most of our perceptual experience is confined to the few degrees subtended by the foveal and parafoveal region. In short, we see what we are looking at. Yet as we move through the world, stepping over curbs, negotiating doorways, and grasping door handles, we often utilize visual information from the far periphery of vision. This differential use of the fovea and peripheral visual fields by perception and action systems may explain why in the monkey there is differential representation of these regions in the ventral and dorsal streams. The receptive fields of cells in the inferotemporal cortex almost always include the fovea and very little of the far peripheral visual fields whereas cells in the posterior parietal cortex have a very large representation of the peripheral visual fields (Baizer et al., 1991). Indeed, in some areas of the dorsal stream, such as the parieto-occipital area, the portion of cortex devoted to the fovea is no larger than would be expected on the basis of the extent of the visual field it subtends; i.e. there is no 'cortical magnification' of central vision (Gattass et al., 1985).

If a similar retinotopic organization of cortical areas exists in the human brain, then one might expect that the visual control of motor behavior might be quite sensitive to differences in visual stimuli presented in the far peripheral visual field whereas perceptual judgements of the same stimuli might be relatively insensitive. In a recent experiment, Goodale and Murphy (1997) presented subjects with five different rectangular objects of the same overall size but different dimensions. These objects were presented randomly at different retinal eccentricities that varied from 5 to 70° and subjects were required to categorize each object into one of five previously learned categories or, in another block of trials, to reach out and grasp the object across its longitudinal axis. As one might expect, the variability of the subjects' perceptual categorizations increased substantially as the objects were presented at more and more eccentric locations. In sharp contrast, the relationship between the aperture of their grasp (before contact) and the width of the object was as well-tuned at 70° as it was at 5°. There was also another striking difference between subjects' perceptual judgements of the width of the objects and the calibration of their grasp. Although the subjects reported that objects did not look as wide in the far periphery as the same objects in more parafoveal regions, the aperture of their grasp was actually larger for objects in the peripheral visual field (even though the grasp continued to be well-calibrated with respect to the object's dimensions). These dissociations between verbal reports and visuomotor control again emphasize the specialization of different parts of the visual system for perception and action.

Another way to demonstrate the distinction between perception and action systems in vision is to look at the way each system deals with objects embedded in pictorial illusions. Pictorial illusions are, of course, favourite ways of illustrating interpretive and context-sensitive aspects of visual perception. Consider the Ebbinghaus (or Titchener Circles) Illusion for a moment. In this familiar illusion, two target circles of equal size, each surrounded by a circular array of either smaller or larger circles, are presented side by side (see Fig. 4a). Subjects typically report that the target circle surrounded by the array of smaller circles appears larger than the one surrounded by the array of larger circles, presumably because of the difference in the contrast in size between the target circles and the surrounding circles. It is also possible to make the two target circles appear identical in size by increasing the actual size of the target circle surrounded by the array of larger circles (see Fig. 4b).

While our perceptual judgements of what we see are clearly affected by the manipulations of the stimulus array, there is good reason to believe that the calibration of size-dependent motor outputs, such as grip aperture during grasping, would not be. After all, when we reach out to pick up an object, particularly one we have not seen before, the visuomotor networks controlling grasping must compute the size (and distance) of the object accurately if we are to pick it up efficiently. It is not

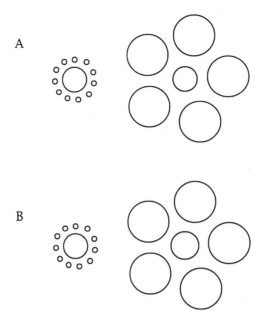

Fig. 4. The 'Ebbinghaus' illusion. The standard version of the illusion, the target circles in the centre of the two arrays appear to be different in size even though they are physically identical, as shown in (A). For most people, the circle in the annulus of smaller circles appears to be larger than the circle in the annulus of larger circles. (B) Shows a version of the illusion in which the target circle in the array of large circles has been made physically larger than the other target circle. The two target circles should now appear to be perceptually equivalent in size.

enough to know that the target object is larger or smaller than surrounding objects; the visuomotor module controlling hand aperture must compute its real size. For this reason, one might expect grip scaling to be refractory to size-contrast illusions.

To test this possibility, Aglioti et al. (1995) developed a three-dimensional version of the Ebbinghaus Illusion in which two thin 'poker-chip' discs were used as the target circles. The disks were arranged as pairs on a standard Ebbinghaus annular circle display (see Fig. 5) drawn on a white background and positioned directly in front of the subject. Trials in which the two disks appeared perceptually identical but were physically different in size were randomly alternated with trials in which the disks appeared perceptually different but were physically identical. The left-right position of the arrays of large and small circles was of course randomly varied throughout. Subjects (all of whom had normal vision) were given the following instructions: if the discs appear equal in size, pick up the one on the right; if they appear different, pick up the one on the left. Subjects used their right hand and grip aperture was tracked using standard opto-electronic recording.

Although there was considerable individual variation, all the subjects remained sensitive to the size-contrast illusion throughout testing. In other words, their choice of disk was affected by the contrast in size between the disks and the surrounding circles. As a consequence, they treated disks that were actually physically different

Fig. 5. A line drawing of our three-dimensional version of the Ebbinghaus illusion. Note the infra-red light emitting diodes (IREDs) attached to the finger, thumb and wrist of the subject.

in size as perceptually equivalent and they treated disks that were physically identical as perceptually different. Remarkably, however, the scaling of their grasp was affected very little by these beliefs. Instead, the maximum grip aperture, which was achieved approximately 70% of the way through the reach towards the disk, was almost entirely determined by the true size of that disk. Thus, on trials in which the two disks were perceived as being the same size, subjects opened their hand wider for the larger disk than they did for the smaller one. An example of such a case in illustrated in Fig. 6a. In fact, as shown in Fig. 6b, the difference in grip aperture for large and small disks was the same for trials in which the subject believed the two disks were equivalent in size (even though they were different) as it was for trials in which the subject believed the two disks were different in size (even though they were identical). In short, the calibration of grip size seemed to be largely impervious to the effects of the size-contrast illusion. This difference in the susceptibility of perceptual judgements and the visual control of prehension was replicated in a recent study in which subjects had no opportunity to compare their hand opening with the goal object during the execution of the movement (Haffenden and Goodale, 1998).

   The dissociation between perceptual judgements and the calibration of grasping is not limited to the Ebbinghaus Illusion. The vertical-horizontal illusion is one in which a vertical line that bisects a horizontal line appears longer than the horizontal line even though both lines are in fact the same length. Vishton and Cutting (1995) have recently demonstrated that even though subjects show the usual bias in their judgements of line length, they did not show a bias when they attempted to reach out and 'grasp' the lines. The relative insensitivity of reaching and grasping to pictorial illusions has also been demonstrated for the Müller-lyer illusion (Gentilucci et al., 1996) and the Ponzo illusion (Ian Whishaw, personal communication).

   But why should perception be so susceptible to these illusions while the calibra-

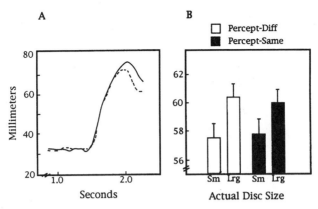

Fig. 6. Graphs illustrating grip aperture in different testing conditions. (A) Representative grip aperture profiles for one subject picking up a large disc (solid line) and a small disc (broken line) on separate trials in which he judged the two discs to be identical in size (even though, of course, the two discs were physically quite different). In both cases, the disc was located on the left hand side of the display. (B)The mean maximum grip aperture for the 14 subjects in different testing conditions. The two solid bars on the right indicate the maximum aperture on trials in which the two discs were judged to be perceptually the same even though they were physically different in size. The two open bars on the left indicate the mean maximum aperture on trials in which the two discs were judged to be perceptually different even though they were physically the same size (either two large discs or two small discs).

tion of grasp is not. Take the Ebbinghaus illusion for example. It is possible that the illusion arises from a straightforward relative-size scaling mechanism, whereby an object that is smaller than its immediate neighbors is assumed to be smaller than a similar object that is larger than its immediate neighbors (for review, see Coren and Girgus, 1978). It is also possible that a computation relating image size and distance is responsible for the illusion. If the array of smaller circles is assumed to be more distant from the observer than the array of larger circles, then the target circle within the array of smaller circles will also be perceived as more distant, and therefore larger, than the target circle of equivalent retinal image size within the array of larger circles. In other words, the illusion might simply be a consequence of the perception system's attempt to make size constancy judgments on the basis of an analysis of the entire visual array (Gregory, 1963).

Mechanisms such as these, in which the relations between objects in the visual array play a crucial role in scene interpretation, are clearly central to the operation of the perception system. As we gaze across the landscape, some of the objects within our field of view will be perceived, in an obligatory fashion, as larger or closer than others. Perception is by its very nature relative. In contrast, the execution of a goal-directed act like manual prehension depends on metrical computations that are centered on the target itself. Moreover, the visual mechanisms within the action system that mediate the control of the grasping movements must compute the real distance of the object (presumably on the basis of reliable cues such as stereopsis and retinal motion). As a consequence, computation of the retinal image size of the object coupled with an accurate estimate of distance will deliver the true size of the object for calibrating the grip – and such computations may be quite insensitive to the kinds of pictorial cues that drive our perception of familiar illusions. Thus, the very act by means of which subjects indicate their susceptibility to the illusion (i.e. picking up one of the two target circles) is itself unaffected by the visual information driving that illusion. This paradox demonstrates that what we think we 'see' is not always what guides our actions. It also provides evidence for the parallel operation of the two kinds of visual processing that we described earlier, each apparently designed to serve quite different purposes, and each characterized by quite different properties.

8. The action/perception distinction in computational vision

We would suggest that the distinction between vision for perception and vision for action is relevant to some aspects of a current debate in the computational vision literature. The debate could be characterized as one between 'behaviorist or purposive' approaches and 'reconstructive' approaches to vision. Here we will make some general remarks that capture only some aspects of the various positions in the debate as there are many theoretical divergences within both 'behaviorist' and 'reconstructionist' proposals that we are overlooking. We are obviously oversimplifying in the belief that such a caricature captures some significant agreement and divergences in general orientation that can be mapped on to the distinctions in perception and action systems that we have proposed. The reader should refer to Tarr and Black (1994) and the accompanying commentaries on that paper for more detail. Other relevant papers that could be consulted are Ballard and Brown (1992), Churchland et al. (1994), Jolion (1994), Sloman (1989) and the collection of papers edited by Aloimonos (1992).

Researchers who espouse behaviorist approaches to vision are often quite sympathetic to the general framework of Gibson (1979) in his emphasis on the active, exploratory nature of perception. As a consequence they concentrate on visual behavior such as obstacle avoidance, reaching and grasping, gaze control, and other aspects of behavior guided by visual input. It is essentially a 'motor' view of perception (Churchland et al., 1994; Watt, 1993). We would suggest that many of the visuomotor transformations that occupy the attention of these researchers are part of the dorsal action system and its associated subcortical and cortical networks. Thus, the preoccupation with visually guided actions that characterizes behaviorist approaches to vision has meant that most of the visual mechanisms that are being studied are those found in the dorsal stream.

In contrast, the reconstructive approach (e.g. Marr, 1982) concentrates on the creation of a replica of the world 'out there' on the basis of the sensory input data present at the retinas. In a sense, the approach of Marr is a 'passive' view of perception in which the representation is central and the external behavior of the organism is largely ignored (Ballard and Brown, 1992). For Marr, vision is 'an information processing task' and visual science is conceived as an 'inquiry into the nature of the internal representations by which we capture this information and thus make it available as a basis for decisions about our thoughts and actions'

(p. 3). This approach to vision need not be seen as opposing the behaviorist approach. Indeed, we would suggest that reconstruction of the external world is exactly the kind of activity which we believe is carried out by the ventral stream. Of course, as noted above, there is considerable debate about the way in which visual mechanisms and stored representations interact in visual perception. Whatever the particular mechanisms might be that underlie recognition and other perceptual/cognitive operations, it is the ventral stream, we believe, that carries them out. Moreover, the 'awareness' that typically accompanies much of visual perception may also depend, in part, on the ventral stream pathways (for some speculative accounts of routes to visual awareness, see Crick and Koch, 1995; Goodale and Milner, 1992; Milner and Goodale, 1995).

Thus, it seems to us that at least some aspects of the arguments about the relative merits of 'behaviorist' and 'reconstructionist' approaches to vision are misplaced. The two approaches are concerned with different visual systems that have different agendas (see also Neisser, 1989, 1994). Of course we realize that the drawing of parallels between 'reconstructionist' and 'behaviorist' approaches and the ventral and dorsal streams of visual processing will in no way settle the many issues that concern researchers in computational vision. Nevertheless, we hope our suggestion will supply some useful distinctions for thinking about these issues.

9. Getting it together: interactions between action and perception

Throughout this paper, we have been advancing the idea that the ventral perception system and the dorsal action system are two independent and decidedly different visual systems within the primate brain. We realize that in doing this we have overstated our position to some extent. This was a deliberate attempt to counter the tendency in object vision research to focus on issues such as recognition and other cognitive operations, without taking into account the actions that are performed on objects and the particular visuomotor transformations necessary for such actions. It is obvious that systems for action and those for perception must interact and cooperate in the control of behavior. Nevertheless, as we have tried to show, the computations carried out by the two systems complement one another.

One way to think about the interaction between the two streams, an interaction that would take advantage of the differences in their computational constraints, is in terms of a 'teleassistance' model. In teleassistance, a human operator uses a symbolic code to communicate with a robot that actually performs the required motor act on the marked goal object (Pook and Ballard, 1996). In terms of this teleassistance metaphor, the perceptual-cognitive system in the ventral stream, with its rich and detailed representations of the virtual scene, would be the human operator. Processes in the ventral stream identify a particular goal and flag the relevant object in the scene, perhaps by means of an attention-like process. Once a particular goal object has been flagged, dedicated visuomotor networks in the dorsal stream (in conjunction with related circuits in premotor cortex, basal ganglia, and brainstem) can then be activated to perform the desired motor act. Mechanisms in the dorsal stream, while not delivering anything like the visual detail provided by perception, do provide accurate information about the goal object in effector-specific frames of reference – and provide this information quickly. This means that a flagged object in the scene will be processed in parallel by both ventral and dorsal stream mechanisms – each transforming the visual information in the array for different purposes.

Thus, once a goal object has been selected for goal-directed action, the two systems process incoming visual information simultaneously – even though the nature of the visual information that is transformed might be rather different. Such simultaneous activation will, of course, provide us with visual experience (via the ventral stream) during the performance of a skilled action (mediated by the dorsal stream). For example, when we reach out to pick up an interesting book, we not only form our grasp according to the dimensions and location of that book but at the same time we might also perceive that it is one we have not seen before. Moreover, certain objects such as tools demand that we grasp the object in a particular way so that we can use it properly. In such a case both streams would have to interact fairly intimately in mediating the final motor output. Certainly there is evidence that, on the neural level, the two systems are interconnected allowing for communication and cooperation between them (reviewed in Goodale and Milner, 1992; Milner and Goodale, 1995). Thus, although there is clearly a division of labour between the perception and action systems, this division reflects the complementary role the two systems play in the production of adaptive behaviour.

Acknowledgements

The preparation of this manuscript was helped in part by grants from the Medical Research Council of Canada to M.A.G. and the Natural Sciences and Engineering Research Council to G.K.H.

References

Aglioti, S., DeSouza, J.F.X., Goodale, M.A., 1995. Size-contrast illusions deceive the eye but not the hand. Current Biology 5, 679–685.

Aloimonos, Y., 1990. Purposive and qualitative active vision. In: Proceedings of the International Conference on Pattern Recognition, Atlantic City, NJ, pp. 346–360.

Aloimonos, Y., 1992. Purposive, qualitative, active vision. CVGIP:Image Understanding 5, 3–129.

Andersen, R.A., 1987. Inferior parietal lobule function in spatial perception and visuomotor integration. In: V.B. Mountcastle, F. Plum, S.R. Geiger (Eds.), Handbook of Physiology, Section 1: The Nervous System, Vol. V, Higher Functions of the Brain, Part 2. American Physiological Association, Bethesda, MD, pp. 483–518.

Baizer, J.S., Ungerleider, L.G., Desimone, R., 1991. Organization of visual input to the inferior temporal and posterior parietal cortex in macaques. Journal of Neuroscience 11, 168–190.

Bálint, R., 1909. Seelenlämung des 'Schauens', optische Ataxie, räumliche Störung der Aufmerksamkeit. Monatschrift für Psychiatrie und Neurologie 25, 51–81.

Ballard, D.H., Brown, C.M., 1992. Principles of animate vision. CVGIP: Image Understanding 56, 3–21.

Biederman, I., Gerhardstein, P.C., 1995. Viewpoint-dependent mechanisms in visual object recognition:

reply to Tarr and Bülthoff, 1995. . Journal of Experimental Psychology: Human Perception and Performance 21, 1506–1514.

Buchbinder, S., Dixon, B., Hyang, Y.-W., May, J.G., Glickstein, M., 1980. The effects of cortical lesions on visual guidance of the hand. Society for Neuroscience Abstracts 6, 675.

Churchland, P.S., Ramachandran, V.S., Sejnowski, T.J., 1994. A critique of pure vision. In: C. Koch, J.L. Davis (Eds.), Large-scale neuronal theories of the brain. MIT Press, Cambridge, MA, pp. 23–60.

Coren, S., Girgus, J.S., 1978. Seeing is Deceiving: The Psychology of Visual Illusions. Lawrence Erlbaum Associates, Hillsdale, NJ.

Crick, F., Jones, E., 1993. Backwardness of human neuroanatomy. Nature 361, 109–110.

Crick, F., Koch, C., 1995. Are we aware of neural activity in primary visual cortex? Nature 275, 121–123.

Edelman, S., Bulthoff, H.H., 1992. Orientation dependence in the recognition of familiar and novel views of three-dimensional objects. Vision Research 32, 2385–2400.

Ellard, C.G., Goodale, M.A., 1986. The role of the predorsal bundle in head and body movements elicited by electrical stimulation of the superior colliculus in the Mongolian gerbil. Experimental Brain Research 64, 421–433.

Ellard, C.G., Goodale, M.A., 1988. A functional analysis of the collicular output pathways: A dissociation of deficits following lesions of the dorsal tegmental decussation and the ipsilateral collicular efferent bundle in the Mongolian gerbil. Experimental Brain Research 71, 307–319.

Ettlinger, G., 1977. Parietal cortex in visual orientation. In: F.C. Rose (Ed.), Physiological Aspects of Clinical Neurology. Blackwell, Oxford, pp. 93–100.

Ewert, J.-P., 1987. Neuroethology of releasing mechanisms: prey-catching in toads. Behavioral and Brain Sciences 10, 337–405.

Gattass, R., Sousa, A.P.B., Covey, E., 1985. Cortical visual areas of the macaque: possible substrates for pattern recognition mechanisms. In: C. Chagas, R. Gattass, C.G. Gross (Eds.), Pattern Recognition Mechanisms. Vatican City: Pontifical Academy of Sciences, pp. 1–20.

Gauthier, I., Anderson, A.W., Tarr, M.J., Skudlarski, P., Gore, J.C., 1997. Levels of categorization in visual recognition studies using functional magnetic resonance imaging. Current Biology 7, 645–651.

Gentilucci, M., Chieffi, S., Daprati, E., Saetti, M.C., Toni, I., 1996. Visual illusion and action. Neuropsychologia 34, 369–376.

Georgeson, M., 1997. Guest editorial: vision and action: you ain't see nothin' yet.… Perception 26, 1–6.

Gibson, J.J., 1979. The Ecological Approach to Visual Perception. Houghton Mifflin, Boston, MA, 332 pp.

Gnadt, J.W., Bracewell, R.M., Andersen, R.A., 1991. Sensorimotor transformation during eye movements to remembered visual targets. Vision Research 31, 693–715.

Goodale, M.A., 1983a. Vision as a sensorimotor system. In: T.E. Robinson (Ed.), Behavioral Approaches to Brain Research. Oxford University Press, New York, pp. 41–61.

Goodale, M.A., 1983b. Neural mechanisms of visual orientation in rodents: targets versus places. In: A. Hein, M. Jeannerod (Eds.), Spatially Oriented Behavior. Springer-Verlag, Berlin, pp. 35–61.

Goodale, M.A., 1988. Modularity in visuomotor control: from input to output. In: Z. Pylyshyn (Ed.), Computational Processes in Human Vision: An Interdisciplinary Perspective. Ablex, Norwood, NJ, pp. 262–285.

Goodale, M.A., 1993. Visual pathways supporting perception and action in the primate cerebral cortex. Current Opinion in Neurobiology 3, 578–585.

Goodale, M.A., 1996. Visuomotor modules in the vertebrate brain. Canadian Journal of Physiology and Pharmacology 74, 390–400.

Goodale, M.A., 1997. Visual routes to perception and action in the cerebral cortex. In: M. Jeannerod (Ed.), Handbook of Neuropsychology, Vol. 11, Elsevier, Amsterdam, pp. 91–109.

Goodale, M.A., Carey, D.P., 1990. The role of cerebral cortex in visuomotor control. In: B. Kolb, R.C. Tees (Eds.), The Cerebral Cortex of the Rat, Ablex, Norwood, NJ, pp. 309–340.

Goodale, M.A., Haffenden, A., (1998). Frames of reference for perception and action in the human visual system. Neuroscience and Biobehavioral Reviews, in press.

Goodale, M.A., Jakobson, L.S., Keillor, J.M., 1994a. Differences in the visual control of pantomined and natural grasping movements. Neuropsychologia, 31, 1994, 1159–1178.

Goodale, M.A., Jakobson, L.S., Servos, P., 1996. The visual pathways mediating perception and prehension. In: R. Flanagan, P. Haggard, A. Wing (Eds.), Sensorimotor Control of the Hand. Academic Press, New York, pp. 15–31.

Goodale, M.A., Meenan, J.P., Bülthoff, H.H., Nicolle, D.A., Murphy, K.S., Racicot, C.I., 1994. Separate neural pathways for the visual analysis of object shape in perception and prehension. Current Biology 4, 604–610.

Goodale, M.A., Milner, A.D., 1982. Fractionating orienting behavior in rodents. In: D.J. Ingle, M.A. Goodale, R.J.W. Mansfield (Eds.), Analysis of Visual Behavior. MIT Press, Cambridge, MA, pp. 267–299.

Goodale, M.A., Milner, A.D., 1992. Separate visual pathways for perception and action. Trends in Neurosciences 15, 20–25.

Goodale, M.A., Milner, A.D., Jakobson, L.S., Carey, D.P., 1991. A neurological dissociation between perceiving objects and grasping them. Nature 349, 154–156.

Goodale, M.A., Murphy, K., 1997. Action and perception in the visual periphery. In: P. Their, H.-O. Karnath (Eds.), Parietal Lobe Contributions to Orientation in 3D Space. Springer-Verlag, Heidelberg, pp. 447–461.

Goodale, M.A., Murphy, K., Meenan, J.-P., Racicot, C., Nicolle, D.A., 1993. Spared object perception but poor object- calibrated grasping in a patient with optic ataxia. Society for Neuroscience Abstracts 19, 775.

Gregory, R.L., 1963. Distortions of visual space as inappropriate constancy scaling. Nature 199, 678–680.

Haaxma, R., Kuypers, H.G.J.M., 1975. Intrahemispheric cortical connexions and visual. guidance of hand and finger movements in the rhesus monkey. Brain 98, 239–260.

Haffendale, A., Goodale, M.A., 1998. The effect of pictorial illusion on prehension and perception. Journal of Cognitive Neuroscience 10, 122–136.

Humphrey, G.K., Goodale, M.A., Gurnsey, R., 1991. Orientation discrimination in a visual form; agnosic: evidence from the McCollough effect. Psychological Science 2, 331–335.

Humphrey, G.K., Goodale, M.A., Jakobson, L.S., Servos, P., 1994. The role of surface information object recognition: studies of a visual form agnosic and normal subjects. Perception 23, 1457–1481.

Humphrey, G.K., Khan, S.C., 1992. Recognizing novel views of three-dimensional objects. Canadian Journal of Psychology 46, 170–190.

Humphrey, G.K., Symons, L.A., Herbert, A.M., Goodale, M.A., 1996. A neurological dissociation between shape from shading and shape from edges. Behavioural Brain Research 76, 117–125.

Hyvärinen, J., Poranen, A., 1974. Function of the parietal associative area 7 as revealed from cellular discharges in alert monkeys. Brain 97, 673–692.

Ingle, D.J., 1973. Two visual systems in the frog. Science 181, 1053–1055.

Ingle, D.J., 1980. Some effects of pretectum lesions in the frog's detection of stationary objects. Behavioural Brain Research 1, 139–163.

Ingle, D.J., 1982. Organization of visuomotor behaviors in vertebrates. In: D.J. Ingle, M.A. Goodale, R.J.W. Mansfield (Eds.), Analysis of Visual Behavior. MIT Press, Cambridge, MA, pp. 67–109.

Ingle, D.J., 1991. Functions of subcortical visual systems in vertebrates and the evolution of higher visual mechanisms. In: R.L. Gregory, J. Cronly-Dillon (Eds.), Vision and Visual Dysfunction, Vol. 2, Evolution of the Eye and Visual System London. Macmillan, Basingstoke, pp. 152–164.

Intraub, H., 1997. The representation of visual scenes. Trends in Cognitive Sciences 1, 217–222.

Jackson, J.H., 1875. Clinical and Physiological Researches on the Nervous System. Churchill, London.

Jakobson, L.S., Archibald, Y.M., Carey, D.P., Goodale, M.A., 1991. A kinematic analysis of reaching an grasping movements in a patient recovering from optic ataxia. Neuropsychologia 29, 803–809.

Jeannerod, M., 1988. The Neural and Behavioural Organization of Goal-directed Movements. Oxford University Press, Oxford.

Jolicoeur, P., Humphrey, G.K., 1998. Perception of rotated two-dimensional and three-dimensional objects and visual shapes. In: V. Walsh, J. Kulikowski (Eds.), Visual Constancies: Why Things Look As They Do. Cambridge University Press, Cambridge, pp. 69–123.

Jolion, J.-M.., 1994. Computer vision methodologies. CVGIP: Image Understanding 59, 53–71.

Kanwisher, N., Chun, M.M., McDermott, J., Ledden, P.J., 1996. Functional imaging of human on visual recognition. Cognitive Brain Research 5, 55–67.

Kanwisher, N., McDermott, J., Chun, M.M., 1997. The fusiform face area: a module in human extrastriate cortex specialized for face perception. The Journal of Neuroscience 17, 4302–4311.

Kawashima, R., Naitoh, E., Matsumura, M., Itoh, H., Ono, S., Satoh, K., Gotoh, R., Koyama, M., Inoue, K., Yoshioka, S., Fukuda, H., 1996. Topographic Representation in Human Intraparietal Sulcus of Reaching and Saccade. NeuroReport 7, 1253–1256.

Klüver, H., Bucy, P.C., 1939. Preliminary analysis of functions of the temporal lobes of monkeys. Archives of Neurological Psychiatry 42, 979–1000.

Logothetis, N.K., Pauls, J., Poggio, T., 1995. Shape representation in the inferior temporal cortex of monkeys. Current Biology 5, 552–563.

Logothetis, N.K., Sheinberg, D.L.., 1996. Visual object recognition. Annual Review of Neuroscience 19, 577–621.

Malach, R., Reppas, J.B., Benson, R.R., Kwong, K.K., Jiang, H., Kennedy, W.A., Leddedn, P.J., Brady, T.J., Rosen, B.R., Tootell, R.B.H., 1995. Object-related activity revealed by functional magnetic resonance imaging in human occipital cortex. Proceedings of the National Academy of Sciences USA 92, 8135–8139.

Matsumura, M., Kawashima, R., Naito, E., Satoh, K., Takahashi, T., Yanagisawa, T., Fukuda, H., 1996. Changes in rCBF during grasping in humans examined by PET. NeuroReport 7, 749–752.

Marr, D., 1982. Vision. Freeman, San Francisco, CA.

McConkie, G.W., Currie, C.B., 1996. Visual stability across saccades while viewing complex pictures. Journal of Experimental Psychology Human Perception and Performance 22, 563–581.

Milner, A.D., Goodale., M.A., 1993. Visual pathways to perception and action. In: T.P. Hicks, S. Molotchnikoff, T. Ono (Eds.), The Visually Responsive Neuron: From Basic Neurophysiology to Behavior, Progress in Brain Research, Vol. 95. Elsevier, Amsterdam, pp. 317–338.

Milner, A.D., Goodale, M.A., 1995. The Visual Brain in Action. Oxford University Press, Oxford.

Milner, A.D., Perrett, D.I., Johnston, R.S., Benson, P.J., Jordan, T.R., Heeley, D.W., Bettucci, D., Mortara, F., Mutani, R., Terazzi, E., Davidson, D.L.W., 1991. Perception and action in visual form agnosia. Brain 114, 405–428.

Mountcastle, V.B., Lynch, J.C., Georgopoulos, A., Sakata, H., Acuna, C., 1975. Posterior parietal association cortex of the monkey: command functions for operations within extrapersonal space. Journal of Neurophysiology 38, 871–908.

Neisser, U., 1989. Direct perception and recognition as distinct perceptual systems. Address presented to the Eleventh Annual meeting of the Cognitive Science Society, Ann Arbor, MI.

Niesser, U., 1994. Multiple systems: a new approach to cognitive theory. European Journal of Cognitive Psychology 6, 225–241.

O'Regan, J.K., 1992. Solving the 'real' mysteries of visual perception: The world as an outside memory. Canadian Journal of Psychology 46, 461–488.

Perenin, M.-T., Vighetto, A., 1988. Optic ataxia: a specific disruption in visuomotor mechanisms. I. Different aspects of the deficit in reaching for objects. Brain 111, 643–674.

Perrett, D., Benson, P.J., Hietanen, J.K., Oram, M.W., Dittrich, W.H., 1995. When is a face not a face? In: R. Gregory, J. Harris, P. Heard, D. Rose (Eds.), The Artful Eye. Oxford University Press, Oxford, pp. 95–124.

Pook, P.K., Ballard, D.H.., 1996. Deictic human/robot interaction. Robotics and Autonomous Systems 18, 259–269.

Price, C.J., Moore, C.J., Humphreys, G.W., Frackowiak, R.S.J., Friston, K.J., 1996. The neural regions subserving object recognition and naming. Proceedings of the Royal Society of London (B) 263, 1501–1507.

Pribram, K.H., 1967. Memory and the organization of attention. In: D.B. Lindsley, A.A. Lumsdaine (Eds.), Brain Function, Vol. IV, UCLA Forum in Medical Sciences 6, University of California Press, Berkley, CA, pp. 79–112.

Puce, A., Allison, T., Asagari, M., Gore, J.C., McCarthy, G., 1996. Differential sensitivity of human faces, letterstrings, and textures: a functional magnetic resonance imaging study. Journal of Neuroscience 16, 5205–5215.

Rensink, R.A., O'Regan, J.K., Clark, J.J., 1997. To see or not to see: the need for attention to perceive changes in scenes. Psychological Science 8, 368–373.

Rock, I., DiVita, J., 1987. A case of viewer-centered object perception. Cognitive Psychology 19, 280–293.

Sakata, H., Taira, M., Mine, S., Murata, A., 1992. Hand-movement-related neurons of the posterior parietal cortex of the monkey: their role in visual guidance of hand movements. In: R. Caminiti, P.B. Johnson, Y. Burnod (Eds.), Control of Arm Movement in Space: Neurophysiological and Computational Approaches. Springer-Verlag, Berlin, pp. 185–198.

Sakata, H., Taira, M., 1994. Parietal control of hand action. Current Opinion in Neurobiology 4, 847–856.

Sakata, H., Taira, M., Kusunoki, M., Murata, A., Tanaka, Y., 1997. The TINS Lecture: The Parietal Association Cortex in Depth Perception and Visual Control of Hand Action. Trends in Neurosciences 20, 350–357.

Schneider, G.E., 1969. Two visual systems: brain mechanisms for localization and discrimination are dissociated by tectal and cortical lesions. Science 163, 895–902.

Servos, P., Goodale, M.A., Humphrey, G.K., 1993. The drawing of objects by a visual form agnosic: contribution of surface properties and memorial representations. Neuropsychologia 31, 251–259.

Sloman, A., 1989. On designing a visual system: towards a Gibsonian computational model of vision. Journal of Experimental and Theoretical Artificial Intelligence 1, 289–337.

Snyder, L.H., Batista, A.P., Andersen, R.A., 1997. Coding of intention in the posterior parietal cortex. Nature 386, 167–170.

Taira, M., Mine, S., Georgopoulos, A.P., Murata, A., Sakata, H., 1990. Parietal cortex neurons of the monkey related to the visual guidance of hand movement. Experimental Brain Research 83, 29–36.

Tarr, M.J., 1995. Rotating objects to recognize them: a case study on the role of viewpoint dependency in the recognition of three-dimensional objects. Psychonomic Bulletin and Review 2, 55–82.

Tarr, M., Black, M., 1994. A computational and evolutionary perspective on the role of representation in vision. CVGIP: Image Understanding 60, 65–73.

Tarr, M.J., Bülthoff, H.H., 1995. Is human object recognition better described by geon structural descriptions or by multiple views? Comment on Biederman and Gerhardstein, 1993. Journal of Experimental Psychology: Human Perception and Performance 21, 1494–1505.

Tootell, R.B.H., Dale, A.M., Sereno, M.I., Malach, R., 1996. New images from human visual cortex. Trends in Neurosciences 19, 481–489.

Ungerleider, L.G., Mishkin, M., 1982. Two cortical visual systems. In: D.J. Ingle, M.A. Goodale, R.J.W. Mansfield (Eds.). Analysis of Visual Behavior. MIT Press, Cambridge, MA, pp. 549–586.

Vishton, P.M., Cutting, J.E., 1995. Veridical size perception for action: reaching vs. estimation. Investigative Ophthalmology and Visual Science 36 (Suppl.), 358.

Watt, R.J., 1991. Understanding Vision. Academic Press, London, pp. 301.

Watt, R.J., 1992. Visual analysis and the representation of spatial relations. In: G.W. Humphreys (Ed.), Understanding Vision. Basil Blackwell, Oxford, 19–38 pp.

Watt, R.J., 1993. Issues in shape perception. Image and Vision Computing 11, 389–394.

Weimer, W.B., 1977. A conceptual framework for cognitive psychology: motor theories of mind. In: R. Shaw, J. Bransford (Eds), Perceiving Acting and Knowing: Toward an Ecological Psychology. Lawrence Erlbaum Associates, Hillsdale, NJ, pp. 267–311.

Index